STRUCTURAL ANALYSIS SYSTEMS

Software — Hardware
Capability — Compatibility — Applications

A. NIKU-LARI
*Director, Institute for Industrial Technology Transfer
24 Rue des Mimosas, Gournay s/Marne
F93460 France*

Volume 4

CAD/CAM
&
STRUCTURAL ANALYSIS
IN INDUSTRY

*Proceedings of the SAS World Conference
Paris, 28–30 October 1986*

PERGAMON PRESS
OXFORD · NEW YORK · BEIJING · FRANKFURT
SÃO PAULO · SYDNEY · TOKYO · TORONTO

U.K.	Pergamon Press, Headington Hill Hall, Oxford OX3 0BW, England
U.S.A.	Pergamon Press, Maxwell House, Fairview Park, Elmsford, New York 10523, U.S.A.
PEOPLE'S REPUBLIC OF CHINA	Pergamon Press, Qianmen Hotel, Beijing, People's Republic of China
FEDERAL REPUBLIC OF GERMANY	Pergamon Press, Hammerweg 6, D-6242 Kronberg, Federal Republic of Germany
BRAZIL	Pergamon Editora, Rua Eça de Queiros, 346, CEP 04011, São Paulo, Brazil
AUSTRALIA	Pergamon Press Australia, P.O. Box 544, Potts Point, N.S.W. 2011, Australia
JAPAN	Pergamon Press, 8th Floor, Matsuoka Central Building, 1-7-1 Nishishinjuku, Shinjuku-ku, Tokyo 160, Japan
CANADA	Pergamon Press Canada, Suite 104, 150 Consumers Road, Willowdale, Ontario M2J 1P9, Canada

Copyright © 1986 Pergamon Books Ltd.

All Rights Reserved. No part of this publication may be reproduced, stored in a retrieval system or transmitted in any form or by any means: electronic, electrostatic, magnetic tape, mechanical, photocopying, recording or otherwise, without permission in writing from the publishers.

First edition 1986

British Library Cataloguing in Publication Data
Structural analysis systems : software,
hardware, capability, compatibility,
applications.
Vol. 4
1. Structures, Theory of—Data processing
I. Niku-Lari, A.
624.1'71'0285   TA647
ISBN 0-08-034918-8

Cover drawing: Centrifugal pump casing.
Manufacturer: C.C.M.-Sulzer, France
Software used: CA.ST.OR

In order to make this volume available as economically and as rapidly as possible the authors' typescripts have been reproduced in their original forms. This method unfortunately has its typographical limitations but it is hoped that they in no way distract the reader.

Printed in Great Britain by Vine & Gorfin Ltd, Exmouth

STRUCTURAL ANALYSIS SYSTEMS

Software — Hardware
Capability — Compatibility — Applications

Volume 4

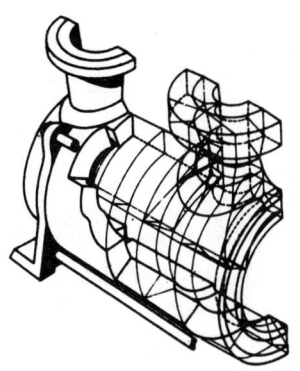

An international series of practical guidebooks
on structural analysis systems and their applications

Other Pergamon Titles of Interest

BATHE	Nonlinear Finite Element Analysis and ADINA 1983
COWAN	Predictive Methods for the Energy Conserving Design of Buildings
CROUCH	Matrix Methods Applied to Engineering Rigid Body Mechanics
GIBSON	Thin Shells
HARRISON	Structural Analysis and Design
HEARN	Mechanics of Materials, 2nd Edition
HOLLAND	Microcomputers and Their Interfacing
JAMSHIDI & MALEK-ZAVAREI	Linear Control Systems
LEININGER	Computer Aided Design of Multivariable Technological Systems
NIKU-LARI	Structural Analysis Systems, Vols. 1, 2, 3 & 5
NOOR & HOUSNER	Advances and Trends in Structural and Solid Mechanics
NOOR & McCOMB	Computational Methods in Nonlinear Structural and Solid Mechanics
PARKES	Braced Frameworks, 2nd Edition
ROZVANY	Optimal Design of Flexural Systems
SPILLERS	Automated Structural Analysis

Pergamon Related Journals (*Free Sample Copy Gladly Sent on Request*)

BUILDING AND ENVIRONMENT

CEMENT AND CONCRETE RESEARCH

CIVIL ENGINEERING FOR PRACTICING AND DESIGN ENGINEERS

COMPUTERS AND GRAPHICS

COMPUTERS AND INDUSTRIAL ENGINEERING

COMPUTERS AND STRUCTURES

FATIGUE AND FRACTURE OF ENGINEERING MATERIALS AND STRUCTURES

INTERNATIONAL JOURNAL OF APPLIED ENGINEERING EDUCATION

INTERNATIONAL JOURNAL OF SOLIDS AND STRUCTURES

JOURNAL OF ENGINEERING AND APPLIED SCIENCES

MATHEMATICAL MODELLING

INTERNATIONAL EDITORIAL ADVISORY COMMITTEE

Dr. T. ANDERSSON, *Sweden*
Prof. J. H. ARGYRIS, *Federal Republic of Germany*
Prof. K. J. BATHE, *USA*
Prof. T. BELYTSCHKO, *USA*
Dr. M. BERNADOU, *France*
Prof. B. A. BILBY, *UK*
Prof. R. D. COOK, *USA*
Dr. T. FUTAGAMI, *Japan*
Dr. S. K. GHOSH, *UK*
Dr. L. ILIE, *France*
Dr. L. IMRE, *Hungary*
Dr. J. C. LACHAT, *France*
Prof. H. LIEBOWITZ, *USA*
Dr. A. NIKU-LARI, *France [Editor]*
Ing. J. MACKERLE, *Sweden*
Ing. W. M. MAIR, *UK*
Dr. G. A. MILIAN, *Mexico*
Dr. D. NARDINI, *Yugoslavia*
Dr. I. PACZELT, *Hungary*
Prof. G. SANDER, *Belgium*
Prof. R. P. SHAW, *USA*
Prof. M. TANAKA, *Japan*
Prof. W. N. WENDLAND, *Federal Republic of Germany*
Prof. G. YOUZHONG, *People's Republic of China*

PREFACE

New challenges dictated by the international competition and the need to save material and energy and to improve product quality and reliability lead engineers to make more and more use of computers in design and manufacturing.

Today, CAD/CAM supported by powerful structural analysis software is finding a wide range of application in all industrial branches such as mechanical and metal working, automotive, aeronautics, nuclear industries, civil engineering, space and military etc. Powerful microcomputers allow small and medium size companies to make use of these new technologies.

We hope that this book will contribute to the transfer of knowledge between research and industry.

This fourth volume of the SAS-international guidebook series contains papers on CAD/CAM and industrial use of structural analysis software, presented at the SAS-World Conference, 28-30 October 1986 in Paris. The conference was sponsored by the French Ministry of Research and Education and was organized by IITT-international* in co-operation with AS & I**.

Papers on other main topics of the SAS-World Conference, FE and BE method as well as Expert Systems, are published in SAS volume five.

I would like to thank all authors and the members of the International Scientific and Advisory Committee for their commitment to the present volume.

Dr. A. KIKU-LARI
Editor

* IITT-International, 24 rue des Mimosas, F-93460 Gournay-sur-Marne, France
** AS & I, péripole 132, 44 rue Roger Salengro, F-94126 Fontenay sous bois, France

EDITORIAL

Structural analysis aims to construct numerical models which represent the best behaviour of the actual engineering material and component. These models are used in research for better understanding of experimental results. In industry the structural analysis models allow both the optimization of design and the prediction of failure.

The structural analysis (SA) is therefore a multidisciplinary problem which demands knowledge of several scientific and industrial disciplines such as, engineering sciences, mechanical or civil engineering, informatics, applied mathematics, computer sciences, etc.

International competition gives to industry the necessary impulse to optimise the design of parts and structures.

The engineer should save material and energy and use new and lighter materials such as composites. No longer is one allowed to over-design parts for "security reasons", and new international criteria have to be considered.

Industry needs to design sophisticated parts working in very special environments, in space, in the human body, in the sea, etc.

The compatibility of the structural analysis systems with modern micro-computers allow small and medium size companies to make use of these new technologies. New super computers help to find rapid solutions to complex industrial design problems.

The evolution of interactive graphics allow the full integration of structural analysis programs in a computer aided design and manufacturing environment. Expert systems, application of artificial intelligence and computer-aided decision making bring new developments in this field.

Structural analysis systems existing in the world market are powerful bridges between research and industry. They bring theory in direct physical contact with the industrial application.

The SA technology is in a rapid evolution. More and more new computers and powerful software appear in the market and the industry faces a new problem - that of selecting the optimum structural analysis system.

The choice of a structural analysis software is an important decision which can often exercise a significant influence over the successful development of a research, manufacture, or design project. Depending on the engineering problem and hardware available, a good choice of the computer program can be both cost and time effective. This new international guidebooks series aims to provide the engineer with the most up-to-date information about structural analysis systems currently available in the world market, and their capabilities.

Editorial

Published under the guidance of a distinguished scientific committee whose members are internationally recognised specialists of finite or boundary element methods, the series should be considered as an essential practical reference tool for the modern engineer involved in such areas as structural, mechanical, civil, nuclear, aeronautical and design engineering, computer science and software development.

Each volume gives detailed information about a wide range of selected software packages describing their purpose, capabilities and limitations and provides several practical examples of industrial applications, often supported by case studies. It also gives to the user the necessary information about postprocessor capabilities, computer-aided design integration and software compatibility with the most commonly used computers.

The guidebooks are industry-oriented and should prove indispensible in helping potential users to select the soft and hardware most suited to their needs. Each volume commences with a program description in tabular form, rapidly directing readers to the program most likely to solve their industrial problems, and concludes with a case-study index.

Main areas covered in the series:

- Finite and boundary element programs
- Finite difference and other methods
- Computer graphics
- Artificial intelligence and expert systems
- Computer-aided decision making in engineering
- Computer-aided design and manufacturing (CAD/CAM)
- Integration of structural analysis and expert systems in engineering CAD/CAM environment
- Hard and software selection
- Micro-computer applications in engineering
- New development in structural analysis software and interactive graphics
- Industrial case study
  . Mechanical engineering
  . Aeronautics and nuclear
  . Biomechanics
  . New materials (composites, plastics, etc)
  . Civil engineering (offshore, seismic, earthquake, etc).

Authors wishing to submit a paper under one of the above headings for possible publication in future volumes are invited to submit their manuscript for editorial consideration of the international scientific committee to the address below.

Dr A Niku-Lari, Director
Institute for Industrial Technology Transfer
I.I.T.T.-international
24 Rue des Mimosas
93460 Gournay-sur-Marne
FRANCE
TEL: (1) 43.05.17.19

CONTENTS

CHAPTER I: INDUSTRIAL CAD/CAM

Industrial CAD/CAM on Microcomputers - Myth Or Fact   3
    J. P. Rammant

Expected-Time Analysis of a Worst-Case Optimal
Hidden-Surface Algorithm   15
    F. Dévai

A New Generation of Computational Tools in
Structural Engineering   25
    L. Ebersolt, P. Verpeaux, M. Farvacque,
    A. Combescure & P. Manigaut

Modified Finite Elements for Efficient Use in CAD-Environment   35
    O. Ohtmer

ANSYS: A General Purpose Finite Element Program
Integrated in the CAD Environment   51
    A. Schaller

GET3D: A Tetrahedral Finite Element Mesh Generator for
the Computation of Electromagnetic Fields   61
    Y. Du Terrail, O. Santana, G. Meunier & J. L. Coulomb

Computer Aided Design and Integral Equations   77
    A. Boyer, G. Caracci & P. Astre

The Introduction Of Display II, an Interactive and
Color Graphics Post-Processing Program   87
    K. S. Kothawala

GRAFEM & IFAD: Predictive Analysis Tools of Applicon   93
    D. Lahoutifard

CHAPTER II: INDUSTRIAL APPLICATION OF SAS SYSTEMS

II-1 MECHANICAL AND METAL WORKING INDUSTRY

Industrial Applications of the Finite Elements and
Boundary Elements Analysis System "CA.ST.OR" 109
    M. Afzali & M. Cristescu

On the Automatic Simulation of Two-Dimensional Metal Forming
Processes by the Finite Element Method 133
    J. C. Gelin & P. Picart

FORGE2: Program for Simulating the Hot-forging of Metals
by Finite Elements 149
    Y. Germain, E. Wey & J. L. Chenot

II-2 NUCLEAR AND CIVIL ENGINEERING

Dynamic Design Optimization of the Base Plate of a
Nuclear Instrumentation Vertical Cabinet 167
    R. Filidoro, C. Pappalettere & N. Pezzella

Static Analysis of Large Frameworks 179
    C. T. F. Ross

Computer Aided Bridges Design 191
    B. Marce & J. P. Chanard

Long Term Static Analysis of Underground Openings
in Creeping Rock 207
    G. Borm

CHAPTER III: MICRO-COMPUTER APPLICATIONS

Vibration of Skeletal Structures via a Microcomputer 219
    C. F. T. Ross

Adaptation of the Computer Code STDYNL to Micro-Computers
and to Vibration in Soils by Dynamic Stress Function 231
    B. A. Ovunc

SAFEpm: Structural Analysis by Finite Elements on Pocket Micros 247
    J. Vykutil

Utilizing the Graphics Capabilities of Microcomputers for
FEM Pre- and Postprocessing 257
    J. F. Stelzer

Subject Index 271

Chapter 1
INDUSTRIAL CAD/CAM

INDUSTRIAL CAD/CAM ON MICROCOMPUTERS - MYTH OR FACTS

J. P. Rammant

SCIW s. v., Steenweg 108, 3912 Herk-de-Stad, Belgium

ABSTRACT

Three application fields are discussed: Steel Construction, Mechanical Design and Civil Engineering. It is shown that, with the use of special software techniques, micro-computers are ready to be applied in interactive graphics, finite element analysis, in design work, in manufacturing preparation and in the numeric control of machinery. Emphasis is on practical examples.

KEYWORDS

CAD-CAM; microcomputers; steel construction; finite element analysis; graphics; civil engineering; mechanical design.

INTRODUCTION

CAD-CAM comprehenses the full design process covering the project design, the stress analysis, the drafting, the manufacturing preparation and the numerical control of production machines. CAD-CAM is oriented towards different industries which means that the software has also to be dedicated. As a software developer we are familiar with 3 professions: Steel Construction, Mechanical Industry, Civil Engineering. In this paper we will show examples that were executed on standard 16 bit micro-computers.

Although the application of CAD-CAM varies to a large extent dependent on the industry, a collection of fundamental software techniques is common:
- interactive draughting
- stress analysis
- bill of material
- database technology

These techniques are permanently in evolution and are strongly related to the hardware evolutions.

A few examples:
- bit mapped graphic screens facilitate the drafting with the help of mouse pointing devices
- the number crunching capability increases permanently (surely in relation to the cost): 32 bit PC's are emerging
- the winchester disk technology is soon to be replaced by faster optical disk systems
- artificial intelligence software tools facilitate the capturing of technological expertise

Developping software is a very lively occupation where R & D are preponderant.

CAD-CAM FOR STEEL CONSTRUCTION

Steel structures are large meccano's with a great variety of elements and connections. Basically standard sections are applied: this facilitates the geometric model: a wire frame representation is a good start. The difficulties are situated in the regulations and codes that have to be respected by the design.

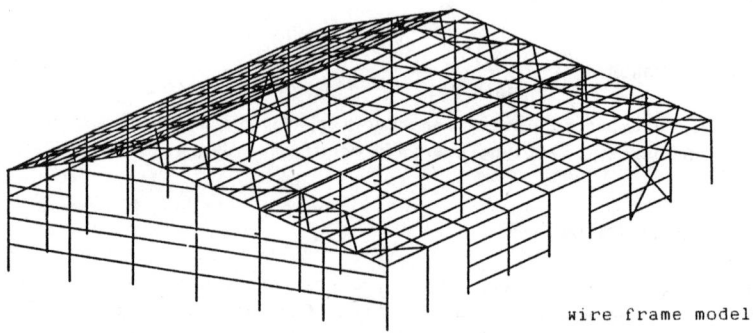

wire frame model

One has to consider: prescribed load-combinations, maximum deformation requirements, stress checking, control of lateral buckling and warping of the elements, determination of the collapse safety factor. Another concern is the design of the connection elements (type, composition) that has to respond to another set of regulations. This results in a necessary strong relation between the set-up of the global steel structure and the design of the various components.

This relation is based upon an integrated modular approach: modules for shape definition, strength analysis, code checking of the members, design of the connections, overview drawings, single element drawings of members and connection components, material lists. One common database accompanies the project.

The integration of the separate modules is illustrated below:

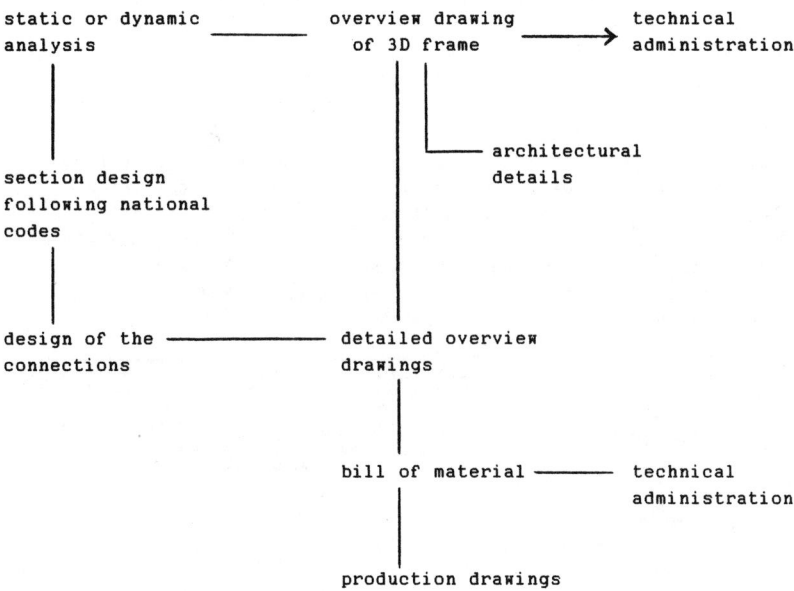

Since data have to be used by different modules a shared data management system with query functions has been developed. This has the additional advantage that data can become selectively maintainable and it provides also a first step towards a knowledge base. The system can be explained by considering a projectfile as a book with texts. The internal memory of the computer contains a buffermemory that can hold several pages of the book. The manager has several catalogues such that he knows the contents of the book and the contents of the pages in memory.

Furthermore, there are operators which allow the data manager to be used as an intelligent softwaretool. This is sketched as follows:

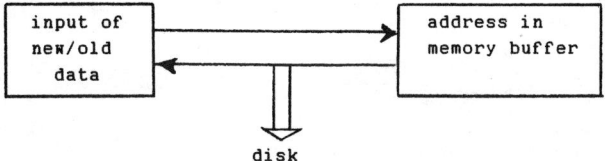

The use of a datamanager decreases the development time of a
software module and facilitates the debugging process. Maintenance
costs are reduced and new modules can be merged easily in the
package. As an illustration, the data needed to generate a detailed
overview drawing cover: coordinates of the nodes, connectivity of
the nodes, section tables with section coordinates, axes, levels
and positions of the members, table of steel connections, etc.
Since these data are becoming available at different stages of the
project, a common database is an essential feature.

Below a few drawings are reproduced to show the results of the
design modules: through standardized connection types, the optimum
connection outline is determined to withstand the internal force
transfers. The bearing capacity of each of the elements of the
connection is checked automatically; the user adapts interactively
the design in such a sense that the strength behavior improves.
Detailed drawings and material lists are automatically extracted
from the design.

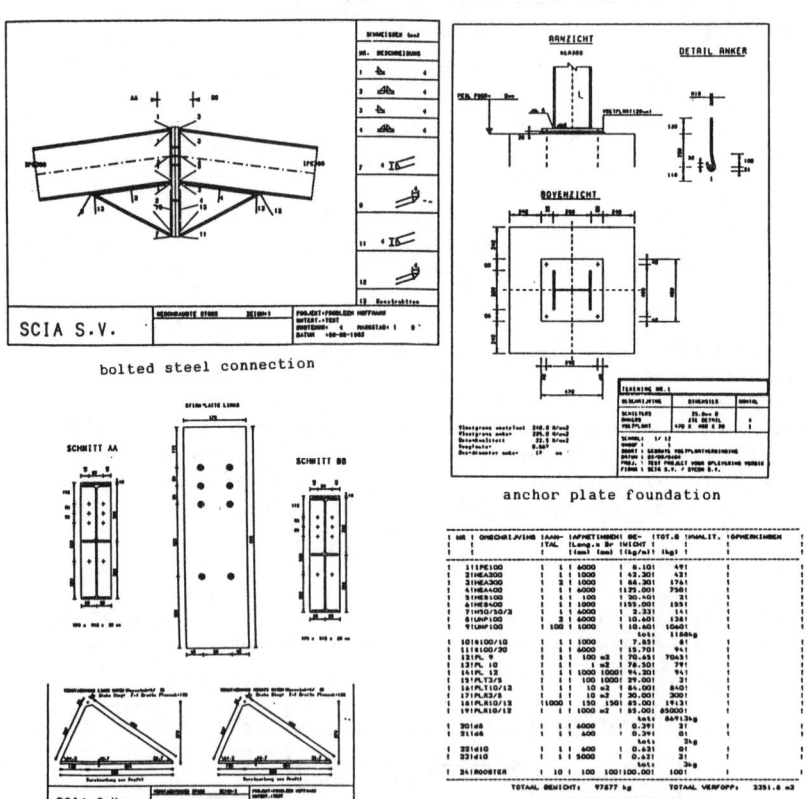

bolted steel connection

anchor plate foundation

detailed drawings of reinforcing steel plates

bill of materials

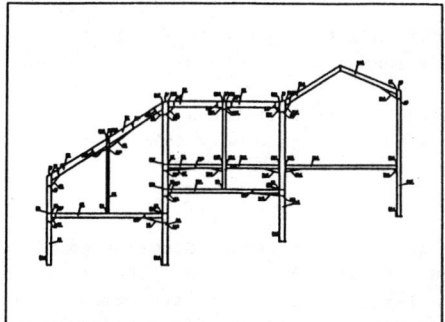

overview drawing of
a portal frame

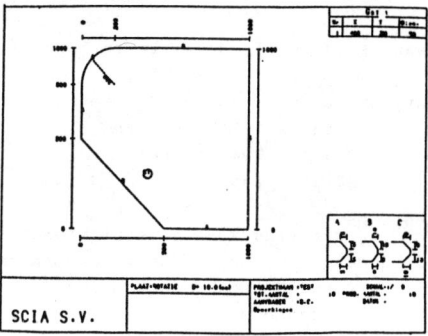

production drawing

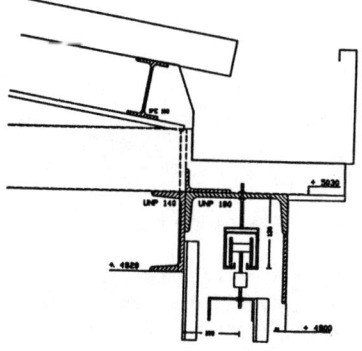

detail of a wall-
roof connection

For non-structural
details the drawing
efforts are minimized
through the use of an
iteractive CAD package.
The example at left is
realised with the AutoCAD
software (from Autodesk
Inc.)

CAD-CAM FOR THE MECHANICAL INDUSTRY

The products of the mechanical industry have a broad spectrum:
- automobile industry, aeronautics
- machine parts
- pressure vessels and nuclear installations
- packing industry (from containers to bottles)
- equipment parts (pumps, ...)

This list is very much incomplete and each of the applications has its specialized area's, see e.g. machine parts. Specialized CAD-CAM software is therefore needed: the efforts to adapt software to a broad application domain are large. This is the main reason that the rapid introduction of CAD-CAM into industry is slown down.

What is currently possible on today's micro-computers?

This question is answered from our experiences:
- 2 and 2 1/2 D drafting
- finite element analysis
- NC steering

For the drafting work several standard packages are available on PC. Some of the better known programs:
- AutoCAD from Autodesk (more than 30,000 installations)
- CADdy from Ziegler Instruments
- EuroCAD from rOtring
- Superdraft
- Micro CADDS from Computervision
- CAD plus

We experienced with the Auto-cad program and found it:
- to be very userfriendly
- having a good execution speed
- reasonable number of functions
- easily to be linked with our own software packages

On the next page a drawing of a part of a mooring hook is represented (by courtesy of STEDITEK n.v., Belgium). Out of the mechanical drawing, the data for the finite element analysis are extracted.

Since 1976 the ESA (Engineering Structural Analysis) finite element package was introduced by SCIA on small computer systems. More than 400 users today are using programme modules out of the package. The finite element method on PC's is offering unlimited design facilities:
- very small purchase level
- complex analysis facilities within reach
- userfriendly PC style with menu driven commands
- graphical support

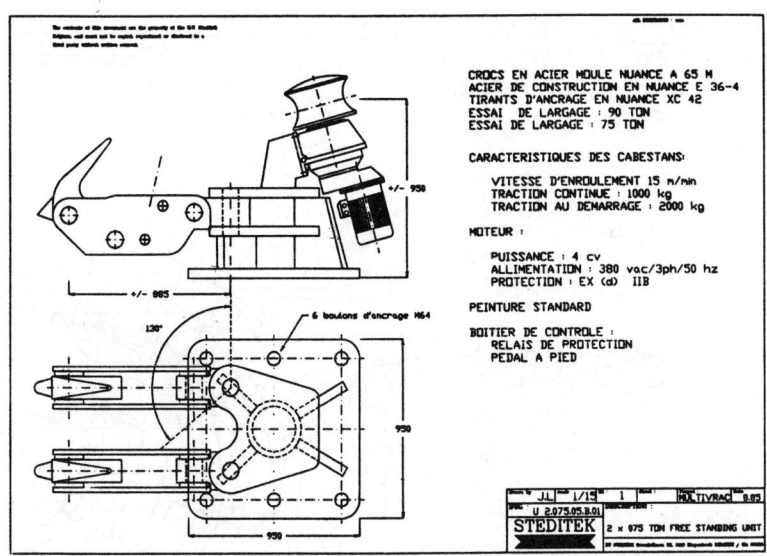

hook structure
(AutoCAD)

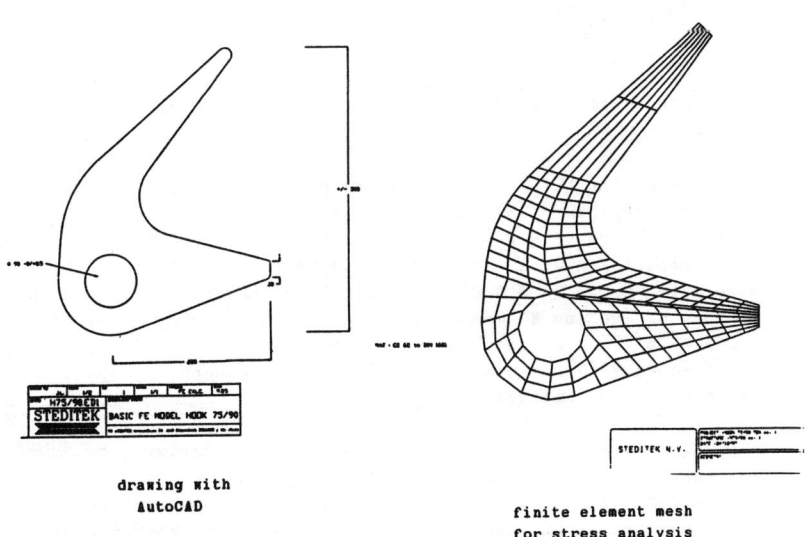

drawing with
AutoCAD

finite element mesh
for stress analysis
E. S. A.

Some examples of structures analysed with the ESA finite element package are shown below:

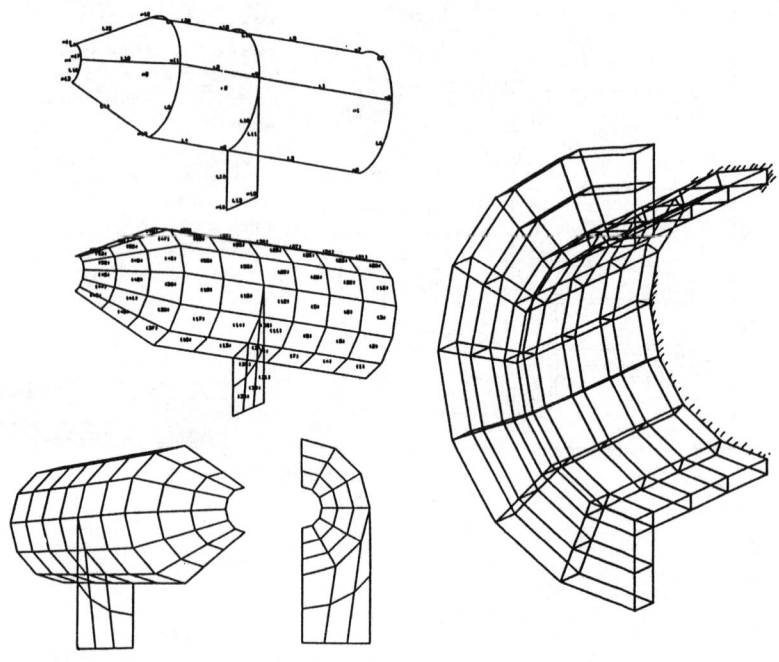

Half model of a pressure vessel   3 D model of a flange

The integration between drafting and design is realized. The further flow towards production preparation is less straightforward. The R & D efforts are known: group-technology for work-preparation, the use of database technology for bill of materials (B.O.M. / M.R.P.), technical administration, integration between design and NC machinery, flexible manufacturing systems. The aim is C.I.M., computer integrated manufacturing.
Starting up with the computerisation of one essential aspect is certainly to be encouraged.

For one project of automation of the production drawings of pressure vessels we used the following software tools:
- SCIA GKS, an implementation of the ISO-norm for interactive graphics on PC. Using the GKS procedures the software develop-

er can generate drawings very fast
- technical data-management system (virtual database system)
- menu-drivers

These production drawings (on large scale) are adapted for optic readers that steer a flame cutting equipment.

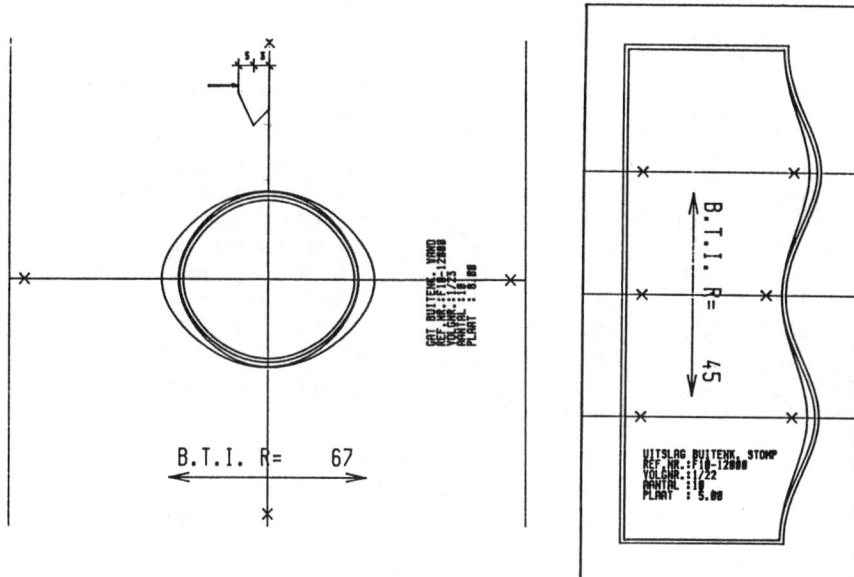

CAD-CAM FOR CIVIL ENGINEERING

The building industry comprehenses several specialisations:
- landsurveying
- road design
- construction of industrial buildings
- housing
- bridges, dams,

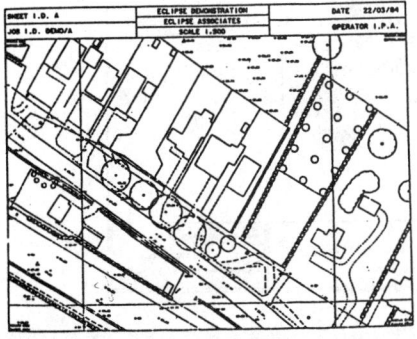

In each field the computer is taking an important part: the landsurveyer will quickly recorder his measurements, calculate the traverse and levels the heights. The detailed drawings are formed and the cartographic heights are indicated. For housing and road design cut and fill calculations are performed on the same model.

During construction of industrial buildings and housings a great variety of problems is encountered: soil mechanic testing, soil resistant constructions (sheetwalls, mud-walls, ...), foundations, steel or reinforced concrete design.

A soil resistant sheetwall has to withstand several excavation phases: with anchors one can reinforce the sheetwall.

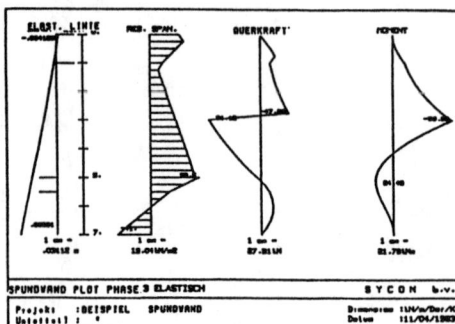

If one takes into account the nonlinear characteristics of the soil and of the wall, one will be able to predict closely the actual behaviour of the structure: this mathematical model can only be solved using an appropriate program.

sheet wall analysis

A reinforced concrete design involves the static (or dynamic) analysis to find the internal forces reacting the external loading. THe organic design (specification of the necessary steel reinforcement) follows immediately the analysis.
Again the finite element method is a powerfull means. Some practical examples are shown below: a foundation plate resting on a soil reinforced with gravel concentrations, secondly a prefab wall element.

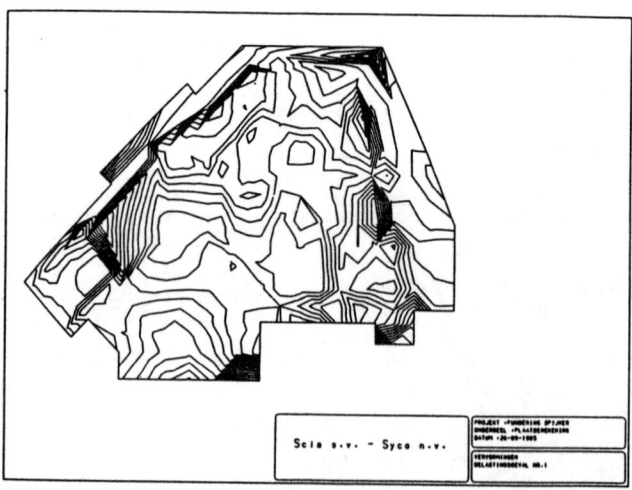

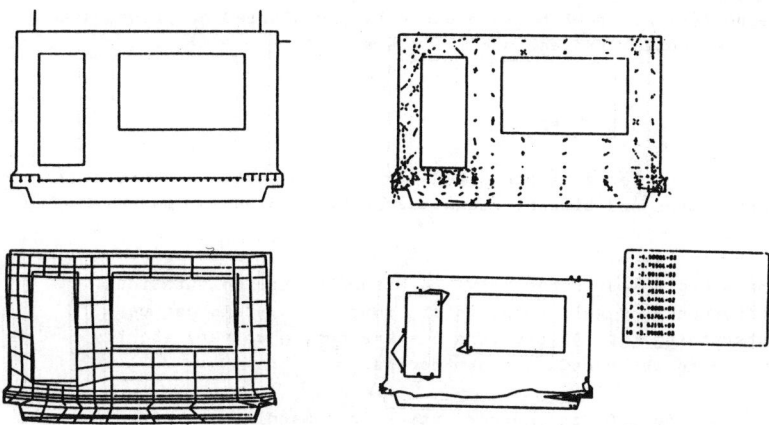

prefab wall element

The organic section design asks for more interaction with the designer: the computer may propose a reinforcement scheme (taking into account a large number of boundary conditions such as minimal reinfement percentages, minimal cover, etc.), it is the designer who decides on the appropriate practical result. He has to interfere with the workers at the building site.

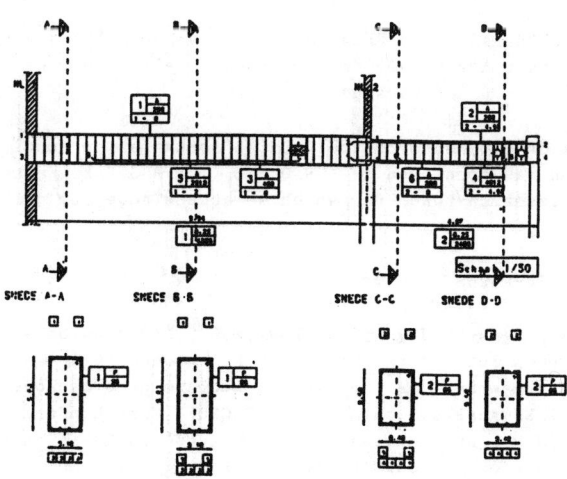

reinforced concrete slab

In the prefab industry a great number of CAD-CAM applications are being applied: prefab floor elements (reinforced or prestressed, wall elements, frames, special slabs, etc.

CONCLUSIONS

The reasons for applying CAD-CAM are clear: a large efficiency improvement and higher technology in the design and manufacturing process.

The micro-computer has grown to maturity: the computational performance of well tuned 16 bit computer systems can be outstanding. The 32 bit versions are coming up very shortly improving the speed with another factor.

However the CAD-CAM implementation is demanding on software development; the software specialist must learn the knowledge from the user and he must implement this knowledge in a comprehensive software product.

ACKNOWLEDGEMENTS

The examples, as represented in this text, are mainly realised with the SCIA software package, thanks to the contribution of our software users.

Two examples (detail of a front and hook) were realized with the AutoCAD program; the survey drawing came from the Eclipse (Eclipse Associates Ltd - U.K.) package.

Part of the developments on the CAD-CAM software for steel construction was sponsored by I.W.O.N.L. - I.R.S.I.A., a belgian government research fund, for which we acknowledge our gratitude.

REFERENCES

(1) Backx E., Rammant J.P., Schymkowitz G., SAP runs on a 16 K desk computer, Proc. 3th SAP user's conf., L.A., June 1978
(2) Backx E., Rammant J.P., A virtual storage data management system for F.E. analysis on micro's, ENGSOFT Conf. London, 1983
(3) Rammant J.P., ESA: Engineering Structural Analysis on personal computers, chapter in book Structural Analysis Systems, ed. A Niku Lari, Vol.2, Pergamon Press, 1985, ISBN 0 08 0325785
(4) Backx E., Rammant J.P., Integrated CAD-CAM software for steel structures on a micro-computer, chapter in book Microcomputers in Engineering Applications, ed. B.A. Schrefler, John Wiley Ltd., 1985

EXPECTED-TIME ANALYSIS OF A WORST-CASE OPTIMAL HIDDEN-SURFACE ALGORITHM

F. Dévai

*Computer and Automation Institute, Hungarian Academy of Sciences,
POB 63, Kende 13-17, H-1502 Budapest, Hungary*

ABSTRACT

Many authors postulate the requirement that the execution times of visibility computations grow linearly with the number of scene data. It is shown that, in general, this requirement cannot be met: An $\Omega(N \log N)$ expected lower bound is provided for scan-line algorithms, i.e. for determining the visibility of N line segments in the plane, assuming the algebraic computation tree model. Intruducing the precise notion of depth complexity, it is demonstrated that the expected running time of a widely used hidden-surface method, the z-buffer algorithm, can be $\Omega(N^2)$. An alternative to the z-buffer algorithm may be the NlogN algorithm that is known to be worst-case optimal, and now it is proved to be also expected-time optimal. If the endpoints of the line segments have integer coordinates, the running time of the NlogN algorithm is $O(N \log D)$ for $D > 1$, where D, $D \leq N/2$, is the average depth complexity of the points of the x-axis corresponding the endpoints of the line segments. If the x-coordinates of the segment endpoints are independent identically distributed random variables with a common density f, the expected time of the NlogN algorithm is still $O(N \log E(D))$ for any smooth f with compact support.

KEYWORDS

Engineering CAD/CAM, interactive graphics, hidden-surface elimination, scan-line methods, NlogN algorithm, z-buffer, depth complexity, expected running time, lower bound, computational geometry

INTRODUCTION

New generations of engineering CAD/CAM systems are facing to deal with hundreds of thousands of parts at a time. Rendering such a scene impose a serious burden on the interactive graphics support of the system. The difficulty is aggravated by the fact that the amount of computational work required by some graphics algorithms grows considerably faster than linearly with the number of data used to describe the scene. Undoubtedly, the most time consuming tasks are visibility computations, such as the elimination of hidden lines or the removal of hidden surfaces.

The methods of visibility computations seem to divide naturally into two classes: *exact* and *approximation* algorithms. Approximation algorithms rather than returning exact picture portions corresponding to visible objects, approximate them by using an integral number of picture elements, called *pixels*. (This classification roughly corresponds to the one described by Sutherland, Sproull and Schumaker (1974), where *image space* algorithms are approximation, and *object space* algorithms are exact algorithms.)

In this paper we are interested in three-dimensional approximation algorithms. Two-dimensional exact algorithms, however, can also be used here as building blocks. Worst-case optimal three-dimensional exact algorithms are given by Dévai (1986) for the hidden-line, and by McKenna (1986) for the hidden-surface problem.

A class of picture generation methods developed for raster displays scan the three-dimensional scene by a sequence of horizontal planes in order to generate the projection of visible points in each plane onto the corresponding scan line. These *scan-line methods* consist of two main phases:

(1) determination of the intersection of objects with scan planes, and

(2) computing the visibility of figures obtained in phase (1).

Phase (2), as shown in Fig.1, requires the solution of a two-dimensional visibility problem for each scan plane.

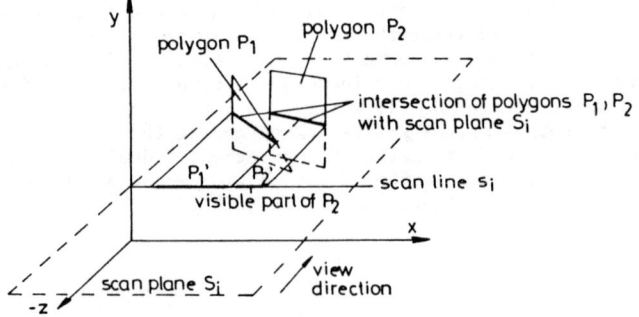

Fig. 1. Scanning the scene by a sequence of horizontal planes

Assuming that the three-dimensional scene is modelled by a set of pairwise disjoint polyhedra (however any pair of polyhedra can be allowed to touch at their surfaces), the worst-case time of phase (1) is $O(N \log N)$,[1] where N is the number of edges in the scene (Dévai, 1985). Phase (2) is more time consuming; until recently all the previously published algorithms (e.g. Bouknight, 1970; Watkins, 1970; Yamaguchi and Tokieda, 1983) take $O(N^2)$ time in the worst case (Beatty, Booth and Mattheis, 1981; Dévai, 1981, 1984).

---

[1] We say that $f(n) = O(g(n))$ ("of order at most $g(N)$") if there exist positive constants c and m such that for all $n > m$, $f(n) \leq cg(n)$. Similarly, $f(n) = \Omega(g(n))$ ("of order at least $g(n)$") if there exist positive constants c and m such that for all $n > m$, $f(n) \geq cg(n)$. Finally, $f(n) = \Theta(g(n))$ ("of order exactly $g(n)$") if there exist positive constants c, d and m such that for all $n > m$, $cg(n) \leq f(n) \leq dg(n)$.

The computational problem of phase (2) can be formulated as follows. Let S be a set of points in the xz plane, and let we denote by V(S,u) the subset of S visible from a given point u. Then

$$V(S,u) = \{x \in S: (u,x) \cap S = \emptyset \}$$

where (u,x) denotes the open line segment defined by the endpoints u and x.

In computer graphics a perspective transformation is usually performed before the visibility computations, so we can assume without loss of generality that the *observation point* u is on the -z axis at infinity, i.e., u = (0,-∞), and all points of the scene have positive x-and z-coordinates. In this way, the visibility problem in two dimensions can be regarded as a projection onto the x-axis, where we require that the images of the line segments bounding our figures be distinguishable, that is, the line segments may have different colours and intensity values.

Many authors postulate the requirement that the execution times of visibility computations grow *linearly* with the number of scene data (Sutherland, Sproull and Schumaker, 1974; Clark, 1976; Hamlin and Gear, 1977; Griffiths, 1979). In the next section we will show that in general, under a wide class of computational models, this requirement cannot be met: An $\Omega(N \log N)$ expected lower bound will be provided under the algebraic computation tree model for determining the visibility of N line segments in the plane.

Then we would like to dispel the delusion that the running time of a widely used hidden-surface method, the z-buffer algorithm, has a constant or at most a linear execution time. Intruducing the precise notion of depth complexity, we will point out that even the expected running time of the algorithm can grow considerably faster than the lower bound.

In the following two sections we analyse a method, called the NlogN algorithm that can be an alternative to the z-buffer algorithm. This method is known to be worst-case optimal, and now it is demonstrated also to be expected-time optimal.

EXPECTED LOWER BOUND

It has been proved that in any model of computation where $\Omega(N \log N)$ is a worst-case lower bound for determining the union of N intervals, $\Omega(N \log N)$ is also a worst-case lower bound for determining the visibility of N line segments in the plane (Dévai, 1981, 1984). Such a model of computation is the *linear decision tree* (Fredman and Weide, 1978; Dobkon and Lipton, 1979), where a linear function of all input variables can be compared at unit cost. Unfortunately, it is not known whether there exists any algorithm for our problem under this model.

Another such model is the *algebraic computation tree* where algebraic operations, root extraction and comparisons are allowed at unit cost (Ben-Or, 1983). Within this model all the known scan-line algorithms can be implemented, so we can conclude that the requirement for a linear run time cannot be fulfilled in the worst case under wide classes of computation models.

Now, we examine the linearity requirement for the expected running time. We will prove an expected lower bound using the *element distinctness problem* that can be formulated as follows.

Given $x_1, \ldots, x_N \in \mathbb{R}$, is there a pair i, j with $i \neq j$ and $x_i = x_j$?

LEMMA 1. Any algorithm that determines the visibility of a planar set of N line segments can be used to solve the element distinctness problem by using O(N) additional algebraic operations.

Proof: Given $x_1, \ldots, x_N$ on the positive x-axis, and an algorithm for line-segment visibility. Place an observer at the point $u = u(a,b)$ with $a > 0$ and $b < 0$, and choose for each x_i, $1 \leq i \leq N$, the point (x'_i, i) where the ray from u through x_i intersects the horizontal line $z = i$. Clearly, this point set can be constructed in O(N) algebraic operations, and $x_i = x_j$ iff one of the points (x'_i, i) and (x'_j, j) obscures the other, $1 \leq i \leq N$, $1 \leq j \leq N$, $i \neq j$, as shown in Fig. 2. Determining the visibility of this point set if the number of visible points is N, the answer is ´no´, otherwise if the number is less than N, the answer is ´yes´ for the element distinctness problem.

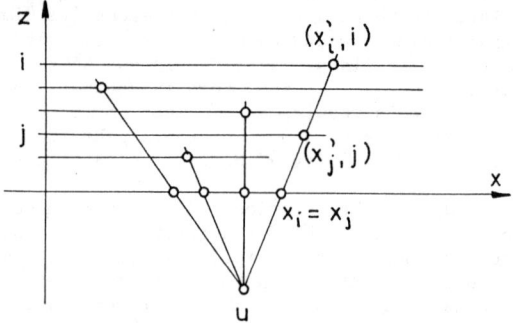

Fig. 2. Element distinctness is reducible to planar visibility

THEOREM 1. Let $x_1, \ldots, x_{2N}$ be independent random variables uniformly distributed in the interval $[0,1]$, then assuming a parallel projection, $\Omega(N \log N)$ is the expected lower time bound on determining the visibility of a planar set of line segments with endpoints (x_i, y_i), (x_j, y_j); $1 \leq i \leq 2N$, $1 \leq j \leq 2N$, $i \neq j$, under the algebraic computation tree model.

Proof: Ben-Or (1983) gives an $\Omega(N \log N)$ expected lower bound with the given conditions for the element distinctness problem. By Lemma 1, element distinctness is O(N) time reducible to planar visibility, and assuming a parallel projection, the theorem follows.

ANALYSIS OF THE Z-BUFFER ALGORITHM

One of the most extensively used hidden-surface techniques is the *z-buffer algorithm* that can be implemented also as a scan-line method. Relying upon estimated timing data of Sutherland, Sproull and Schumaker (1974), both Newman and Sproull (1979) and Foley and van Dam (1982) conclude that the algorithm takes constant time. Perhaphs one reason for its popularity is this good promise of performance.

As we proved, we cannot get better than a $\Theta(N \log N)$ expected time under the algebraic computation tree model. Nevertheless, one may think that assuming a different model of computation, some improvement might be possible.

Sublinear behaviour, however, is not even in the average case possible, since any algorithm for determining the visibility of N objects takes at least N steps under any reasonable single-processor model of computation.

To clear up the commom fallacy regarding the the performance of the z-buffer algorithm we will give a precise analysis of its running time. Being an approximation method, the algorithm assumes *integer coordinates*. Now, let N line segments be given in the scan plane by their endpoints, and let l_i and r_i, respectively, denote the x-coordinates of the left and right endpoints, $0 \leq l_i \leq R$, $0 \leq r_i \leq R$, where R is the number of picture elements in the scan line.

We need the N-element vectors XL, ZL, XR, ZR that contain the x- and z-coordinates of the left and right endpoints, respectively. Also we need an R element vector ZBUFFER initialized to the largest possible z-value and a *refresh buffer* in which the intensity values are stored for each pixel to be displayed. The refresh buffer is initialized to the background intensity value. Then the algorithm can be implemented as follows.

```
for i := 1 to N do
    z := ZL[i];
    dz := (ZR[i] - ZL[i])/(XR[i] - XL[i]);
    for j := XL[i] + 1 to XR[i] do
        z := z + dz;
        if z < ZBUFFER[j] then
            ZBUFFER[j] := z;
            put the intensity value corresponding to segment i
            to the appropriate place in the refresh buffer
        endif
    end
end
```

Let d(x) be the number of line segments intersected by the half line starting from the viewing point and going through the point x of the x-axis of the coordinate system. The quantity d(x) will be called the *depth complexity* of the point x.

Assume that the line segments in the xz plane are half-open: the left endpoint does not belong to the segment. Then the *average depth complexity* A over the scan line is

$$A = \frac{1}{R} \sum_{i=1}^{R} d(x_i) = \frac{1}{R} \sum_{j=1}^{N} (r_j - l_j).$$

The number of comparisons performed by the if statement of the program is

$$C = \sum_{j=1}^{N} (r_j - l_j) = RA.$$

If only arithmetic operations taken on data are considered, the running time of the z-buffer algorithm is

$$T(N,R) = aN + bRA,$$

where the constants a and b, respectively, account for the time required by the arithmetic operations performed by the outer and the inner loop of the algorithm.

The *worst-case time* $T_w(N,R)$ occurs if $A = N$:

$$T_w(N,R) = N(a + bR) = O(NR).$$

Since there exist such a scene that each segment is converted into exactly R pixels, we can write

$$T_w(N,R) = \Theta(NR).$$

Forrest (1980) claims that the worst-case time of the algorithm is linear, since we can regard R as constant. If, however, we want to be able to distinguish the N objects, which is a reasonable requirement, R cannot be less than N. Expressing the worst-case time as a function of N, the best we can obtain is $T_w(N) = \Omega(N^2)$.

To carry out an *expected-time analysis*, suppose that the x-coordinates of the endpoints of each segment are choosen uniformly and independently at random from the interval $[0,R]$. Then there are $(R+1)^2$ possible ways to choose integer pairs: we can obtain R+1 pairs with distance zero, and $2(R+1-k)$ pairs with distance k, $1 \leq k \leq R$.

The expected number of C

$$E(C) = \sum_{j=1}^{N} E(r_j - 1_j) = \sum_{j=1}^{N} \frac{1}{(R+1)^2} \sum_{k=1}^{R} 2(R + 1 - k)k$$

$$= N \frac{R(R + 2)}{3(R + 1)},$$

and the *expected running time*

$$T_e(N,R) = aN + bN \frac{R(R + 2)}{3(R + 1)}.$$

It is remarkable that the expected time is only about three times less than the worst-case time. Expressing the former as a function of N, we obtain $T_e(N) = \Omega(N^2)$ which grows with N considerably faster than the lower bound.

THE N LOG N ALGORITHM

An alternative to the z-buffer algorithm can be a method called the *NlogN algorithm*. It has been proven that given N non-intersecting line segments in the xz plane, this algorithm takes $O(N \log N)$ time in the worst case (Dévai, 1981, 1984). As we said before, $\Omega(N \log N)$ is the lower bound for the problem, so the algorithm is *worst-case optimal* under the algebraic tree model of computation.

The algorithm can be implemented by using an N-element heap. A convenient data structure for a heap is an array H, such that

$$H[i] \leq H[2i], \quad \text{and} \quad H[i] \leq H[2i+1]$$

for $3 \leq 2i+1 \leq N$. Each line segment in H will be represented by a pointer to a record containing the parameters of the appropriate line equation, and the x-coordinate of the left and that of the right endpoint. Upon insertion and deletion in H these line equations will be evaluated, and the obtained z-values will be used as keys. Then the NlogN algorithm can be implemented as follows.

(1) Sort the x-coordinates of the endpoints of the segments in increasing order: $x_i \leq x_{i+1} \leq \ldots \leq x_{2N}$
(2) <u>for</u> i := to 2N - 1 <u>do</u>
    <u>if</u> x_i is the left endpoint of a line segment L <u>then</u>
        insert L in H
    <u>else</u>   {x_i is the right endpoint of L}
        delete L from H
    <u>endif</u>;
    report H[1] as visible
<u>end</u>

Simple but efficient algorithms for heap insertion and deletion have been given by Knuth(1973), page 158, exercises 5.2.3.16 and 5.2.3.19.

ANALYSIS OF THE N LOG N ALGORITHM

Assume, first, *integer coordinates*, as in the case of the z-buffer alborithm. Then the sorting in step (1) can be implemented in O(N) time by using a *bucket sort* (Aho, Hopcroft and Ullman, 1975).

As for step (2), let Q(x) be an upper bound on any heap operation at point x. Then there exists a positive constant c such that

$$Q(x) \leq c \log d(x)$$

whenever $d(x) > 1$; otherwise $Q(x) = 0$. (All logarithms in this paper are to the base 2.) Then the running time of step (2)

$$T_2(N) \leq \sum_{i=1}^{2N} Q(x_i) \leq c \sum_{i=1}^{2N} \log d(x_i).$$

Since

$$\sum_{i=1}^{2N} \log d(x_i) = \log \prod_{i=1}^{2N} d(x_i)$$

$$= 2N \log \left(\prod_{i=1}^{2N} d(x_i) \right)^{\frac{1}{2N}}$$

$$\leq 2N \log \left(\frac{1}{2N} \sum_{i=1}^{2N} d(x_i) \right) = 2N \log D,$$

we can write

$$T_2(N) \leq 2 c N \log D,$$

where

$$D = \frac{1}{2N} \sum_{i=1}^{2N} d(x_i)$$

is the average depth complexity over the set of x-coordinates of the segment endpoints. The maximum possible value of D is the sum of the sequences 0, 1, ..., N-1 and N, N-1, ..., 1, divided by 2N, which is N/2.

Taking account the running time of step (1), we can conclude that if the endpoints of the line segments have integer coordinates, the running time of the NlogN algorithm is $O(N \log D)$, where $1 < D \leq N/2$.

The NlogN algorithm can also be used as a building block of three-dimensional exact visibility algorithms (Dévai, 1981), so the expected behaviour of these algorithms also depends on the expected running time of the NlogN algorithm. In this case the set of x-coordinates are *real numbers*, and using any comparison based sorting algorithm, the expected running time of step (1) is $\Theta(N \log N)$.

There is a class of sorting methods, however, called distributive sorting algorithms, with better than $\Theta(N \log N)$ expected running time (Dobosiewicz, 1978; van der Nat, 1985). Such a method is *distributive merge sorting* (DMS) that has a linear expected time for a wide class of input distributions, while retaining an $O(N \log N)$ worst-case time (Dévai and van der Nat, 1986). As opposed to other distributive methods, DMS retains the $O(N \log N)$ worst-case time without diminishing the expected performance.

We say that a function f(x) has *compact support* if there exist a constant K such that $f(x) = 0$ for all $x \notin [-K,K]$. For N records with key values independently drawn from a distribution with compact support, the expected time complexity of DMS is at most $c(f)N$, with a constant $c(f)$ depending on the probability density function f.

A uniform distribution obviously has compact support, so assume again that the x-coordinates of the endpoints of each segment are chosen uniformly and independently at random from the interval $[0,R]$, but now allowing real x-values.

First we determine $d(x_i)$ for $1 \leq i \leq 2N$. For any one of the i-1 points left to x_i, it holds that the segment incident on the point intersects the line $x = x_i$ with probability

$$\frac{2N - i + 1}{2N - 1} = p.$$

Then $d(x_i)$, for any fixed i, has a *binomial distribution*

$$P(d(x_i)=k) = \binom{i-1}{k} p^k (1-p)^{i-1-k}, \quad 0 \leq k \leq i-1.$$

The expected value of $d(x_i)$ is

$$E(d(x_i)) = (i - 1)p = (i - 1)\frac{2N - i + 1}{2N - 1},$$

and the expected value of D,

$$E(D) = E(\frac{1}{2N}\sum_{i=1}^{2N} d(x_i)) = \frac{1}{2N}\sum_{i=1}^{2N} E(d(x_i))$$

$$= \frac{1}{2N}\sum_{i=1}^{2N} (i - 1)\frac{2N - i + 1}{2N - 1} = \frac{2N + 1}{6}.$$

By similar reasoning as before, and substituting $E(D)$, we have

$$E(T_2(N)) \leq 2 c N \log E(D) = 2 c N \log((2N + 1)/6).$$

Although the expected running time of step (2) is $O(N \log N)$ for the above case when every endpoint is connected to any other with the same probability by a segment, for special cases, say if $E(D) = O(\log N)$, we should like to retain the overall $O(N \log E(D))$ expected time for the whole algorithm, including step (1). As we have seen, this is possible by using distributive sorting.

THEOREM 2. *Let the x-values of the segment endpoints be independent identically distributed random variables with a common density f, then the expected time of the NlogN algorithm is $O(N \log E(D))$ for any smooth f with compact support.*

We remark that distributive sorting algorithms assume a model of computation, called real RAM or N-tree, that is more powerful than the algebraic computation tree.

Sutherland, Sproull and Schumaker (1984), implicitly assumes constant average depth complexity for a hypothetical scene. Although we do not know whether this assumption is realistic in the practice, in this case both the z-buffer, and the NlogN algorithm would have linear expected time. It should be noted, however, that while the running time of the z-buffer algorithm grows linearly with the avarage depth complexity, the run time of the NlogN algorithm grows only logarithmically.

CONCLUSIONS

The expected running times of two scan-line algorithms are analysed assuming a uniform distribution of the x-coordinates of N line segments in the scan plane. While the expected time of the z-buffer algorithm can grow at least as fast as the function N^2, the expected time of the NlogN algorithm is best possible according to the $\Omega(N \log N)$ lower bound under the algebraic tree model of computation.

We pointed out that the number R of the picture elements in the scan line cannot be regarded as a constant, but rather as a parameter of the z-buffer algorithm. We claim that it is fair to assume that R is of order N, since R cannot be less than N if we want to be able to distinguish N objects.

REFERENCES

Aho, A.V., J.E. Hopcroft and J.D. Ullman (1975).*The Design and Analysis of Computer Algorithms*. Addison-Wesley, Reading, Mass.

Beatty, J.C., K.S. Booth and L.H. Mattheis (1981). Revisiting Watkins' algorithm. *Proc. 7th Canadian Man-Computer Communications Conference*, Toronto, Canada, 359-370.

Ben-Or, M. (1983). Lower bounds for algebraic computation trees, *Proc. 15th ACM Annual Symp. on Theory of Computing*, 80-86.

Bouknight, W.J. (1970). A procedure for generation of three-dimensional half-toned computer graphics presentations. *Commun. ACM*, 13,9, 527-536.

Clark, J.H. (1976). Hierarchical geometric models for visible surface algorithms. *Commun. ACM*, 19, 10, 547-554.

Dévai, F. (1981). *Complexity of visibility computations*. Dissertation for the degree of Candidate of Sciences. Hungarian Academy of Sciences, Budapest, Hungary, (In Hungarian).

Dévai, F. (1984). Complexity of two-dimensional visibility computations. *Proc. 3rd European Conference on CAD/CAM and Computer Graphics*, Paris, France, MICAD'84, Vol. 3, 827-841.

Dévai, F. (1985). A digital signal processor architecture for real-time image synthesis. *Proc. IEEE Int. Symp. New Directions in Computing*, Trondheim, Norway, 371-376.

Dévai, F. and M. van der Nat (1986). Distributive merge sorting. In M. Arató, I. Kátai and L. Varga (Eds.), *Topics in the Theoretical Bases and Applications of Computer Science*. Akadémiai K., Budapest, pp. 331-338.

Dévai, F. (1986). Quadratic bounds for hidden-line elimination. Accepted for presentation at the *1986 ACM Symposium on Computational Geometry*, Yorktown Heights, New York, USA.

Dobkin, D.P. and R.J. Lipton (1979). On the complexity of computations under varying sets of primitives. *J. Comput. & Syst. Sci. 18*, 86-91.

Dobosiewicz, W. (1978). Sorting by distributive partitioning. *Inf. Process. Lett. 7*,1, 1-6.

Foley, J.D. and A. van Dam (1982). *Fundamentals of Interactive Computer Graphics*. Addison-Wesley, Reading, Mass.

Forrest, A.R. (1980.) Recent work on geometric algorithms. In K.V. Brodlie (Ed.), *Mathematical Methods in Computer Graphics and Design*. Academic Press, London, pp. 105-121.

Fredman, M.L. and B. Weide (1978). On the complexity of computing the measure of U[ai,bi]. *Commun. ACM, 21*,7, 540-544.

Griffiths, J.G. (1979). Eliminating hidden edges in line drawings. *Comput. Aided Des. 11*,2), 71-78.

Hamlin, G. and C.W. Gear (1977). Raster-scan hidden surface algorithm techniques. *Comput. Graphics 11*,2, 206-213.

Knuth, D.E. (1973). *The Art of Computer Programming*, Vo. 3: Sorting and Searching. Addison-Wesley, Reading, Mass.

McKenna, M. (1986). *Worst-case optimal hidden-surface removal*. Report JHU/EECS-86/05, The Johns Hopkins University, Baltimore, Maryland.

van der Nat, M. (1985). Expected time complexity of a new class of distributive partitioning sort algorithms. In: *Two papers on distributive sorting*. Working P. GT/10, Comput. & Autom. Inst., Hung. Acad. Sci., Budapest, 3-8.

Newman, W.M. and R.F. Sproull (1979). *Principles of Interactive Computer Graphics*, 2nd ed. McGraw-Hill, New York.

Sutherland, I.E., R.F. Sproull and R.A. Schumaker (1974). A characterization of ten hidden-surface algorithms. *Comput. Surv. 6*,1, 1-55.

Watkins, G.S. (1979). *A real-time visible surface algorithm*. Computer Science, University of Utah, UTEC-CSc-70-101, Salt Lake City.

Yamaguchi, F. and T. Tokieda (1983). A solid modelling system: FREEDOM-II. *Comput. & Graphics 7*,3-4, 225-232.

A NEW GENERATION OF COMPUTATIONAL TOOLS IN STRUCTURAL ENGINEERING

L. Ebersolt, P. Verpeaux, M. Farvacque and A. Combescure

CEN Saclay DEMT/SMTS, 91191 Gif sur Yvette, France

P. Manigaut

Informatique Internationale, Agence de Saclay, Boîte Postale 24, 91190 Gif sur Yvette, France

The new concepts of operators and typed objects changed considerably the programming capacities for the finite element method in structural engineering.

Their greater versatility offers many advantages, especially the user's ability to modify or improve an algorithm merely by changing the dataset, without the involvement of the development team.

INTRODUCTION

Over the past twenty years, the finite element method has revolutionized the methods and concepts of structural design. Many finite elements have been developed and used successfully. Programs based on this method have virtually proliferated, but these programs often had capacities limited to a few elements or a few specific problems, and required the use of preprocessors (meshing) and post-processors (graphic plot).

The Castem 2000 structural design program under development is aimed to unify and homogenize a broad class of problems deriving from the theory of finite elements <6,7>. In terms of data processing, this effort was made possible through the concepts of operators and typed objects, and the use of an ESOPE FORTRAN precompiler designed for dynamic management of the memory. This data processing architecture offers many advantages providing an example of the application of the recent concepts of software engineering.

In the presence state of its development, the Castem 2000 structural engineering computation program has proved its capacities concerning:

- standard elements (two- and three-dimensional massive elements),
- elastic problems with different load cases (thermal, pressure),

- non-linear methods (large shell displacements),
- 'original' elements such as the Linespring model.

This paper focuses on the following points:

- concepts of operators and typed objects,
- software advantages of these concepts,
- mechanical advantages of these concepts,
- example of a non-linear algorithm,
- example of computation with the Linespring model.

CONCEPT OF OPERATORS AND TYPED OBJECTS

The operators act on typed objects

The concept of operators is intimately linked with that of typed objects. Castem 2000 handles typed objects by means of operators, and the objects are created at the user's discretion by means of an operator library.

An operator performs three tasks:

- acquisition of argument objects of the operator: thanks to the typing of these objects, it can check the validity of the operator's syntax,
- actual computations,
- writing of the result object.

In other words, each operator acts independently of the others, both for computation and for error management.

What objects?

The different objects are classed in two categories.

- Objects required for the mesh:
    - POINT
    - ELEMENT

The objects of the POINT type store the point coordinates, while the objects of the ELEMENT type store the data concerning a mesh.

Objects required for numerical computation:
- AFFECTE
- CHPOINT
- CHAMELEM
- RIGIDITE
- SOLUTION

Objects of the AFFECTE type specify the type of finite element to be used.

Objects of the CHAMELEM type store the data whose geometric supports are objects of the ELEMENT type.

Objects of the CHPOINT type store the data whose geometric supports are objects of the POINT type.

Objects of the RIGIDITE type store the rigidity and mass matrices.

Objects of the SOLUTION type store all the intermediate results in an iterative computation.

Which operators?

Various categories of operator are available:
- mesh operators,
- mechanics operators,
- 'utility' operators.

The main mechanics operators are:
- AFFECT   declaration of the finite element formulation,
- RIGI   computation of rigidity matrices,
- MASSE   computation of mass matrices,
- RESOU   inversion of a matrix,
- SIGMA   stress computations,
- BSIGMA   stress divergence computations,
- VIBRAT   eigenvector computations.

To give an example, the main steps in an elastic computation may be:
- specification of a certain number of POINT,
- ELEMENT mesh,
- declaration of the finite element formulation (AFFECT operator),
- mechanical properties (CRECHA operator),
- loading and boundary conditions (FORCE and BLOQUE operators),
- computation of the rigidity matrix (RIGI operators),
- resolution of $Ku = F$ (RESOU operator),
- stress computations (SIGMA operator).

The main steps of an eigenmode search computation are identical to those listed above, apart from the last three:

- RIGI operator,
- MASSE operator,
- VIBRAT operator.

The main steps in a buckling mode search computation will be:

- RIGI operator,
- KSIGMA operator,
- VIBRAT operator.

Software advantages

The concepts of operators and typed objects offer the user a number of advantages.

- First, a LIST operator exists, which prints an object: this considerably reduces the amount of paper unnecessarily printed, because the user chooses the data he wishes to see.

- The versatility of the operators helps to develop a true interactive finite element program: the user decides to use certain operators (error messages may or may not appear on the screen) and the machine responds at the end of the execution of each operator. The Castem 2000 system can therefore be learned rapidly, since the machine responds immediately.

- Also available is the possibility of performing a symbolic computation to generate CHPOINT type objects, varying with the polynomial functions of the coordinates.

The user can make a preliminary computation by finite elements (patch test) and then, by another sequence of operators, retrieve these results, which serve to validate the finite element computations very quickly.

EXAMPLE OF A NON-LINEAR ALGORITHM

Mechanical problem

The mechanical problem is that of a computation with large shell displacements. This requires computations of the equilibrium equations on the deformed configurations <8>.

The BSIGMA operator performs this function and, by calculating this divergence on different configurations, serves to evaluate the forces due to the change in geometry.

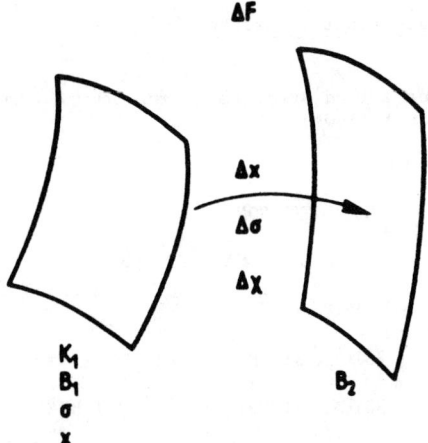

Figure 1 Non-linear algorithm with large shell displacements

For a load increment ΔF applied to configuration 1, the algorithm is written:

$$K_1 \, \Delta x_{n+1} = \Delta F$$

$$\Delta \sigma = D \, B_1 \, \Delta x_{n+1}$$

$$F_1 = {}^t B_1 \, (\Delta \sigma + \sigma_1)$$

$$F_2 = {}^t B_2 \, (\Delta \sigma + \sigma_1)$$

$$\Delta F = \Delta F + F_1 - F_2$$

$$\text{if } ||\Delta x_{n+1} - \Delta x_n|| \lesssim \varepsilon \quad \text{end}$$

with the following notations:

- $x,\ \ , K\ , B$ coordinates of configuration 1, stresses, rigidity matrix, divergence operator

- B_2 divergence operator of configuration 2

- $\Delta x_n,\ \Delta x_{n+1},\ \Delta F,\ \Delta \sigma$ increments of force displacements and stresses.

Transcription of the algorithm in Castem 2000

In Castem 2000, and for a load step, the algorithm in terms of operators is written as follows:

```
REPETER PAS 5

DXNP1   =  RESOU KNA FON

DSIGN   =  SIGMA DXNP1 MAT1 EPA1 X

SIGNP1  =  DSIGN + SIG

FOR1N   =  BSIGMA SIGNP1 X EPA1

FOR2N   =  BSIGMA SIGNP1 (X + DXNP1) EPA1

FORN    =  FOR1N - FOR2N

FON     =  FORN + DFORCE

XNORM   =  XTX (DXN - DXNP1)

TANT QUE (XNORM < PREC)
```

The following should be noted.

The use of the operators REPETER and TANT QUE, which serve to execute a sequence of instructions as often as desired, which is vital for iterative algorithms.

The use of the standard operator XTX, which helps the user to modify the convergence tests and to improve the algorithm.

The typed objects employed correspond closely to the mathematical notations in the previous section:

K_1	KNA	This algorithm was used for the computation of a flawed ring subjected to external pressure. Figure 5 compares the computation with the analytical solution for a mesh of 40 DKT type shell elements.
ΔF	FON	
σ	SIG	
$\Delta\sigma_n$	DSIGN	
$\Delta\sigma_{n+1}$	DSIGNP1	
x	X	
Δx_n	DXN	
Δx_{n+1}	DXNP1	

EXAMPLE OF COMPUTATION WITH THE LINESPRING MODEL

The Linespring model

The Linespring model is a three-dimensional model with four nodes and 24 degrees of freedom modelling a partly through crack and calculating the stress intensity factor at the crack front <5,9>.

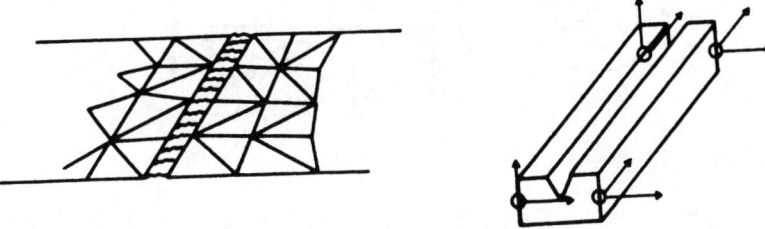

Figure 2   Linespring model

The Linespring model was tested on configurations of different complexities:

.   first on plates under bending or tensile stress,
.   then on cylinders with a circumferential crack of constant depth <10>,
.   and on cylinders under internal pressure with an elliptical longitudinal crack.

The calculated value of K approaches to within 10% of the analytical value at the notch root.   The value in the neighbourhood of the skin of the shell is less accurate, as may have been expected, given the assumptions in the formulation of the model.

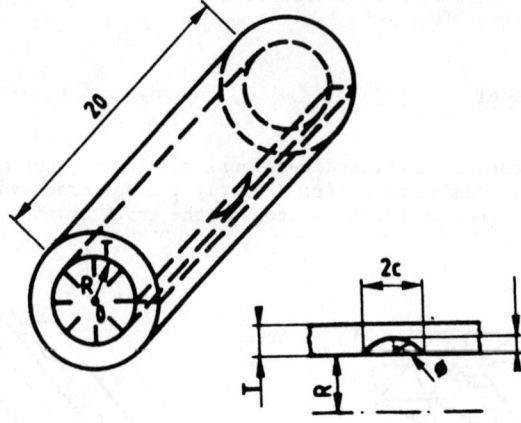

Figure 3   Cylinder under internal pressure with elliptical crack

The primary value of this model resides in the small number of unknowns used in comparison with the massive element models required for the previous analyses, therefore helping to cut computation costs considerably.

Virtual extension method

The Linespring model computes the stress intensity factor along a direction perpendicular to the plane of the plate. This leaves the question of computing the stress intensity factor parallel to the plane of the plate at point B, because this concept is absent from the formulation of the model.

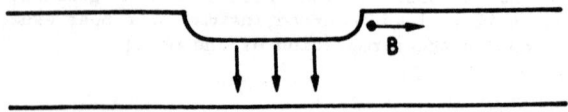

Figure 4   Stress intensity factor at point B

One possibility is nevertheless available, by using the operator concept. The stress intensity factor at point B is written:

$$\frac{1 - \nu^2}{E} K_{B^2} = {}^t u \, dKu$$

where u is the displacement field, and dK the variation in the rigidity matrix in a virtual extension of the crack.

In the Castem 2000 program, this expression is calculated with three lines:

    K1 = RIGI MAT CAR

    K2 = RIGI MAT CAR DE1

    DELTA = XTMX DE1 (K1 - K2)

Note the close analogy between the algebraic expression and its transcription in the data language of Castem 2000.

CONCLUSION

In the past year, the Castem 2000 system has witnessed extremely promising development, eighteen elements having been completed in the elastic region during this period, together with the implementation of non-linear algorithms for shell elements.

The structuration of the program and its great versatility offer considerable advantages both for development and maintenance, as well as for the development of new algorithms.

Future development trends are aimed to integrate plasticity for different types of behaviour, as well as a wider range of finite elements.

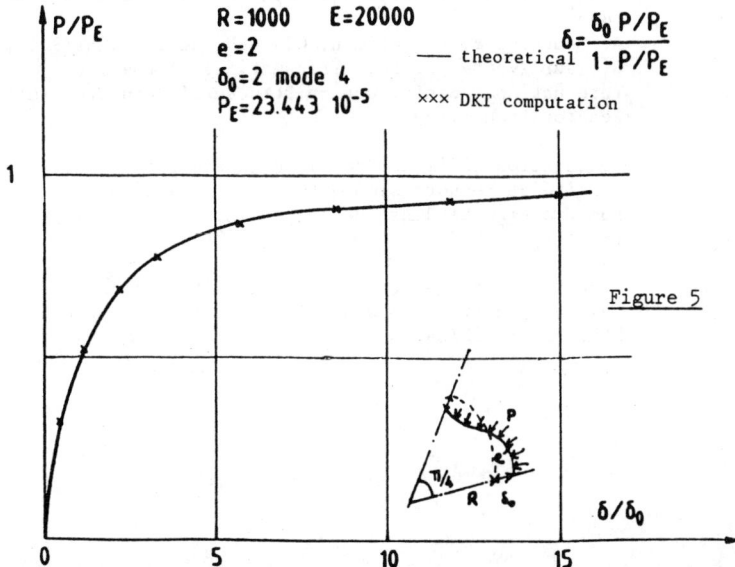

Figure 5

REFERENCES

<1>   Compendium of stress intensity factors
      Rooke, Cartwright

<2>   Elastic plastic analysis of surface flaws using a
      simplified Linespring model
      R.D. King, Engineering Fracture Mechanics, $\underline{18}$ (1)
      217-231 (1983)

<3>   Stress intensity factors for internal surface cracks
      in cylindrical vessels
      Neuman, Raju, Transaction of the ASME, VOL.102,
      November 1980, 343-346

<4>   Elastic surface crack analysis using a shell Linespring
      Model
      Kuman, Cerman, Schumacher, EPRI Report EPRI/NP/3607,
      August 1984, Advances in Elastic/Plastic Fracture
      Analysis

<5>   Mécanique de la rupture
      Bui

<6>   The finite element method
      O.C. Zienkiewicz, McGraw-Hill

<7>   Finite element procedures in engineering analysis
      Klaus Jürgen Bathe, Prentice Hall, 1982

<8>   Non-linear analysis of shells (large displacements),
      Use of the equilibrium equations based on the deformed
      body
      A. Combescure, A. Hoffman, CEA/CEN Saclay, DEMT/SMTS,
      Gif sur Yvette, France, Transactions of the 5th
      International Conference on Structural Mechanics in
      Reactor Technology

<9>   Formulation bidimensionnelle d'un élément 'Linespring' ou
      densité de ressort simulant l'ouverture d'une fissure
      non traversante dans une coque mince
      DEMT Report 85/163

<10> Rapport de validation de l'élément 'Linespring',
      Cylindre en traction avec fissure circonférentielle
      DEMT Report 85/247

MODIFIED FINITE ELEMENTS FOR EFFICIENT USE IN CAD-ENVIRONMENT

O. Ohtmer

California State University, Long Beach, CA 90840, USA

ABSTRACT

The aim is to integrate Finite Element (FE) software in Computer Aided Design (CAD) software in order to simplify the usage at an engineers workstation.
Solid models, which provide even more complete mathematical information than wireframes are proposed as the foundation for drafting. The database for solid models is also used for Finite Element analysis of structural and thermal properties as well as for NC-(numerical control) machine tools and robotics manufacturing cells.
Not only the generation of solid models is suggested to integrate FE-Analysis in CAD-Environment. In addition several new, numerical algorithms and procedures in FE-analysis are discussed for efficient use in CAD-environment.

KEYWORDS

Finite Elements; Boundary Elements; Computer Aided Design Software; Engineers Workstation; Hard-Software supported Education; Equilibrium Models in Closed Meshes; Optimisation Procedures; Solid Modelling; Conformal Mapping; Animations; Simplified Input Commands; Automatic Conversion to special FE-and CAD- Software- Packages.

1. INTRODUCTION

Today many FE- (Finite Element) Software-Packages (STRUDL, NASTRAN, ANSYS, ADINA, etc.) are available to calculate linear or nonlinear problems in many different areas (static-, dynamic-, and buckling analysis; heat transfer-, network-, and flow analysis). In addition several general purpose CAD -(Computer Aided Design) Software Packages (CADAM, EUCLID, CD2000, CATIA, MOVIE etc.) are widely used at universities and industries to generate all kinds of design draftings.
During, the last years many attempts were made to integrate Finite Element calculations in CAD -Environment. Indeed, CAD-, and Finite Element (FE) Software Packages must be available at the engineers workstation.

The question is only how to integrate the named software packages that their application is very easy and efficient [5].
If a plate bending-, plane stress-or shell problem has to be designed, the engineer can not take advantage of a common data base because of a few characteristical geometric data required for the CAD-Program systems; while the standard FE-Program Systems need many input data (joint coordinates and element incidences specifying a fine idealization of the structure) for calculation of displacements and stresses within reasonable accuracy.

A more general approach will be discussed in this paper to simplify the designing procedure. We are considering methods which are under research work today and already applied in many cases.

Not only FE- procedures can be changed to simplify the usage in an CAD-environment. The CAD- Software itself should be modified in the sense that solid models become the foundation for drafting. Only solid models contain complete mathematical information. Only solid models create the illusion of a part, allowing the engineer to quickly understand the part geometry and eliminating the ambiguities that arise when working with wireframes.

Nine different numerical algorithms and procedures for efficient use in CAD-environment are going to be discussed below.

o Implementation of an efficient solution of large linear systems of equations with arbitrary bandwidth.
o Implementation of special Boundary Elements in Finite Element Software Packages.
o Implementation of Equilibrium Models applied in Closed Meshes in a Finite Element Analysis.
o Implementation of Structural Optimization Procedures.
o Optimized mesh generation of substructures by conformal mappings.
o Using a deformed structure model to modify a generated mesh.
o Solid modelling as the foundation for drafting and FE -calculation.
o Standard simplified input-output-operation - commands for FE -and CAD -Software packages.
o Animations of moving structures and mechanisms.

2. IMPLEMENTATION OF AN EFFICIENT SOLUTION OF LARGE LINEAR SYSTEMS OF EQUATIONS WITH ARBITRARY BANDWIDTH.

The Gauss-or Cholesky-elimination procedure implemented in FE-Systems is efficient only for minimized bandwidth [14,][13]. By applying the Cuthill-Mckee algorithm reordering the joint numbers the bandwidth can be minimized. Applying Irons' frontal solution method, a minimized bandwidth can be obtained reordering the Finite Element numbers [15]. Often within the bandwidth many zeros are occurring which should also be ignored during the elimination procedure. In Figure 1 a large sparse matrix with minimized bandwidth is listed. The "2" on the main-diagonal represents squared submatrices of "matrix size" $\approx$ 45. The "rows" represent rows of submatrices. The "1" is a rectangular submatrix containing non-zero values, the "0" is a rectangular submatrix with only zero values. The whole stiffness matrix of a shaker conveyor has about 10000 degrees of freedom. The marked hyperrow within the bandwidth for example contains 20 submatrices, only 5 of them are non-zero.

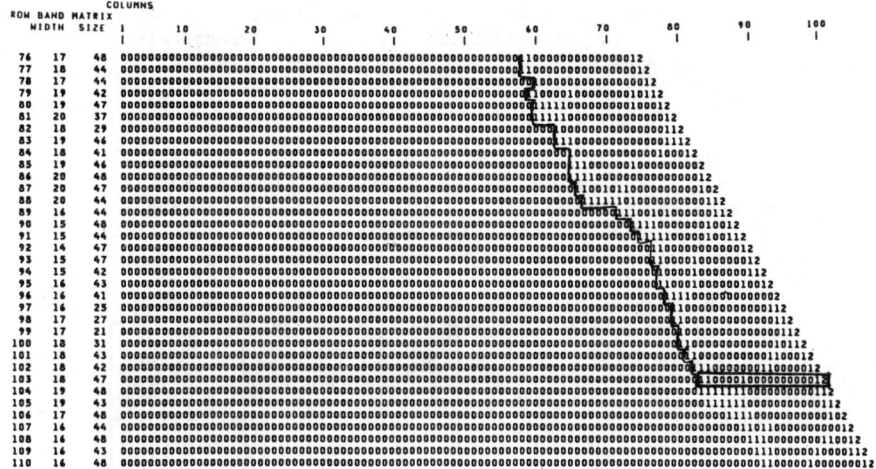

Figure 1 partitioned stiffness matrix in submatrices.

An efficient elimination algorithm for an arbitrary bandwidth without renumbering can be implemented by performing a variable partitioning of the global stiffness-and mass matrix. Only the non-zero submatrices in each hyperrow are stored during the assembling procedure [14]. In Fig. 2 a simple plane TRUSS-structure is shown consisting of 5 joints A,B,C,D and E, (10 degrees of freedom 1 to 10) and 4 elements (K1 to K4). On the main-diagonal the quadratic submatrices are named [KD](i), the non-zero off-diagonal rectangular submatrices are named [KO] (i,j). It does not matter, that the off-diagonal submatrices originally are arranged a little bit different. In general a submatrix contains the degrees of freedom of more than one joint.

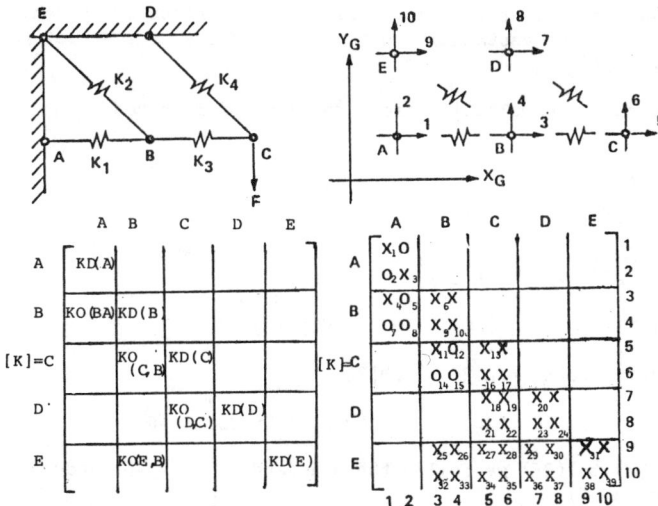

Figure 2. Assembling the Global Element Stiffness Matrices

In (1) a linear system of equations is written in matrix notation with the stiffness matrix [K] as coefficient-matrix. As demonstrated in Figure 2 only the nonzero submatrices [KO](i,j) are stored.

$$[K] * \{X\} = \{F\} \tag{1}$$

The Cholesky elimination procedure for symmetric matrices is applied in partitioned form. The generation of the "LOWER TRIANGLE" matrix [L] can easily be explained multiplying [L] with its transpose triangle matrix $[L]^T$. The product is equal to the given matrix [K] which is stated in the Cholesky-Method.

$$[L] * [L]^T = [K] \tag{2}$$

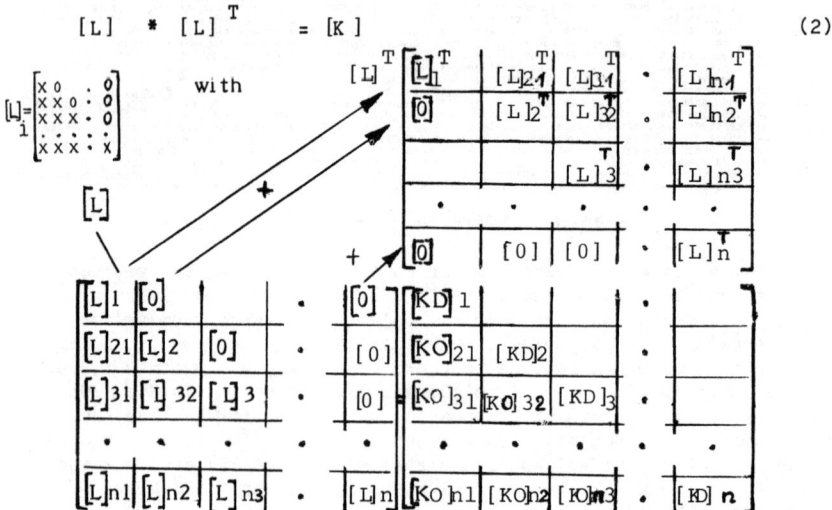

The unknown submatrices $[L]_i$ are triangle submatrices of the shown structure $[L]_{i,j}$ are rectangular submatrices of the same structure as $[KO]_{i,j}$.

The errows show the multiplication procedure of matrices.
We obtain:

$$[L]1 * [L]1^T = [KD]1 \tag{3a}$$

$$[L]21 * [L]1^T = [KO]21 \tag{3b}$$

$$[L]21 * [L]21^T + [L]2 * [L]2^T = [KD]2 \tag{3c}$$

$$[L]31 * [L]1^T = [KO]31 \tag{3d}$$

$$[L]31 * [L]21^T + [L]32 * [L]2^T = [KO]32 \tag{3e}$$

$$[L]31 * [L]31^T + [L]32 * [L]32^T + [L]33 * [L]33^T = [KD]3 \tag{3f}$$

To solve (3a) to (3f) we follow the standard cholesky-procedure [16] p. 155) given in (4).

$$L_{ii} = (KD_{ii} - \sum_{k=1}^{i-1} L_{ik}^2)^{\frac{1}{2}}; \quad L_{ij} = (KO_{ij} - \sum_{k=1}^{j-1} L_{ik} * L_{jk})/L_{jj} \quad \text{for } j<i) \quad (4)$$

Applying the equations in (3) to solve the example in Figure 2 with (3a) and (4) we obtain $[L]_A$, applying (3b) and (4) $[L]_{BA}$ can be calculated. (3d) states that $[L]_{CA}$ is zero because $[KO]_{CA}$ is zero. $[L]_{DA}$ and $[L]_{DB}$ are zero because $[KO]_{DA}$ and $[KO]_{DB}$ are zero. Applying the same procedure to the hyperrow E in Figure 2 we realize that the positioning of the submatrices in [K] and [L] are not identical. Only the submatrices $[L]_i$ and $[KD]_i$ are always nonzero.

$[L]_{EA} = 0$; $[L]_{EB} \neq 0$; and also $[L]_{EC}$ and $[L]_{ED}$ are now nonzero although $[KO]_{EC}$ and $[KO]_{ED}$ are zero. Calculating the submatrices in the hyperrows 1 to n we must store the positions of nonzero submatrices $[L]_{i,j}$.

The multiplication of nonzero submatrices can be written in the following FORTRAN notation which is a modified version of Cholesky-procedure for submatrices (see [16] p.155).

```
C   [L]1*[L]1ᵀ = [KD] 1      solve for [L]1, applying (4)
    DO 1 I=2, N
    IB = IBAND (I) -I
    DO 2 J = IB, I
    JB = IBAND(J) - J
    LB = MAXO(IB,JB)                                                  (5)
C   [X]= [KO](I,J)  store submatrix [KO](I,j) in matrix [X]
    NN = IG (I,J)
    DO 3 K = 1,NN
    KK = IA(I,K)
C3  [X] =    [X] - [L](I,KK) *[L] (J,KK)
C   multiplication of submatrices and adding to [X]; inverting triangle
C   matrix [L](J,J) and multiplying with [X] applying (4).
C2  [L] (I,J)  =    [X] * [L](J,J)
C1  [L](I,I) * [L]ᵀ(I,I) = [X]        solve for [L](I,I)
```

IBAND (I) specifies the bandwidth of matrix [K] measured in hypercolumns. IG (I,J) specifies the number of hypercolumns KK with nonzero submatrices [L](j,kk) in the hyperrow I. <u>Hypercolumn J is excluded.</u> [IA](I,K) specifies the associated hypercolumn to K.
The whole procedure is visualized in Figure 3. Given is the stiffness matrix [K] in partitioned form. The lower triangle matrix [L] is generated.

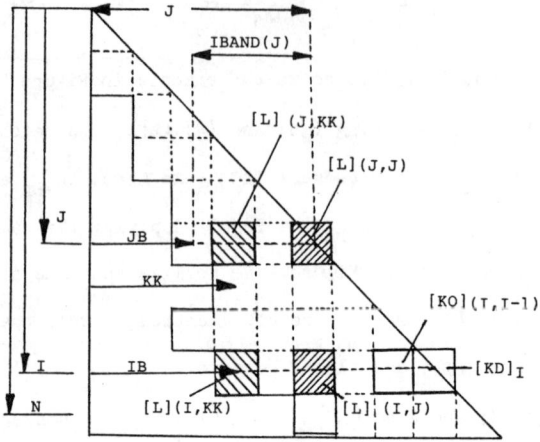

Fig. 3 Visualising the partitioned Cholesky Method for arbitrary bandwidth.

As shown in (3) only the submatrices of the triangle matrix [L] in the same hypercolumn are multiplied. [L] is generated hyperrow-wise which is stated in (5) and [17].
In Figure 3 the first hypercolumn considered is IB; the last one in this case IB + 1. (3) proves that hypercolumn J is excluded. The Cholesky-backsubstitution can be performed with the known lower triangle matrix [L] in partitioned form [17].

In general rearranging the partitioned triangle matrix [L] or [K] in Figure 2 and store them row-wise in blocks is not very time consuming due to [14]. A block then contains a specified number of rows. If the submatrices [KD](i) and [KO](i,j) in Figure 2 are stored blockwise in hyperrows (in this case two rows per block) in the submatrices [A](i) the values X_i in Figure 2 are reordered as shown in (6).
This procedure being similar to the one given in [16] p. 155 is only recommendable if the bandwidth is minimized.

$\{A\}(1) = \{X_1 \blacksquare 0_2 X_3 \blacksquare\}$

$\{A\}(2) = \{X_4 \ 0_5 \ X_6 \ \blacksquare 0_7 \ 0_8 \ X_9 \ X_{10} \ \blacksquare\}$

$\{A\}(3) = \{X_{11} \ 0_{12} \ X_{13} \ \blacksquare 0_{14} \ 0_{15} \ X_{16} \ X_{17} \blacksquare\}$ (6)

$\{A\}(4) = \{X_{18} \ X_{19} X_{20} \blacksquare X_{21} X_{22} X_{23} X_{24} \blacksquare\}$

$\{A\}(5) = \{X_{25} X_{26} \ 0_{27} 0_{28} 0_{29} 0_{30} X_{31} \blacksquare X_{32} \ X_{33} \ 0_{34} 0_{35} 0_{36} 0_{37} X_{38} X_{39} \blacksquare\}$

IAG (1) = 1; IAG(2) =3; IAG(3) =6; IAG(4) = 10; IAG (5) = 13; IAG(6) = 17; IAG (7) = 20; IAG(8) = 24; IAG(9) = 31; IAG(10) =39

The integer array IAG (i) indicates the addresses of the diagonal values in [K] in Figure 2.

3. IMPLEMENTATION OF SPECIAL BOUNDARY ELEMENTS IN FINITE ELEMENT SOFTWARE PACKAGES.

For so-called boundary elements the stress-and displacement-distribution can be expressed by analytical functions. Therefore, the area integrals in the Hybrid-Stress Functional containing the parameters of variation in quadratic form are zero. The first and second variation are applied only to boundary integrals to generate the element stiffness matrix. Within these elements the equilibrium and compatibility equations are fulfilled continuously. Therefore, it is no longer necessary to idealize domains by a relative fine grid to obtain accurate results. Considering the above the problem can be described by a system of equations of relative small size [2].

Figure 4 shows a plane stress problem. The crack requires a special Finite Element Idealisation consisting of a singular boundary element, isoparametric elements and special quadrilateral boundary elements. The isoparametric elements are used because their edges may be curved.

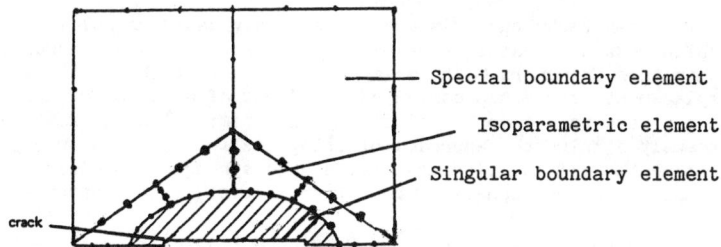

Figure 4 Practical Idealization of a structure with singularities

4. IMPLEMENTING EQUILIBRIUM MODELS APPLIED IN CLOSED MESHES IN A FINITE ELEMENT ANALYSIS.

Most finite element programs applied to structural analysis use displacement models and treat mode displacements as the primary unknowns. However, in many cases, the designer would prefer to work directly in terms of stress resultants and stress fields which satisfy completely the equilibrium conditions. The stress resultants can be treated as element unknowns, and the model can be analyzed using the flexibility method also known as the force-or mesh method. The computation of closed meshes (solution of a topological problem in graph-theory) is not a time consuming procedure. Rigid elements can easily be taken into account. One-two-and-three-dimensional elements can easily be coupled. Multi-connected areas are detected during the definition of closed meshes.

Since the input can be specified as for displacement models, it is possible to perform the analysis using force-or displacement models. Both methods are converging against the exact solution from different sides, lower and upper bounds are specified. Therefore, it is possible to estimate the accuracy of the approximated finite element solution by bracketing the exact solution [3], [4].

In Figure 5 a standard Finite Element Idealisation of a plane stress problem by triangle elements is given. (Idealisation by quadrilateral elements is also possible.) In Figure 6 six closed meshes are automatically analysed. Basic stress resultants are introduced at the cut edges (marked by dashed lines). The cut forces are interpreted as loadings on the remaining "TREE-Structure."

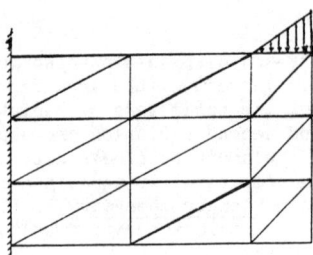 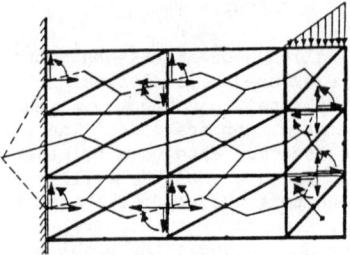

Fig. 5 Finite Element idealisation of a cantilever and load pattern

Fig. 6 Interior graph with a tree emphasised.

5. IMPLEMENTATION OF STRUCTURAL OPTIMIZATION PROCEDURES.

Optimization techniques discussed are mainly based on solving a displacement-constrained problem with stress constraints accomodation within this framework. The main drawback is that the finite element displacement method has dominated the field of analyis for many years and has been used almost exclusively in optimization work. While extremely simple, the approach of using the force method concept to overcome the difficulties associated with strength optimization of redundant systems appears to be entirely novel, (see Chapter 4.)

At the present it seems that for combining generality with computational efficiency the best approach is to modify and augment the finite element packages for providing derivative (also called sensitivity) calculations needed in the structural optimization procedure. Since engineers aim is to produce efficient designs, an important contribution in this area is made by optimization theory and the computer based methods which result from the practical application of this theory. The named procedures enable the engineer to design structures very efficiently because the manual iteration procedure applying conventional Finite Element Programs is now replaced by fully automated internal iterations within the optimization.

Twenty years ago a special procedure was already implemented in STRUDL [14]. It makes sense to implement today other more sophisticated optimization algorithms in FE - Systems. The optimization procedure sometimes is very time-consuming proportional the square of the number of unknowns. Therefore it is recommendable to apply the optimization algorithm to boundary elements proposed in [2]. Working with boundary elements instead of displacement models we obtain good approximations already for a small number of unknowns. Due to the displacements, stresses, or eigenvectors a different design sensitivity analysis is performed. With u_j^i the displacement constraint value for the j-th degree of freedom under the i-th loading condition and $\bar{u}_j$ the allowable dispalcement we specify:

$$u_j^i - \bar{u}_j \leq 0; \quad j = 1,2,\ldots n_d; \quad i = 1,2,\ldots n_c \qquad (7)$$

n_d = number of displacements; n_c = number of loading conditions

With σ_j^i, the element stress constraint value for the j - th critical point under the i-th loading condition and $\bar{\sigma}_j$ the allowable stress we can define:

$$\sigma_j^i - \bar{\sigma}_j \leq 0 \quad ; \quad j = 1,2,\ldots n_s; \quad n_s = \text{number of stresses} \quad (8)$$

A more general function constraint ψ_j may be introduced:

$$\psi_j(\{b\}, \{u^i\}) \leq 0 \quad ; \quad j = 1,2,\ldots n(i); \quad i = 1,2,\ldots n_c \quad (9)$$

$\{u^i\}$ = computed displacement vector.
$\{b\}$ = design variable vector
n_c = number of loading conditions.
$n(i)$ = number of constraints

A design variable can be as simple as the cross-sectional area of a rod element or the modulus of elasticity of a specific element to a complex linking of many individual element cross-sectional properties (such as the area and second moments for beam type elements) along with a complex linking together of many individual finite element properties (thickness). The constraint values themselves are determined from the relationship:

$$\psi_i = \frac{(\text{Constraint value})^o}{|\text{Limit}|} - 1. * \text{sgn(Limit)} \quad (10)$$

In the Finite Element Formulation we define the "First Variation" as:

$$\frac{\partial \Pi}{\partial \{u\}^T} = 0 \quad (11)$$

Associated linear System of Equations

$$[K] \cdot \{u\} = \{F\} \quad (12)$$

Π = total potential energy; $\{u\}$ = global displacement vector
$[K]$ = global stiffness matrix; $\{F\}$ = load vector

The "Second Variation" known as Iterative Solution of Nonlinear Equations may be written in the notation:

$$\frac{\partial ([K])}{\partial \{u\}} \cdot \{u\} + [K] \cdot \frac{\partial \{u\}}{\partial \{u\}} = \frac{\partial \{F\}}{\partial \{u\}} \quad (13)$$

or

$$[K] \cdot \{\Delta u\} = \{\Delta F\} - [\Delta K]\{u\} \quad (14)$$

According to the "Second Variation" the Design Sensitivity Solution in statics is specified in (15) following a proposal in [13]:

$$\delta v_i^{(k)} = \left\{ \left\{ \frac{\Delta v_i^{(k)}}{\Delta b_j} \right\}^T + \left\{ \frac{\Delta v_i^{(k)}}{\Delta u_j} \right\}^T \left[\frac{\Delta u_j}{\Delta b_j} \right] \right\}^T \{\delta b_j\} = \{A_{ij}^{(k)}\}^T \{\delta b_j\} \quad (15)$$

ψ_i = i-th constraint; b_j = j-th design variable

Λ_{ij}^k = derivative of ψ_i with respect to the j-th design variable for the k-th physical load condition (a term of the design sensitivity matrix).

The components Λ_{ij} of the design sensitivity matirx are called the sensitivity coefficients of the constraint ψ_i with respect to the corresponding design variables. These derivatives represent the effect of a design change on a constraint. Specifically, if the component Λ_{ij} is positive, an increase in b_j will increase ψ_i. If Λ_{ij} is negative, an increase in b_j will decrease ψ_i. Also, the order of magnitude of the various sensitivity coefficients Λ_{ij} determine which design variables have a significant effect on ψ_i. For a more detailed overview the following publications are highly recommended: [7], [8], [9], [10], [11], [12].

6. OPTIMIZED MESH GENERATION OF SUBSTRUCTURES BY CONFORMAL MAPPINGS.

Conformal mappings are not only useful to delete geometric singularities (see chapter 3), they can also be applied to optimise the Finite Element mesh generation. In Figure 7 the Joukowski Transformation (17) is applied to generate an FE - Idealisation around an aerofoil **or circle**.

$$\zeta = Z + a^2/Z \qquad (17)$$

ζ, Z = complex variables, a^2 = real constant

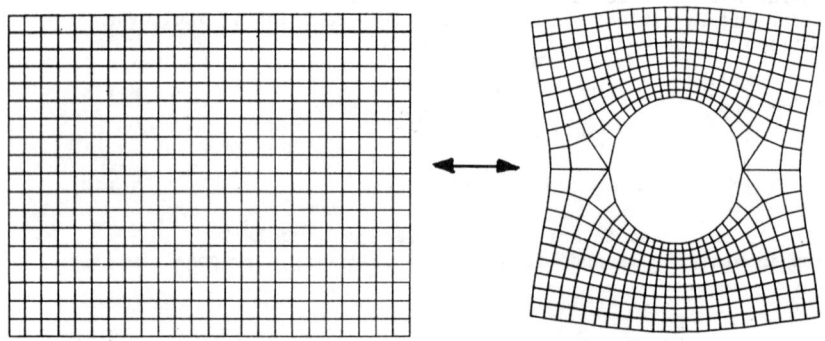

Fig. 7. Finite Element mesh generation by conformal mapping around a circle.

The demonstrated method is not restricted to plane structures.
Optimised meshes can also be obtained for cylindrical-, spherical-and
torus- surfaces because the named surfaces can be transformed to plane
surfaces by conformal mappings.

7. USING A DEFORMED STRUCTURE MODEL TO MODIFY A GENERATED MESH

In standard FE programs you may specify displamcements or forces as
loadings. The deformed frame plate-or shell structure is a smooth
structure in the sense of an approximation by cubic spline functions.
Indeed, it can be shown that the deformed structure is identical with
the one obtained by applying 1D - 2D - or 3D- spline functions to
generate a smooth curvature or surface through the given joints defined
by the deformation of the structure. Therefore it is recommendable to
implement in FE -systems a command to add computed deformations to the
joint coordinates of the undeformed structure. A large variety of modified structures can then be generated without changing the element
incidences. In Fig. 8 a cylindrical shell is fixed supported at the
left hand side and subjected to given displacements at the right hand
side.

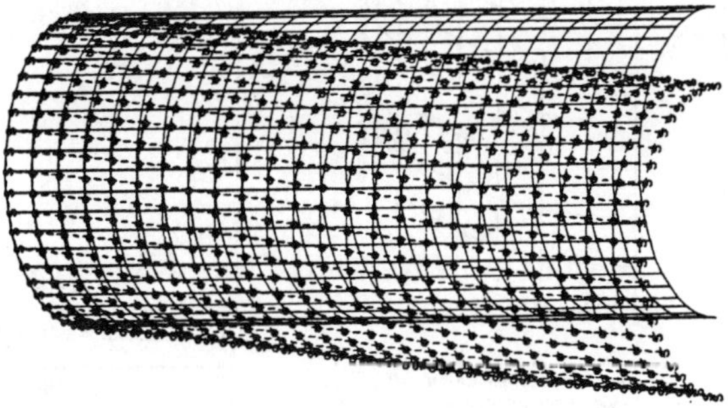

FIG. 8 Deformation of a cylindrical cantilever shell subjected to given displacements.

8. SOLID MODELLING AS THE FOUNDATION FOR DRAFTING AND FE - CALCULATION.

Most computer-aided drafting packages have 2D databases, although many
packages are now based on 3D-wireframes. Experts predict, however, that
soon solid models, which provide even more complete mathematical
information will replace wireframes as the foundation for drafting. The
following statement is given in [18]. "Solid models create the
illusion of a part allowing the engineer to quickly understand the part
geometry and eliminating the ambiguities that arise when working with
wireframes." Because solids contain a more complete description of a
part, the database can be used in other engineering functions.
Engineering analysis of thermal and structural properties can take
advantage of solid model data. NC machine tools and even robotics
manufacturing cells can use the part geometries generated by a solid
modeler. In Fig. 9, a cylindrical wall is generated by GTSTRUDL in a
command language which is self-documenting.

STRUDL - Input
STRUDL 'CYLTRI'
UNITS DEGREE
GENE 10 JOI CYL ID 1 INC 1 R 0.525 INC 0.0 THETA 0.0 INC 10.
REPEAT 9 TIMES ID INC 10 LY INC 0.1
REPEAT 2 TIMES ID INC 100 RADIUS INC -0.025
TYPE TRIDIMENSIONAL
GENERATE 9 ELEMENTS ID 1 INC 1 FROM 1 INC 1 TO 2 INC 1 TO 102 INC 1 -
TO 101 INC 1 TO 11 INC 1 TO 12 INC 1 TO   112 INC 1 TO   111 INC 1
REPEAT 8 TIMES ID INC 9 FROM INC 10 TO 10
REPEAT 1 TIME ID INC 81 FROM INC 100 TO 100

Graphical representation only
contour lines drawn.
(rotated about x-axis by $\varphi_x = 30°$).

FINISH

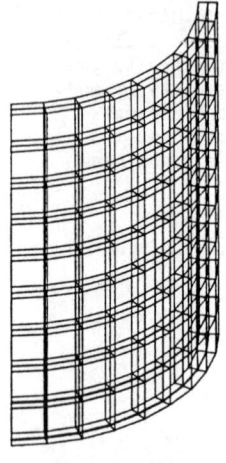

Graphical representation without
hidden lines removed.
(rotated about x-axis by $\varphi_x = 30°$)

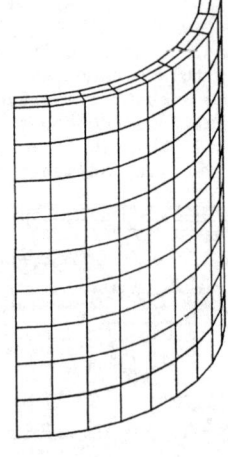

Graphical representation with
hidden lines removed.
(rotated about x-axis by $\varphi_x = 30°$)

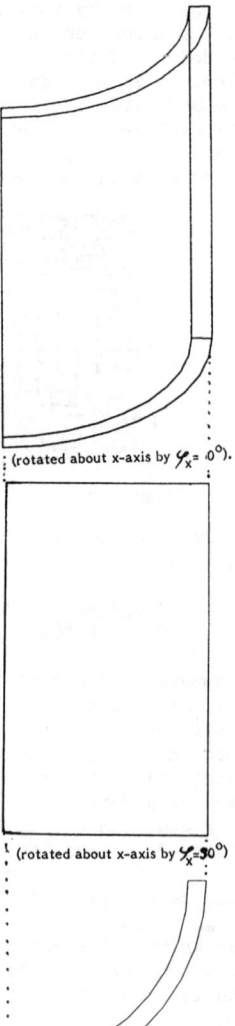

(rotated about x-axis by $\varphi_x = 0°$).

(rotated about x-axis by $\varphi_x = 90°$)

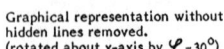

 x

The graphical representations $\varphi_x = 0$. and $\varphi_x = 90°$.

(only contour lines drawn) are the wireframes, the draftsman has
to create. It is obvius that more information is presented by the
other drawings. The work left is to dimension and annotate the
generated wireframes.

Figure   9

The following graphical representations are in Fig. 10 given for
demonstration.

FIG. 10

9. STANDARD SIMPLIFIED INPUT-COMMANDS FOR ALL FE-AND CAD-SOFTWARE PACKAGES.

There is no doubt, that an up-to-date engineering education must include
digital simulation techniques in the future. The digital simulation
must be very easy to handle for an engineer, otherwise the student at
the university and later in industry learns mainly the syntax to communicate with the computer instead of concentrating on the design and
optimisation of engineering machinery or the maintenance and improvement
of manufacturing processes. As hardware configurations only 32 bit word
computers having the power of a supermini or a mainframe are applicable.

32 bit word machines are necessary to be able to adapt existing software packages. A software platform must be established instead programming in FORTRAN from scratch.   5 An engineer of today in industry has very seldom to write in FORTRAN his own program. In general he has to use an available software package or he has to maintain and modify a sofware developed by others. To perform digital simulations a so called engineering workstation must be installed consisting of a supermini or mainframe and alphanumerical as well as graphical terminals. In addition to the named hardware a powerful software platform must be accessible. The application software systems mainly written in FORTRAN and machine language are very complex, heterogeneous and therefore difficult to apply.

More and more designing codes require the verification of the results of one software by applying a second independent software package, a fact which causes further complications. Not only the named software packages (Finite Element-(FE) and Computer Aided Design (CAD)-Systems are important for computer simulations. Planning for the future we have also to consider robotics and artificial intelligence software packages (AI). The engineer must have access to FE-, CAD-, and AI-software systems at one workstation. Two main problems must be solved in the near future to be able to apply digital simulation techniques within the engineering curriculum:

a. The named software packages must be integrated.
b. The communication with the computer applying the named software must be simplified.

NASTRAN is a well known FE-Program system, CADAM and CATIA are also widely used as CAD-software packages. These software packages as typical examples. The integration of NASTRAN and CADAM or CATIA and the simplification of its applications cannot be performed modifying both systems. Due to several reasons we have to use the software packages unchanged. Therefore it is suggested to write input commands which are very easy to understand for an engineering student. The integration of a finite element system as NASTRAN and a CAD-system as CATIA can be realized creating mathematical models of the real engineering environment by generating joints and connecting the joints by 1D-, 2D-, or 3D-elements, that means substructures. In general only a subset of the features of CATIA is applied but all capabilities available for special applications.

The following examples may explain the proposal. Whenever we specify joints, points or nodes the joint location information is given by the following JOINT COORDINATES command in a COBOL notation. A unique joint name and the coordinate location of each joint must be given in one basic global coordinate system.

Command: $\left\{\begin{array}{l}\underline{\text{JOINT}}\\ \underline{\text{NODE}}\end{array}\right\}$ COORDINATES

$\left\{\begin{array}{l}i_1\\ a_1'\\ \vdots\end{array}\right\}$ ([$\underline{X}$COORD] v_x [$\underline{Y}$COORD] v_y [$\underline{Z}$COORD] v_z)

In a mathematical model joints are connected by 1D-, 2D-, or 3D-elements. The element connectivity information is given by applying the following ELEMENT INCIDENCES-Command in a COBAL notation.

Command: <u>ELEMENT</u> <u>INCIDENCES</u>

$$\left\{ \begin{array}{c} i_1 \\ 'a_1' \end{array} \right\} \text{ node list}$$
A unique element name must be defined and associated with the names of the connected joints.

The software to read the named information is available in source code as a software platform. Only two very simple subroutines have to be changed to create the associated NASTRAN-or-CATIA-Input. The same procedure is applicable to specify inputs to other FE- and CAD-systems. Other input-informations are handled in the same way. By this we create an engineer command language used to communicate with the computer at a workstation. We are free to change the self documenting commands to an other language than english.

A circle can be drawn specifying the location of its center and the radius. Then internally joints on the circle are generated for drawing purposes. Following the named proposal a circle is specified generating joints on the circle and connecting the joints by curved 1D-elements. Sometimes a circle is drawn as a polygon because a very simple but fast plot-subroutine is used. In addition, polygons are easier to handle if the hidden line removal procedure is applied.

10. ANIMATIONS OF MOVING STRUCTURES, MECHANISMS, STREAMLINES, STRESS-PRESSURE-AND TEMPERATURE DISTRIBUTIONS.

Visualizing the real moving piston connected with moving rod being connected with rotating crank-shaft (hidden lines removed) in slow motion is for sure, the easiest way to make students understand how engines work. This simulation of the real engine is more instructive than to watch a real engine working, because one can cut parts to have a look inside during the motion. [5]. Analyzing a complex vibration problem it is possible to watch the deformations or stress flow during the movement in slow motion. In a 3D fluid flow problem the velocities of the particles on their paths called streamlines can be visualised. A transient heat transfer problem can easier be explained if students can watch moving contourlines (lines having constant temperature).

For demonstration a moving four-barmechanism is visualized in Fig. 11 on a hard copy of a Tektronix 4114 terminal withouth a refresh-unit.

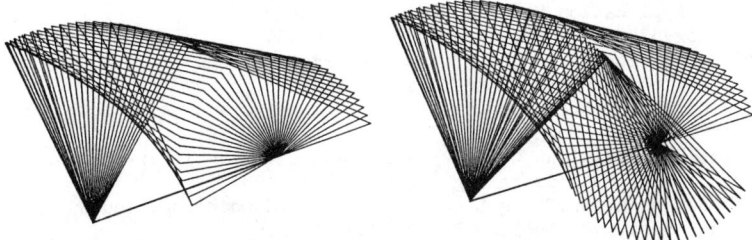

Fig. 11 Visualising the moving of a four-bar-mechanism.

LITERATURE

[1] O. Ohtmer
Efficient nonlinear computation of very large complex structures by automatic partitioning. Proceedings Second Intern. Conference on Numerical Methods for nonlinear problems, Barcelona, April 1984

[2] O. Ohtmer
Appliying analytical functions to define special boundary elements in an elasto-plastic problem with singularities idealized by Finite Elements Proceedings 5th International Conference on Boundary Elements, Hiroshima, November 1983 Springer Verlag.

[3] O. Ohtmer
Equilibrium models applied in closed meshes in a Finite Element Analysis Proceedings XII Finite Element Kongress Baden-Baden, November 1983.

[4] O. Ohtmer
Computation of lower and upper bounds to estimate the accuracy of a Finite Element Analysis.
Proceedings International Conference on accuracy estimates and adaptive Refinements in Finite Element computations Lissabon, 1984.

[5] O. Ohtmer
Hard-Software supported education in Mechanical Engineering Proceedings ASEE Annual Conference Atlanta, June 1985.

[6] O. Ohtmer
Modified Finite Elements for efficient use in CAD-Environment. International Conference on the Use of Computers in Civil Engineering, Toronto August 1985.

[7] H. Hornlein
Abriss der Strukturoptimierung MBB-Bericht, Munchen April 1984.

[8] Arora, J.S., Haug E.J.
Efficient Hybrid Methods of Optimal Structural Designs, Journal of Eng. Mech. Div. Proc. of ASCE, Vol. 103, No. EM3 1978. pp 603-680.

[9] Haug E. J., Arora, J.S.
Applied Optimal Design: Mechanical and Structural Systems
John Wiley & Sons, 1979.

[10] Arora J.S., Haug, E.J.
Methods of Design Sensitivity Analysis in Structural Optimization AIAA Journal, Vol. 17, No. 9, 1979.

[11] Haug, E.J., Arora, J.S.
Designed Sensitivity Analysis of Elastic Mechanical Systems, Computer Methods in Applied Mechanics and Engineering, 15, 1978.

[12] Morris, A.J.
Foundations of Structural Optimization: A Unified Approach
John Wiley & Sons, 1982.

[13] NASTRAN, User's Manual Vol. 1
MacNeal-Schwendler Corp. 185 Colorado Blvd, Los Angeles.

[14] O. Ohtmer
STRUDL Application Manual, ICES-User's Group 1976,
P.O. Box 8243, Cranston, Rhode Island 02920

[15] ANSYS Theoretical Manual, Swanson Analysis Systems
P.O. BOX 65, Houston, Pennsylvania 15342.

[16] A. Jennings, Matrix Computation for Engineers and Scientists, John Wiley and Sons, New York 1977.

[17] O. Ohtmer, Efficient Cholesky - Procedure for arbitrary Bandwidth. Journal Num. Methods in Eng. John Wiley, 1987.

[18] R.G. Bowerman, Drafting Links up with Solid Modeling, Journal Machine Design, Sept. 12, 1985, A Penton Publication.

ANSYS[R]: A GENERAL PURPOSE FINITE ELEMENT PROGRAM INTEGRATED IN THE CAD ENVIRONMENT

Axel Schaller

Analyse de Systèmes et Informatique*, France

Swanson Analysis Systems, Inc. (SASI) has been providing industry with top-quality finite element computer tools for engineering analysis since 1970. ANSYS and ANSYS-PC programs have been intentionally designed as general purpose FEA programs, with capabilities flexible enough that they can be tailored to a wide range of applications such as, nuclear, aerospace, offshore, transportation, medical, steel, railroad, packaging or civil construction.

SASI's FEA products are available for use on Systems ranging from supercomputers to PC's to match virtually any requirements and budget and interface with many CAD systems.

The product description on the following pages provide a brief overview of ANSYS and ANSYS-PC products. Another paper presented by L. ILIE and L. VADEZ (A.S. & I) focus on industrial applications of the program.

* A.S. & I is one of the european ANSYS Support Distributors (ASD)
ANSYS is a registered Trademark of Swanson Analysis Systems, Inc.

ANSYS CAPABILITIES:

Perhaps the greatest advantage ANSYS offers its users is its incredible wide range of capabilities. ANSYS not only provides all functions that engineers and scientists expect in an analysis program - such as a variety of analysis types, material representations and a comprehensive library of elements - it offers much more. Some of the extras you might not expect include pre and post processing, on-line documentation, design optimization, solid modeling and 3-dimensional graphics.

The following analysis capabilities are available in ANSYS.

<u>Statics</u> : solves for the displacements and stresses in a structure subject to applied loads

- Linear Statics assumes that the structural equilibrium equations and material properties are linear.

- Nonlinear Statics allows for nonlinear behavior in both geometry and/or material. Large deflections, stress stiffening, plasticity, creep, and interface (gap) conditions can be included in an analysis.

<u>Dynamics</u> : Determines the time history response of a structure to transient loading conditions.

- Linear Transient Dynamics efficiently solves for the response of a linear structure.

- Nonlinear Transient Dynamics incorporates material, geometric, and/or interface nonlinear effects.

- Spectrum Analysis envelops the dynamic response to random vibration or seismic loading.

- Harmonic Response determines the steady-state response of a linear structure subjected to harmonically time-varying loads.

<u>Mode Frequency</u> : computes the natural frequencies and associated mode shape of a linear, undamped structure.

<u>Stability Analysis</u> : determines the load capacity of a structure

- Linear Eigenvalue Buckling determines the critical loads (bifurcation points) and the associated buckled shapes for a linear structure.

- Large Deflection analysis determines the limit load, whether failure occurs by bifurcation or snap-through buckling.

<u>Heat Transfer</u> : Solves for the temperature distribution and heat flow within a body. The temperature results can be used as boundary conditions to a structural analysis.

- Linear Heat Transfer assumes non-temperature-dependent material properties.

- Nonlinear Heat Transfer can have temperature-dependent material properties (including phase change effects) and can include radiation and temperature-dependent convection boundary conditions.

- Transient Heat Transfer solves for the time-dependent temperature distribution within a body. Non-linear effects may be included

<u>Magnetostatics :</u> Solves for the intensity and flux density of a magnetic field due to current sources and/or permanent magnetic materials.

<u>Coupled Field analysis</u> : Simultaneously solves for interacting multiple field effects including two or more of the following : structural displacements and forces, temperature and heat flows, electrical voltage and current, magnetic intensity and flux, and confined fluid flow pressure and velocity

<u>Global/local Modeling</u> : Used to improve the running logistics or modeling efficiency of the previously-mentioned analysis procedures.

- Substructuring physically portions out a piece or multiple pieces of a model and generates corresponding substructures for use in the full analysis - at substantial cost savings.

- Submodeling uses the results of a coarsely-modeled structure to obtain an accurate solution of a locally-refined submodel.

A wide variety of material representations are possible with ANSYS. Material properties may be temperature-dependent, isotropic, orthotropic, or anisotropic. Non-linear material behavior such as plasticity, creep, swelling, and nonlinear elasticity are available in both static and dynamic analyses Plasticity material options include.

- The von Mises yield criterion coupled with kinematic hardening which represents most metal behavior very well in plastic range.

- Anisotropic Plasticity which allows for different stress-strain behavior in different directions as well as different behavior in tension and compression. This option can be used for composites or metals in which the yield strength is affected by processing (i.e. rolling).

- Drucker-Pager in which the material strength is dependent on the confinement pressure, such as for granular materials (i.e. dry soils, rock)

The ANSYS program contains a library of more than 70 different elements. In addition, many of the elements have options which allow numerous other possibilities to be used in an analysis.

The element library includes :

• Structural Elements such as spars (trusses), beams, piping, membranes, plates, thin and thick shells, layered shells, conical axisymmetric shells, axisymmetric solids, 2-D and 3-D solids, and 3-D solids with reinforcing materials. Inertial, thermal, stress stiffening, and large rotation effects are included with these elements.

• Heat Transfer Elements including conduction, convection, and radiation links, thick and thin shells, 2-D, Axisymmetric, and 3-D solids. Thermal mass and heat generation effects are included in these elements.

• Thermal Electric Line Elements including 2-D, axisymmetric, and 3-D solids as well as magnetic-thermal-electric solid elements.

• Other elements include matrix elements, substructures, control elements, and immersed pipe or cable elements.

• Other effects which can be modeled include gaps, friction, viscous dampers, cables, plastic hinges, crack tips, fluid and thermal flow in pipes, and nonlinear force-deflection curves.

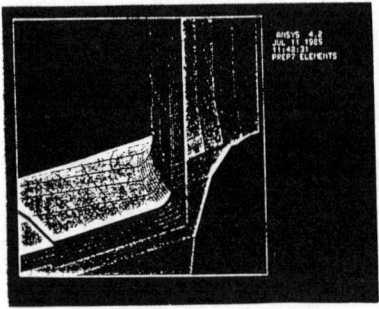

Figure 1 : Hidden line plot of a 3 D finite element model of a pipe junction

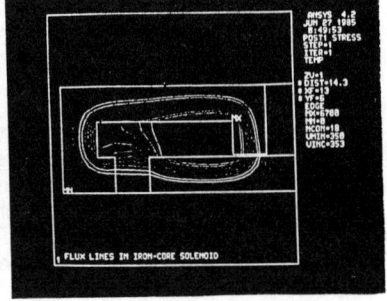

Figure 2 : Magnetic flux in a 1/2 symmetry model of an iron-core solenoid with a moveable plunger

SOLID MODELING AND MESH GENERATION

Until recently, the geometry and finite element mesh of an FEA model have been defined simultaneously. Now, however, ANSYS contains a versatile and sophisticated solid modeler which creates the geometry of a part or structure independently of the finite element mesh. With ANSYS, this portion of an FEA analysis requires less of the analyst's time.

The ANSYS solid modeler is based upon the Boundary Representation (B - rep) method of modeling. With this method, vertices, edges, and faces of volumes are represented with Keypoints, line segments and areas. A given volume is represented in the geometry database by a tree-like list of the entities (keypoints, line segments, areas, or volumes) it consists of. Each of the entities is stored in the database individually along with pointers to the other entities which makes it up.

This entities are defined with appropriate one-, two-, or three-dimensional cubic polynomial. This presents a clear advantage over Constructive Solid Geometry (CSG) modelers in that edges and Surfaces of general and arbitrary shape can be represented. The model does not have to be made up well-defined "regular" geometric shapes. With the ANSYS modeler, complex edges and surfaces are approximated with parametric cubic functions. The price paid for the flexiblility of the B-rep method, however, is a larger data storage requirement than a CSG modeler.

The ANSYS solid modeler is intended to provide the features desirable for and necessary to creating finite element models. Certain general Solid Modeling characteristics, such as interference calculation, are not available. However, the finite element analyst will find mass property calculations such as moments of inertia, total volume, and centroid location.

More than 70 commands are available in the ANSYS PREP7 Mesh module for the construction and definition of the model. These are in addition to the hundreds of commands in the remainder of PREP7 used for additional analysis specifications ranging from load definition and printout controls to commands used for piping system definition. The Mesh module commands allow definition, listing, plotting, modification, deletion, etc., of the geometric entities. Besides these basic commands, many commands perform specialized functions.

Most of thes commands are used to manipulate line segments, the most powerful of the entities. Two "crossing" line segments may be intersected with automatic redefinition of the existing two line segments into four. Also available are commands which allow definition of full circular arcs or portions there of. Lines tangent to a keypoint and a line can be defined as well as lines tangent to two lines. Along the same vein, straight lines which "hit" one or two other lines at some specified angle(s) are also able to be generated with a single command.

Dragging operations can be used to create areas or volumes by "dragging" lines or areas, respectively, through space along a series of line segments. In a similar manner, areas and volumes can be generated by rotating lines or areas about a specific axis. In each of these cases, complex and extensive geometries can be created with a minimal effort.

Fillets between intersecting lines or areas can also be defined. Simple specification of the lines, for instance, and the radius of the fillet are all that are required. In the case of a line fillet, the existing lines are automatically redefined and shortened to maintain model integrity.

Once a Solid Model has been created, it can be meshed automatically with, in the simplest case, a single command. The nodes and elements so defined can be quads (2D) or bricks (3D) for regularly shaped areas or volumes. In the case of areas and volumes with extreme angles, or triangular or tetrahedrally shaped ones, a special feature of the solid modeler is available. The mesh generator is able to create triangular or tetrahedrally shaped elements. Such meshes can be used to analyse arbitrary areas and volumes that previously were extremely difficult or impossible to mesh. The modeling time spent by the analyst is reduced by shifting the task to the machine.

An extremely important feature of ANSYS solid modeler is its ability to handle parametric imput. Parametric input allows the specification of model parameters, such as length, radius, or Young's modulus as variables. Simple assignment of values to the variables then allows a rapid mean of generating many models of different sizes but of the same family. This capability also carries over to material specifications, load specifications, etc. In fact, any user-input quantity may be specified as a vareible in the ANSYS program. A model so defined can then be analyzed with the ANSYS Optimization routine which is able to intelligently vary the parameters to minimize a user-specified objective function , such as weight.

ANSYS INTERFACES WITH CAD SYSTEMS

Although ANSYS contains a powerful Solid Modeler, the program also interfaces with a number of CAD programs. This ability makes ANSYS an even more valuable tool in the computer-aided engineering field. ANSYS features an auxilary routine that contains a number of data translators. The translators convert a coded output file from various CAD programs to ANSYS preprocessing input commands.

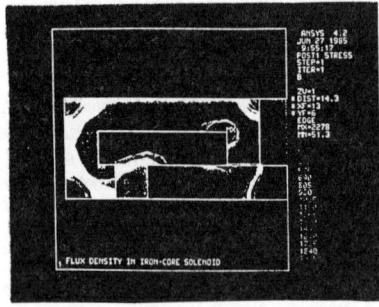
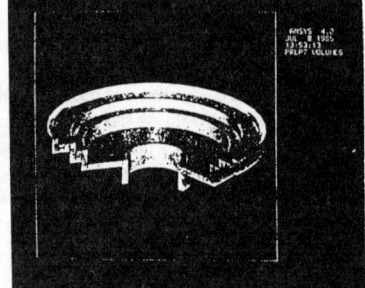

Figure 3 : Contour plot of the magnitude of the flux density in the iron-core solenoid shown in figure 2. The flux density in the air gap between the core and the plunger can be used to calculate the magnetic force acting on the plunger.

Figure 4 : Shaded Solid model of a spindle

PROGRAM   COMPANY

ANVIL ™   Manufacturing & Consulting Services, Inc.
AUTOTROL R   Autotrol Technology
FEMGEN   FEGS International, Ltd.
GRAFTEK   Graphics Technology Corp
IGES   US Dept. of Commerce, Nat. Bureau of Stds.
MEDUSA ™   Prime Computer
PATRAN ™   PDA Engineering
SUPERTAB ™   General Electric, CAE International

Additionally some CAD programs are desinged to write ANSYS preprocessor commands automatically. These includes Computervision's CADDS FEM, Mc. Auto's UNIGRAPHICS program, among others.

DESIGN OPTIMIZATION

Until recently, finite element analysis has been used almost exclusively for the analysis of a user-designed model. With the new design optimization capabilities of ANSYS, however, the computer itself can now be used as an active participant in the design of a model. This Technique enables the computer to generate a series of designs which are checked for feasibility, and which improve as the series progresse until a "best" design is obtained. Shape optimization, as well as optimization of parameters such as area, moment of inertia and thickness is possible.

Design optimization in the ANSYS program utilizes parametric input, but now the imput parameters are used as design variables. The optimization module acts as a controller that uses the finite element program. It sends information in the form of design variables and receives results called state variables and the objective function. The user must define the design and state variables, including limits of each, and the objective function. The optimization module selects and tests new design variables on an iterative basis as it attempts to minimize the objective function. This iterative process is shown in Figure 5.

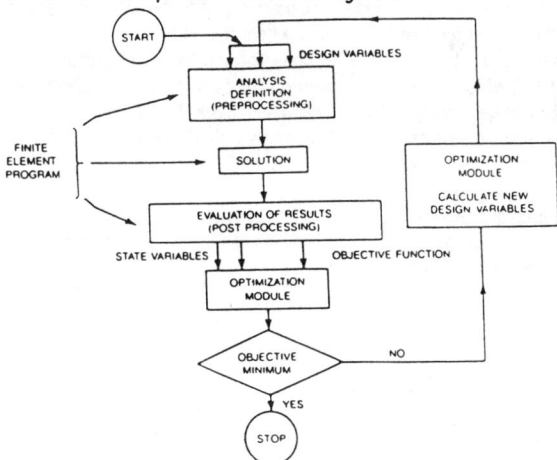

Figure 5 : Design optimization flow chart. Results are tested after each run ot determine needs and variables for subsequent run.

The nature of the optimizing Technique is such that it may be used for any of the element types and analysis procedures available. Since it is an approximate method, there is no need for the engineer to know or provide explicit expressions for the objective function or the constraint functions. For example, the optimizing method used will work for fully-stressed structural analysis, heat transfer shape optimization, vibration analysis, magnetics design, or stress concentration minimization.

ANSYS RUNS ON MOST MAJOR BRANDS OF HARDWARE

To offer the advantages of ANSYS to the widest possible range of users, the program can be leased on the following computers:

Alliant, Amdahl, Apollo, Bull, Cyber, Celerity, Computervision, Convex, Cray, Data General, DEC, ELXSI, Floating Point System, Fujitsu, Harris, Hewlett Packard, IBM, Prime, Ridge, Sun, Univac.

SASI is currently supporting and maintaining the program on approximately 30 different operating systems from about 20 different vendors.

This wide range of computers offers the ANSYS program to engineers with all levels of computing power.

ANSYS IS AVAILABLE ON PC'S TOO

Even if you dont't have access to a mainframe or a mini-computer, you can still have the advantages of using ANSYS. A family of PC products, all rigidly-defined subsets of the full ANSYS program are available. The programs are designed to operate on personal computers such as the IBM^R PC/XT, PC/AT, or similar compatibles.

The current offerings on the PC consist of ANSYS-PC/LINEAR which is a complete program including preprocessing and postprocessing, linear static and modal analysis ; ANSYS-PC/THERMAL which is a complete program including preprocessing, steady-state or transient heat transfer analysis including non-linear effects, and postprocessing ; ANSYS-PC/SOLIDS which contains virtually all the Solid Modeling capabilities in ANSYS as well as the full ANSYS preprocessor, PREP7. ANSYS-PC/SOLID is a preprocessing package which is designed to prepare analysis data for ANSYS, ANSYS-PC/LINEAR, or ANSYS-PC/THERMAL ; ANSYS-PC/OPT is the design optimization of the ANSYS-PC family.

Because each of these ANSYS-PC products are subsets of the full ANSYS program, the command input is the same as full ANSYS and data can be transferred from the PC to the full ANSYS program for analysis on larger computer when the engineer feels this is necessary.

QUALITY ASSURANCE - ANSYS IS STILL THE LEADER

An FEA prgram is only as useful and valuable as it is reliable, so as ANSYS has changed and developed through the years, SASI's quality assurance program has evolved right along with it.

SASI's Quality Assurance program began as a limited series of internal verification problems, designed to test the efficiency and occuracy of the ANSYS program's operation. Today, SASI employs a full-time quality assurance staff and the ANSYS program goes through an exacting Q.A. procedure including more than 2000 verification problems before being approved for release. SASI engineers compare ANSYS-calculated solutions with known theoretical solutions and results calculated in the previous ANSYS release. All to ensure that users have a dependable and efficient FEA program.

IBM ^{R} PC/XT and PC/AT are registered Trademarks of International Business Machines Corporations.

CONCLUSION

There are good reasons why ANSYS is one of the most widely recognized large-scale, general purpose finite element programs for engineering analysis available today. Since 1970, when Swanson Analysis Systems, Inc. began operations, the ANSYS program has undergone continuous revision and upgrading to keep pace with the rapid evolution of computer hardware. This ongoing series of enhancements ensures that ANSYS' uses and capablilities stay current with and often anticipate the needs of the market place. SASI continue to explore the capabilities of new hardware such as parallel processors, microcomputers and enhanced graphics display devices. Future ANSYS updates will continue to use the most advanced proven technology available to provide its users with the finest in FEA capabilities.

ANSYS and the ANSYS-PC products are installed at approximately 1000 sites worldwise including more than 230 universities. Customer support services include a variety of seminars for training, a telephone hotline, extensive documentation and consulting services.

ANSYS support Distributors (ASD's) provide licensing and other assistance in major cities in the United States, Canada, Western Europe (appendix A), Israel and the Far East.

REFERENCES :

(1) DeSalvo, Gabriel J. and John A. Swanson (1985) ANSYS User's Manual : Swanson Analysis Systems, Inc.

(2) Kohnke, Peter C. (1985), ANSYS Theoretical Manuel ; Swanson Analysis Systems, Inc.

(3) Ketelaar C., ANSYS : Engineering Software with the design and analysis Answers (1986) Structural Analysis Systems, Pergamon Press;

(4) Debaecker H., Schaller A. (1986) : ANSYS, une approche CAO de l'optimisation des structures : Proceedings of the 5 th European Conference on CAD/CAM and Computer Graphics, Hermes Micado.

APPENDIX A

ANSYS Distributor and Support in Europe.

ANKER-ZEMER Engineering A/s : Scandinavia

A.S. & I. : France, Belgium, Netherlands, Spain and Portugal

CADFEM GmbH : Germany, Austria, Swiss, Netherlands

S.I.Me.C Srl. : Italy

Structures and Computers Ltd. : United Kingdom, Netherlands

GET3D: A TETRAHEDRAL FINITE ELEMENT MESH GENERATOR FOR THE COMPUTATION OF ELECTROMAGNETIC FIELDS

Y. Du Terrail, O. Santana, G. Meunier and J. L. Coulomb

Laboratoire d'Electrotechnique de Grenoble, ENSIEG, BP. 46, 38402 St. Martin d'Hères, France

ABSTRACT

The application of the finite element method to electromagnetic computation, needs a particular approach because the objects but also the surrounding space have to be taken into account.

The original approach used by the package GET3D, allows to mesh **globally** a tridimensional domain **without** the usual but tedious preliminary subdivision in basic volumes.

The first part will be dedicated to the presentation of algorithms. The second part will be devoted to the introduction of the various steps of the use of GET3D; namely: the geometric modelling and the mesh generation of volume and boundary finite elements. Some examples of realistic mesh production will be shown.

I. INTRODUCTION

The two-dimensional computation of magnetic fields is nowadays a basic tool for the designer of electrical devices. Nevertheless, some studies need also three-dimensional analysis.

A three-dimensional C.A.D. finite element package is composed of three parts : the preprocessor, the processor and the post-processor. The present paper is devoted to the first one.

The literature gives many three dimensional mesh generation methods, mainly developed by mechanical and thermical engineers. Generally, the proposal algorithms are restricted to simply connected objects where only the inner volume needs to be discretized. With electromagnetic problems, an additional difficulty arises due to the presence of outer volume of air where the magnetic field exists. This air region, which has frequently a very complex shape, must be discretized in finite elements compatible with the mesh of the object.

II. PRESENTATION OF ALGORITHMS

II.1 Delaunay's algorithm

It consists of finding, for a given set of nodes X_i in a domain D, a set of tetrahedra which connect these nodes all together [5].

First, a Dirichlet decomposition on D allows to define intermediate Voronoï's polyhedra V_i such that :

$$V_i = [X \in D, \forall j \neq i, 1 \leq j \leq n, d(X,X_i) < d(X,X_j)]$$

where d() means the Euclidian distance and n the number of nodes. The obtained polyhedra V_i are convex and non empty and cover entirely the domain D.

Delaunay's polytopes are generated by connecting each node inside Voronoï's polyhedra attached to a same vertex. These polytopes are decomposed in tetrahedral elements.

The mesh obtained is non-unique and the circumscribed sphere of any Delaunay's tetrahedron never contains another node; its faces are as equilateral as possible (Figure 1).

The algorithm is the following:

- *Initialization of the decomposition : the initialization of the mesh is realised by creating a box composed with 8 auxiliary nodes outside of the domain and 6 first tetrahedra. This tetrahedral discretization of the surrounding box insures that any node X_i of the domain will be included inside an already existing tetrahedron.This initial mesh is called Π_8.;*
- *Insertion of the remaining nodes:*
  <u>do for</u> $i = 9,10,11,....,n$
   insert the node X_i into the mesh Π_{i-1} to obtain the mesh Π_i (all the elements of Π_{i-1} whose circumscribed sphere contains X_i are eliminated; X_i is then connected to the faces of the created hole).
  <u>end do;</u>

In GET3D, this basic algorithm is used for the geometrical definition of objects (see §II.2) and for the generation of the finite element mesh (see §II.4.1 and §II.4.2).

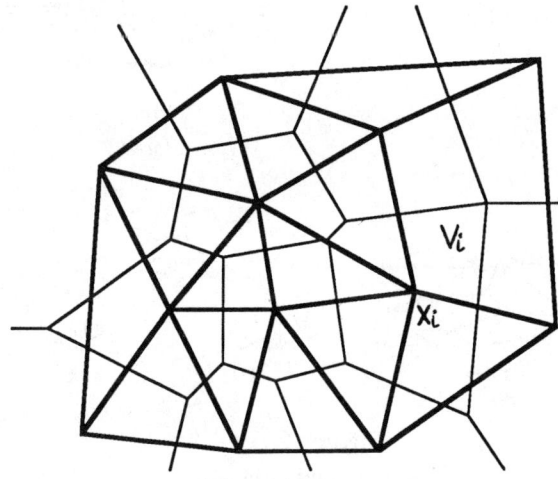

Figure 1.
Voronoï's polyedra and Delaunay's triangulation (2D examples).

II.2 Definition of solid objects

The Delaunay's algorithm generates a convex volume from a set of points. When the object is not convex, the decomposition obtained is an overabundant outer layer. By modifying this mesh (suppression and addition of tetrahedral elements in a mesh using interactive algorithms), we can sculpture the desired object (Figure 2).

The general procedure of an object creation is the following:

- *interactive creation of points;*
- *automatic tetrahedral decomposition (eventually overabundant);*
- *while the object is not well decomposed :*
    visualisation of the outer layer of the mesh;
    interactive suppression and addition of tetrahedra;
  end while;
- *recording the sets of points and tetrahedra defining the geometry.*

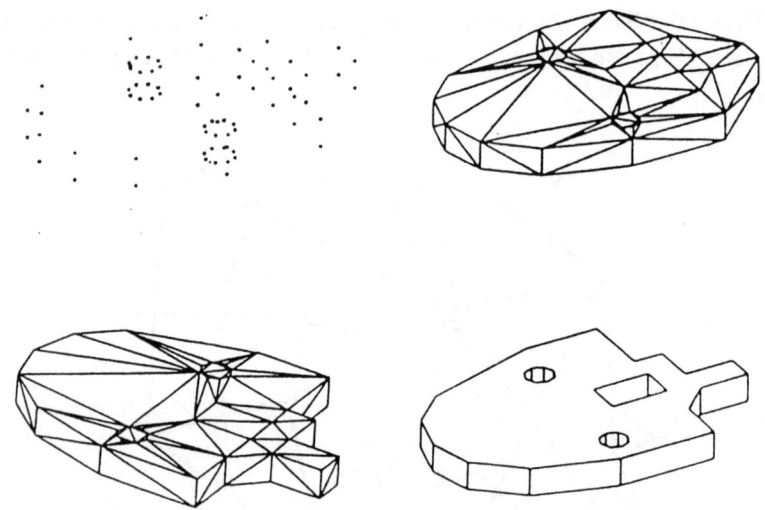

Figure 2.
Building and object.

II.3 Definition of domain

Electromagnetic domains are generally made up of few parts, different or identical, distributed inside a "box" of air (figure 3).

The studies done on a given device may depend of the relative positions of the different components (i.e. influence of the angular position of the rotor on the electromagnetic torque).

From these observations, we deduce the folowing rules :

1) Several occurrences of the same object can be present at different places in the same domain.
2) The position of an occurrence of an object is defined relatively with regard to the previously positioned objects in the domain.
3) A new domain can be obtained from a previous one by addition or suppression of an object.

In order to satisfy the rule (1), we define the entity **volume** as an occurrence of an object in the domain. An object can be at the origin of several volumes.

The rule (2) justifies the posibility modifying the place of already positioned volumes using geometrical transformation.

Addition and suppression commands allow to satisfy the rule (3).

II.4 Discretization

The mesh of a domain is performed in three steps:
- initial automatic mesh generation using predefined boundary nodes;
- automatic generation of nodes and elements inside volumes;
- automatic improvement of tetrahedron shapes.

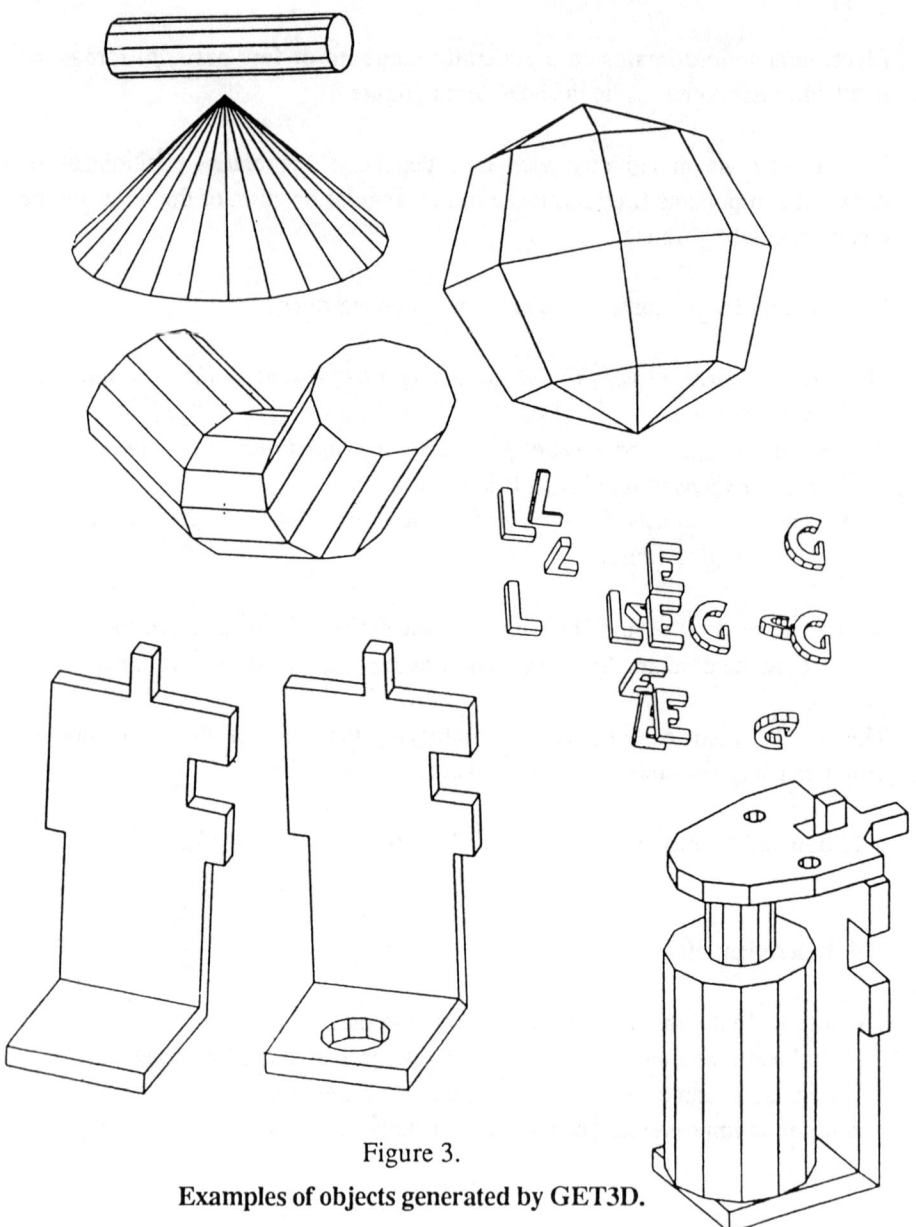

Figure 3.
Examples of objects generated by GET3D.

II.4.1 Initial boundary mesh

Our implementation of Delaunay's algorithm needs a preliminary set of nodes on the boundaries of the volumes.

The user has the possibility to create interactively these nodes using classical geometric transformations (translation, rotation, ...).

Before starting the Delaunay's algorithm, a box including the domain, made of 8 nodes and 6 tetrahedra, is created. At the end of the mesh generation, this box is eliminated.

The technique allows the creation of a first tetrahedra set built with only the boundary nodes. In order to obtain well shaped tetrahedra, other nodes must be created inside volumes.

The porcupine effect

*The Delaunay's algorithm leads to the creation of tetrahedral elements whose faces are as equilateral as possible; for that reason, elements will not necessarly respect the boundaries of each object. We called it the **porcupine** effect (figure 4). It may appear in two cases:*
  - mesh obtained from only the corners of the domain.
  - proximily of faces with ill compatible distribution of nodes.
The porcupine effect can be corrected by imposing node refinement on the concerned boundaries.

II.4.2 Automatic generation of internal nodes and elements

The mesh refinements doesn't perform subdivision of the large elements into smaller ones, but insert new nodes at judicious places and apply the Delaunay's algorithm on them [5].

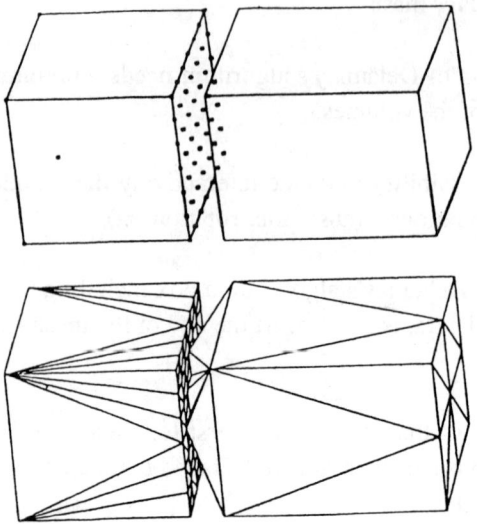

Proximity of discretized and non discretized boundaries

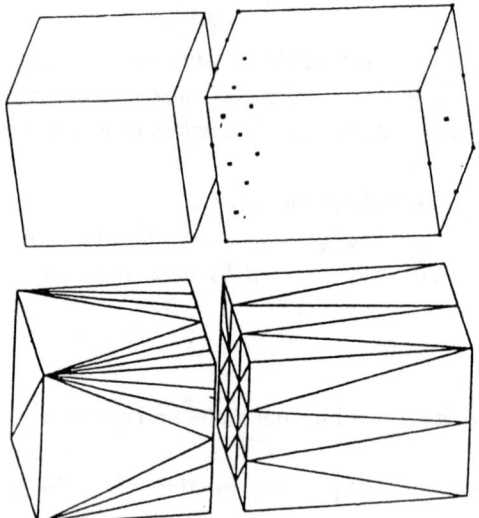

Correction of the previous mesh by transmission of the discretisation from one boundary to the other

Figure 4.
The **porcupine** effect.

This iterative process is composed of two steps:

- allocation of weigth P_N to each boundary node. The weigth P_N is the arithmetical average of the length of the boundary edges connected to the node N.
- detection of too large tetrahedra by considering the weigth W_K of the tetrahedron T_K.

$$W_K = [\prod_{i=1,4} P_{Ni}]^{1/4} \text{ with } T_K = (N_1, N_2, N_3, N_4)$$

and its volume:

$$V_K = 1/6 \begin{bmatrix} 1 & 1 & 1 & 1 \\ X_{N1} & X_{N2} & X_{N3} & X_{N4} \\ Y_{N1} & Y_{N2} & Y_{N3} & Y_{N4} \\ Z_{N1} & Z_{N2} & Z_{N3} & Z_{N4} \end{bmatrix}$$

If $|V_K| > W_K^3$, then T_K is a too large tetrahedron and a new node N is created. Its coordinates are:

$$(X)_N = \sum_{i=1,4} (X_{Ni} P'_{Ni}) / \sum P'_{Ni}$$

where

$$P'_{Ni} = \sum_{1 \leq j \neq i \leq 4} P_{NjP} / (3 \sum_{1 \leq j \leq 4} P_{Nj})$$

and its weight is $P_N = W_K$
This method allows to propagate a density of boundary nodes inside the volume.

II.4.3 Automatic improvement of tetrahedra shape

We applied the Laplace's algorithm [5]. Each internal node (non-located on a boundary) is moved to the barycenter of connected nodes. This procedure is very simple and quick (three or four iterations).

Finally several methods allow to detect the elements definitively ill-shaped (two acute angles, two flat tetrahedra):

- A quality coefficient of a face can be defined as the ratio of diameter of the circumscribed circle versus diameter of the inscribed circle [8].
- A quality coefficient of a tetrahedron can be defined as the ratio of diameter of the circumscribed sphere versus diameter of the circumscribed sphere [8].
- A density coefficient of a tetrahedron can be defined as the ratio of tetrahedron volume versus domain volume [8].

II.5 Mesh visualization

We use two algorithms to visualize a set of triangular faces (the exterior faces of a set of tetrahedra, figure 5).

The first one determines and draws the visible portion of edges of triangles. This vector algorithm can be time consuming for a large mesh (a quadratic function of number of triangles), but it is suitable for any display terminal.

The second one, on the other hand, uses specificities of raster display. The triangular faces are preliminary sorted out by depth and visualized in the processed order. The visualization time is a linear function of the number of faces.

II.6 Element generation

Finite elements of order one (4 nodes) or two (10 nodes) are created automatically when all operations of mesh have succeeded. In the case of finite element of order two, new nodes are created at the middle of each edge of tetrahedra.

Boundary elements are identified interactively by grouping triangles faces placed on volumes surfaces and by assigning them a boundary name.

Physical regions are defined interactively by giving to the volumes a region reference (i.e. conductor, pole, ...).

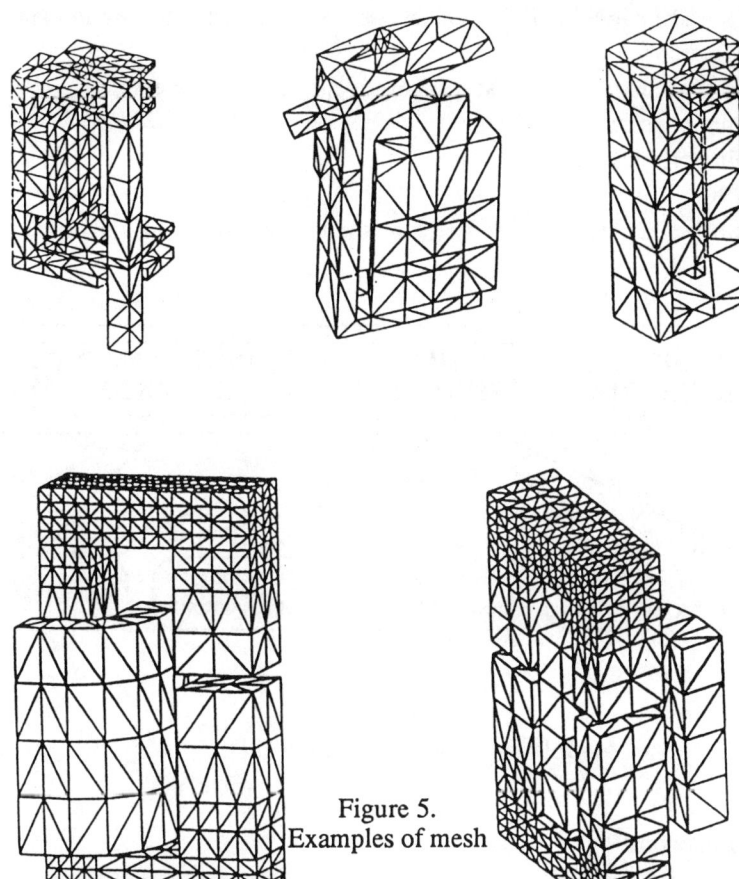

Figure 5.
Examples of mesh

III. PROGRAM ARCHITECTURE

III.1 Modules

GET3D, written in Fortran77, is divided in three modules as shown in figure 6.

The SOLID MODELER allows to define the "Macro Mesh" of each object (using Delaunay's algorithm).

The MESH GENERATOR has three tasks:
- creation of the geometric domain by transferring and positioning objects;
- automatic initial boundary mesh generation;
- automatic internal mesh refinement.

The FINITE ELEMENT GENERATOR prepares datas for the finite element processor, like:
- building first order linear or second order curvilinear elements,
- describing physical boundaries,
- describing physical regions.

The fundamental algorithms used by each module are shown in figure 6.

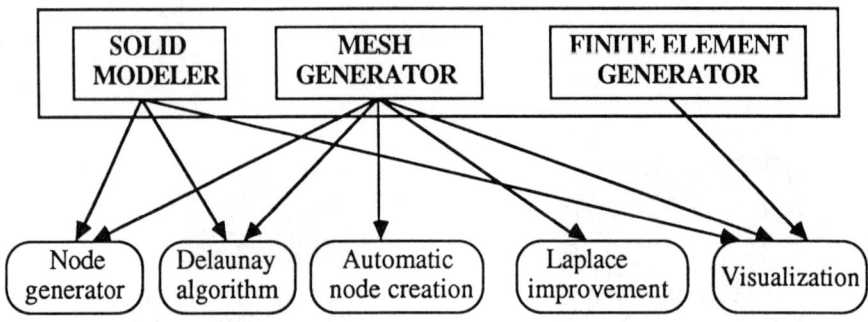

Figure 6.
Modules and algorithms of GET3D.

III.2 Data structure

Such a package needs very structured datas, in order to allow enhancement and improvement of the program functions, but also easy adaptation to the size of problems.

For these reasons, *memory management programs* have been developed. They work directly on Fortran tables and bring up to table, linear file or pile structures. *Direct management programs* permit to create, destroy, consult and register each entity (i.e. a node, a tetrahedron, ...). *Interactive management programs* insures communication between the user and some information he can control.

III.3 Interactive programs

The design process is never composed of sequential tasks linked together in a definite manner. On the contrary, the various modules and tasks can be activated in any order.

For this reason, we use interactive and graphical tools in order to command algorithms and visualize results quickly.

These libraries are *Bib-dialog [7]* for alphanumeric interaction, *Bib-diagra* for basic graphical management and *Bib-ds3d* for tridimensional visualisation. These tools have been developed in the *Laboratoire d'Electrotechnique de Grenoble*. Note that *Bib-diagra* provides the compatibility with many graphic systems (Tektronix, Ramtek, Apollo, ...).

IV. CONCLUSION

IV.1 Advantages of this mesh generator

The choice of generation of tetrahedra allows to separate the geometric description and the discretization. For instance it is possible to couple together GET3D with a solid modeller.

The creation of a finite element model is completely achieved by GET3D. It realizes the different steps of geometry design, mesh generation and finite element preparation.

The Delaunay's algorithm is a good choice to obtain global meshes for objects and air volumes. This point is very important for electromagnetic problems.

IV.2 Disadvantages

Lot of nodes when using order two elements are generated. Generally, an equivalent brick discretization (same number of nodes) gives better final numerical results.

Manual correction of the *porcupine* effect becomes a tedious task with large problems.

IV.3 Future developments and investigations

Many techniques yet applied in 2 dimensions may be considered with interest to improve the actual program. Particularly, automatic adaptation of a Delaunay 's mesh to a given geometry, automatic adaptation to a physical problem [4] and automatic adaptation of a mesh to geometrical modifications could be integrated in GET3D. The first point induces the writing of an algorithm of automatic correction of the porcupine effect and the second point a direct link with the finite element processor. The third one can be treated using geometrical data parametrizations [1], [2], [8].

AKNOWLEDGEMENTS

We would like to thank the Telemecanique Society (France) as well as the Laboratoire d'Electrotechnique de Grenoble wich supplied this study.

REFERENCES

[1] Y. Du Terrail, "GET3D - A 3D mesh generator for finite element analysis of electrical devices", CAPE'86, Copenhague, Mai 1986.

[2] Y. Du Terrail, G. Meunier, J.L. Coulomb, "Deux approches de maillages paramétrés tridimensionnels pour la modélisation des champs magnétiques par la méthode des éléments finis", MICAD'86, Paris.

[3] Mark A., Yerry and Mark S. Shepard, "Automatic Three-dimensional Mesh Generation by the Modified Octree Technic", International Journal for Numerical Methods in Engineering, vol.20, pp. 1965-1990, 1984.

[4] Z.J. Cendes, D. Shenton, H. Shahnasser, "HYDRA-A Three Dimensional Magnetics Program based on Delaunay Tasselation and Complementary Finite Element Methods", *Proceeding of COMPUMAG*, Fort-Collins, USA, 1985.

[5] F. Hermeline, "Triangulation automatique d'un polyèdre en dimension N", *RAIRO Analyse Numérique*, Vol. 16, no. 3, pp. 211-242, 1982.

[6] P. Rafinejad, J.L. Coulomb, "Interactive computer Techniques in Three Dimensional Modelisation of Field Problems by Finite Element Method", *Proceedings of COMPUMAG*, Grenoble, FRANCE, 1978.

[7] J.L. Coulomb, BIB-DIALOG, Bibliothèque FORTRAN-77 d'interactivité alphanumérique. Rapport interne du 1/12/84, LEG, ENSIEG.

[8] Yves Du Terrail, "Modélisation géométrique et topologique en 3 dimensions pour l'application de la méthode des éléments finis en électromagnétisme", Thèse de Docteur à l'INP de Grenoble, Octobre 1985.

COMPUTER AIDED DESIGN AND INTEGRAL EQUATIONS

A. Boyer, G. Caracci and P. Astre

Institut National des Sciences Appliquées, Toulouse, France

SUMMARY

The knowledge of the structural distortion of plastic materials under load is very important for determining their dimensions. Using the method of integral equations, we have studied this distortion for a gearwheel made from a plastic material. Using various visual plots, we were able to determine new profiles and the relief angles required for meshing under load, without any dynamic loading.

Key words : distortion – integral equations.

A knowledge of the distortion of spur gears under load is fundamental for gears made from plastic. In particular, it allows solutions to be found for problems of the calculation of the relief angle at the tip, and homokinetics, the risk of interference during movement, ect, to be studied. All the studies concerned with this subject, excepting that carried out by CETIM (Centre Technique des Industries mecaniques), using the method of finite elements (1), are essentially experimental.

2. CHOICE OF THE METHOD FOR CALCULATING THE DISTORTIONS

The analysis of a spur gear tooth is a typical case of a plane problem. Apart from the calculation of the contact pressure, one of the essential problems in deciding the dimensions of the gear is the determination of the deflection of the tooth under load. This deflection may be evaluated by the integral equation method.
The integral equation method is very suitable for this type of problem (2), since the unknowns in relation to the volume are in this case of no concern. Only the displacements at the contour have to be determined.
   It should nevertheless be noted that, in the integral equation method, the problem covers two fields :
      – The stress field at the contour
      – The displacement field at the contour (3),
while the classic finite element method is in general a single – field problem : that of displacements.
In addition, certain subjects (for example, the calculation of the contact pressure between two distorting solids (4)) involve the notion of volume and distortion energy. The finite element method, while completely appropriate, nevertheless contains a certain number of disadvantages.
      – The presentation and checking of the data is long and complex, despite the development of automatic matrix of programs.
      – Very high resolution time.
      – The formula known as " displacements " gives good results for the displacements, but a lower accuracy for the stresses. It seemed to us that the integral equation method could deal with certain of these limitations. The principal advantage of this technique is the very simple division of the surface. A three – dimensional problem is replaced by a two – dimensional one, greatly simplifying the insertion of the data and the use of the results.
The program which generates the distortion of the gear tooth has an automatic data generation program which is entirely in a dialogue mode (5).
By means of these subroutines (MAIBI, CARIE, ect), we were able, very quickly and with a short calculation time, to modify the matrices so as to define the contour of the structure, the number of points on the matrix and their positions, and finally their influence on the results obtained.

3. DEFINITION OF THE CONTOUR OF THE STRUCTURE

In this phase, we " optimised " the contour to give sufficient accuracy, while holding the calculation costs down to a reasonable level. A study (6) carried out using the finite element method showed that, if zero displacements are imposed at the contour in figure 1, the displacements of the contour PQ and SR will not exceed 3,5% of the maximum displacement of the structure, with an applied force F at the tip of the tooth.

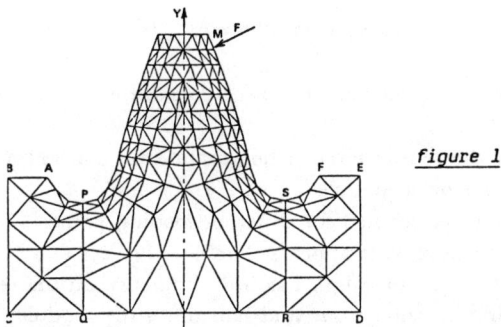

figure 1

It thus seemed reasonable to impose conditions such that the displacements were zero along the contour PQRS.

The tooth profile obtained with the program MAIBI is defined by 47 matrix points (figure 2).

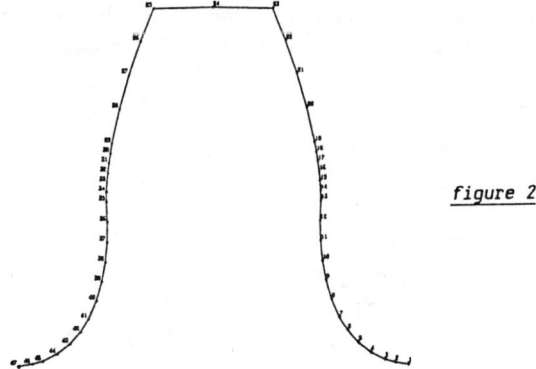

figure 2

We varied the values of :
- the built – in depth, from once times the module to three times the module (figures 3a and 3b)
- the number of matrix points on this built – in portion (figure 3c and 3d)

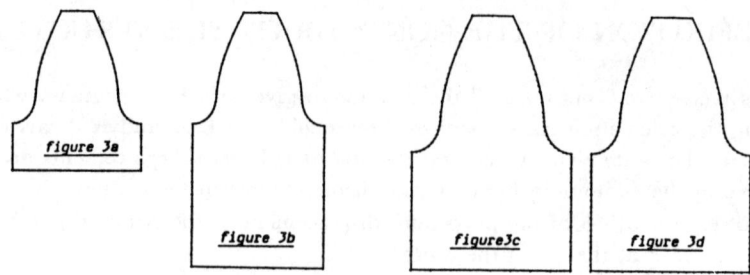

The boundary conditions were as follows :

- for the displacements : zero displacements on the built – in segments
- for the tensile forces : horizontal unit concentrated force applied at a point on a module.

Several runs were performed for different loading points. From the results presented in appendix 1, it appears that :

- the built – in length has little influence on the result obtained, beyond a minimum value : one and half times the module.
- the number of built – in segments, which considerably increases the calculation time, has a negligible influence, beyond twelve built – in segments.
- the deflection at the loading point can be measured with greater accuracy at the matrix point situated on the opposite corresponding plane of the tooth, in order to avoid the peculiarity due to the concentrated force. This peculiarity is clearly illustrated on the plot of the tooth distortion (figure 4). We shall take a tooth which has eighteen built – in segments.

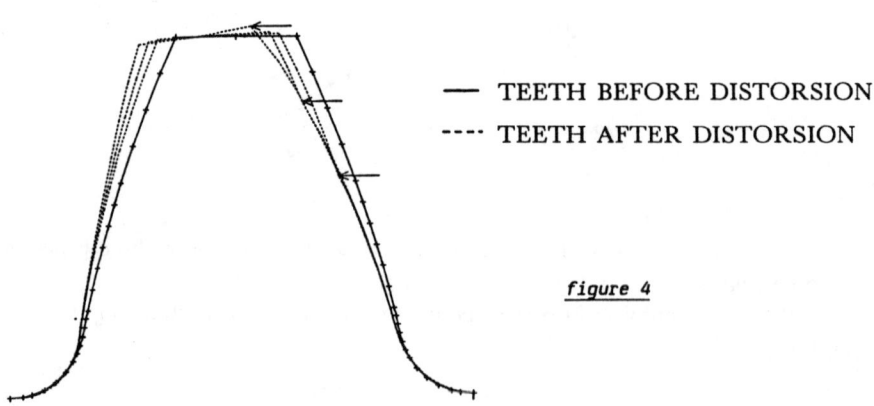

4. STUDY OF DEFLECTION OF A TOOTH DURING MESHING

Using the preceding model, we determined the deflection at the point of application of the load on a tooth (figure 5)

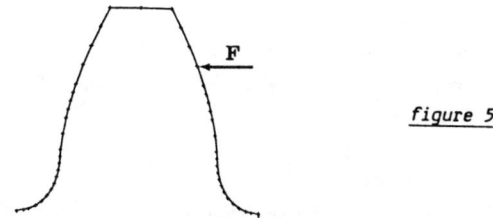

figure 5

Let f0 be the unit deflection for a tangential force of 1 daN and a tooth width of 1mm.

In the elastic range, the value of the deflection will thus be : $f = f0*Ft/b$, with Ft in daN and b in mm.

By means of integral equations, we calculated the unit deflections for different values of :
- the number of teeth and the undercut : we covered the standard range for gears with 15, 50, 100 teeth and -0.5, 0, $+0.5$ for the undercut.
- the type of material
  . steel E = 210000 MPa
  . plastic (7) E = 500 - 1000 - 3000 MPa.

The results obtained are presented on the curves in appendix 2. The results are given in numerical form and the equations for the curves were obtained by smoothing (the method of least squares).

Let us calculate the distribution of the forces on the teeth during meshing (8). Let a pair of teeth D1 D2 in contact at M and the following pair D'1 D'2 be in contact at M' (fig. 6)

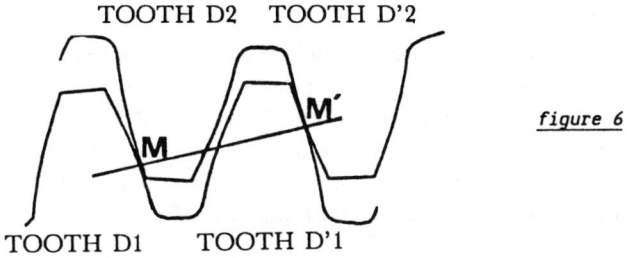

figure 6

This hyperstatic problem (2 teeth in contact) is resolved by making use of the distortion of solids in contact with one another.

Let : F be the load on pair D1 D2 along the line of action
F' be the load on the pair D'1 D'2 along the line of action
For a unit couple Co = 1 m daN
we have F + F' = Co/rb

The compatibility of the displacement fields at M and M' means that the displacement at M with a load F, and at M' with a load F', must be equal, along the straight line MM'
$$\delta M = \delta M'$$
Thus, after resolution, we have

$$F = \frac{\cos \theta_{1M'} \cdot f'_1 + \cos \theta_{2M'} \cdot f'_2}{(\cos \theta_{1M} f_1 + \cos \theta_{2M} f_2) + (\cos \theta_{1M'} f'_1 + \cos \theta_{2M'} f'_2)} \cdot \frac{c}{rb}$$

$$F' = \frac{\cos \theta_{1M} f_1 + \cos \theta_{2M} f_2}{(\cos \theta_{1M} f_1 + \cos \theta_{2M} f_2) + (\cos \theta_{1M'} f'_1 + \cos \theta_{2M'} f'_2)} \cdot \frac{c}{rb}$$

The results obtained are shown on the curves (figure 7).

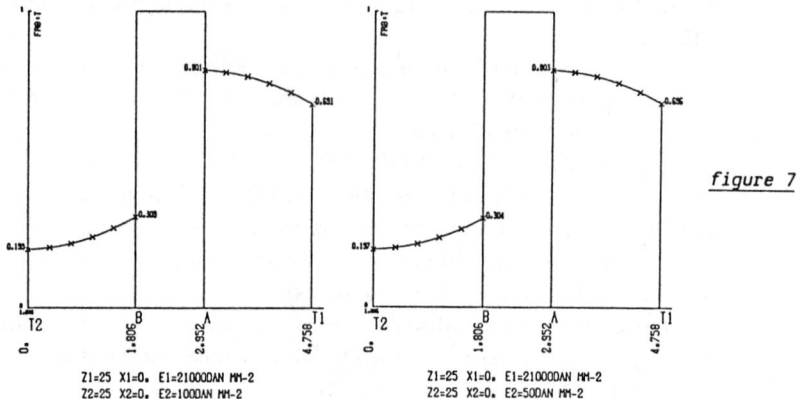

figure 7

For a steel – plastic gear, we may note that :

– when the load is distribution between the two pairs f teeth, the variation of Frb/T is parabolic. Nevertheless, the sum of the values of Frb/T at two points remote from the pitch is equal to the total load.

– it appears that the plastic tooth transfers the force only when the contact is close to the base of tooth. When the contact is at the tip of the plastic tooth, the latter deflects and transmits only a small proportion of the couple.

Let us apply these results to the study of the relief angle at the tip of the tooth (figure 8).

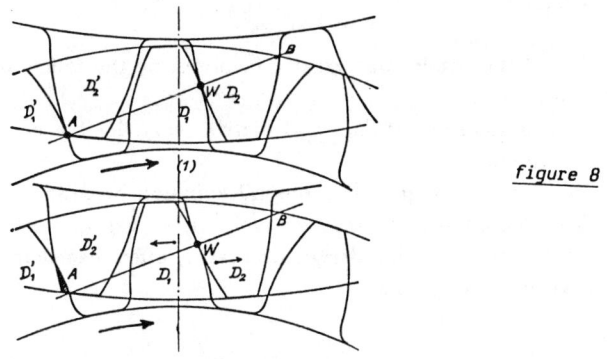

figure 8

The teeth D1 and D2 are in contact, and the following pair D'1 and D'2 are starting to mesh.

If the teeth were not loaded, contact at tl would take place without any dynamic loading.

Conversely, in the case of meshing with loading, the teeth D1 and D2 deflect, resulting in a dynamic loading as the pair D'1 and D'2 start to mesh.

This clearly prejudicial dynamic loading (source of noise, breakdown of the lubrication film) must be eliminated by incorporating a slight relief angle at the tip of the tooth.

This relief angle is complex to determine by calculation (intersection of the distorted profiles on the involute), but can be easily found by graphical simulation on a screen.

We divided up the rotation of the gear and, at each position, on a digitiser, we determined the relief angle necessary for the satisfactory functioning of the gear (figure 9).

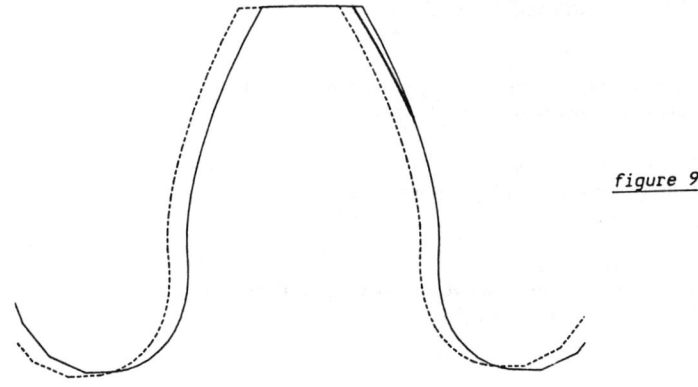

figure 9

5. CONCLUSIONS

The achievement of the results was greatly favoured by the following features :
 – automatic preparation of data and matrix, very flexible in use, entirely in a dialogue mode.
 – low cost of the running of the integral equation program.
 – a CAD – calculation link – up, relatively little used at present, which, by means of effective, variable design programs, offers excellent results by dynamic visual simulation.

REFERENCES

1. MATHIS
   Study of the stresses and distortions in gear teeth
   CETIM Technical memorandum N 18

2. LACHAT – WATSON
   Application of the integral equation method to structural calculations
   CETIM Technical memorandum N 25

3. SALOMON
   Linear elasticity
   Masson 1968 pp 448 – 489

4. CARACCI – ASTRE – LAFITTE
   Analysis of the contact pressures in a plastic gear

5. BOYER – CARACCI – ASTRE – LAFITTE
   Design and use of C.F.A.O programs by mechanical engineering students.
   3rd Conference on C.F.A.O MICAD 84 Paris

6. CHABERT – DELFOSSE – MATHIS
   Evaluation of the bending stresses in spur gear teeth under load
   CETIM Technical memorandum N 15

7. BORD – GIALLONARDO
   Guide to plastic materials in mechanical engineering
   CETIM volume 2

8. BOYER – ASTRE – CARACCI
   Bending of spur teeth – influence on various meshing characteristics.
   2nd World Gearing Congress Paris 1986

APPENDIX 1

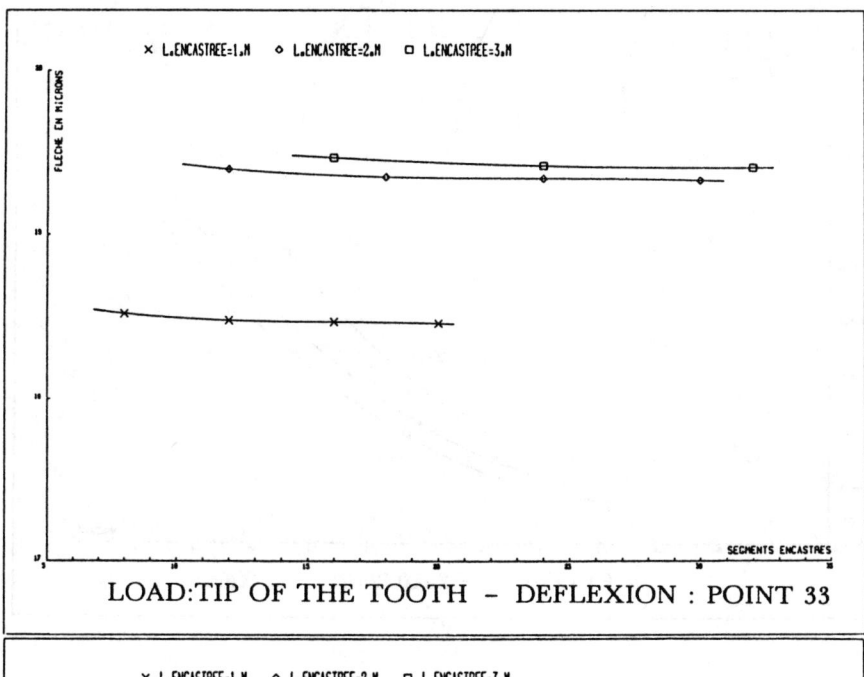

LOAD:TIP OF THE TOOTH – DEFLEXION : POINT 33

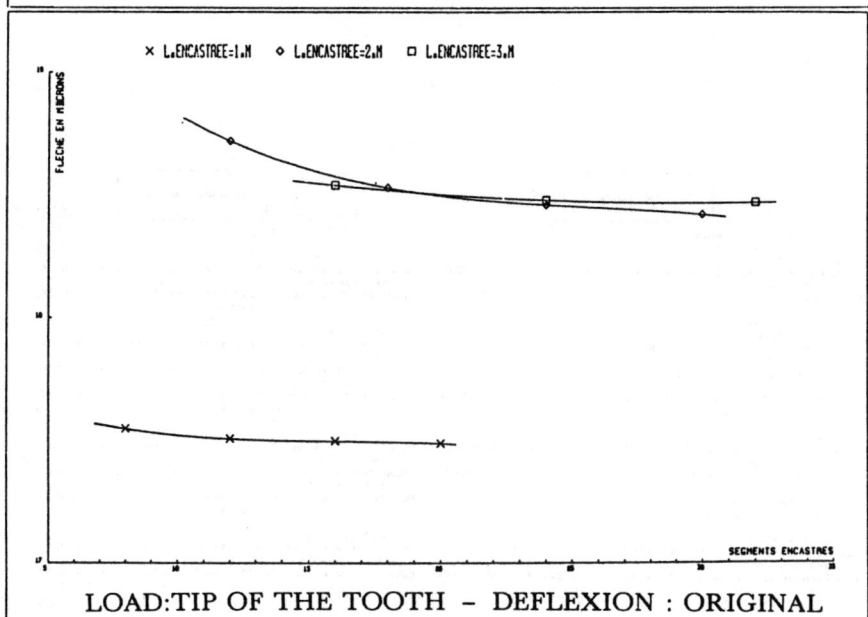

LOAD:TIP OF THE TOOTH – DEFLEXION : ORIGINAL

APPENDIX 2

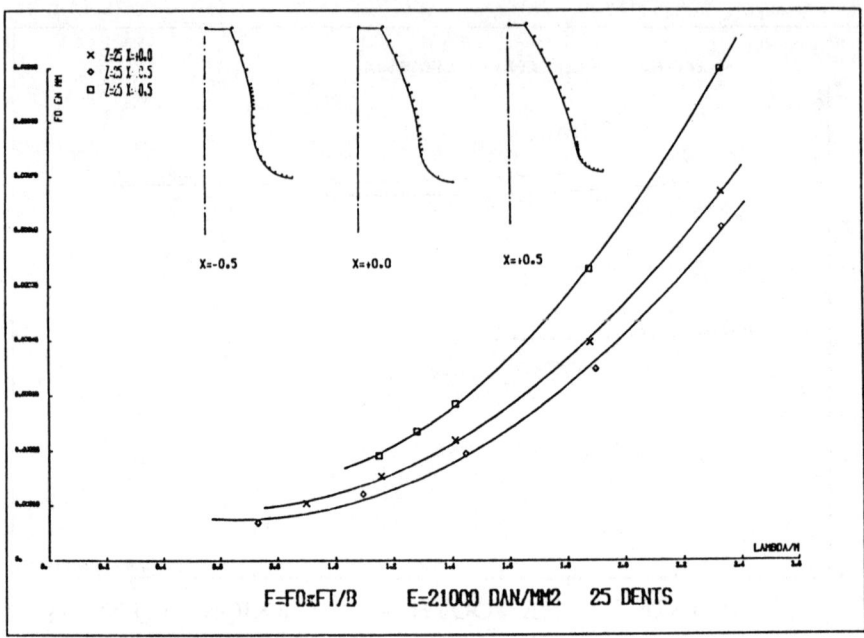

$F = F_0 \times F_T / B$ $E = 21000 \ DAN/MM2$ 25 DENTS

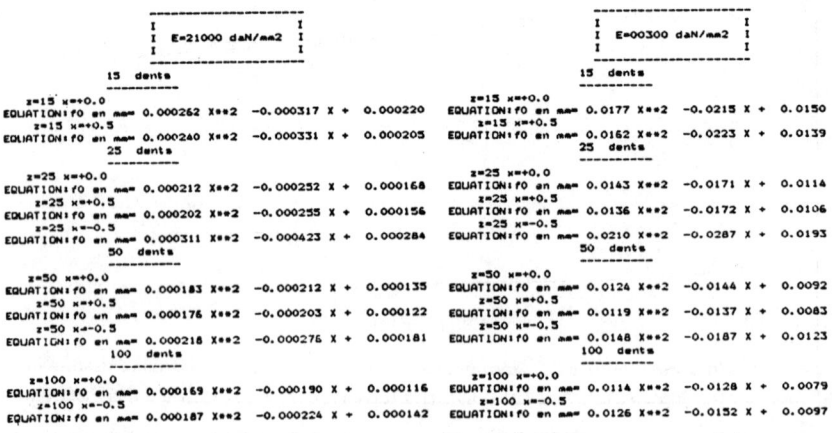

THE INTRODUCTION OF DISPLAY II, AN INTERACTIVE AND COLOR GRAPHICS POST-PROCESSING PROGRAM

Kant S. Kothawala

Engineering Mechanics Research Corporation, 1707 W. Big Beaver, Troy, MI 48084, USA

ABSTRACT

DISPLAY II is an interactive and color graphics software program which uses the latest state-of-the-art graphics techniques. DISPLAY II is a very powerful program for interactive post-processing and graphical portrayal of finite element related data, including model geometry and results of analyses.

KEYWORDS

Post-processing, interactive and color graphics, parallel processing, finite element modelling and mesh generation.

INTRODUCTION

An international center for engineering technology, EMRC's finite element modelling program DISPLAY has been improved significantly over the last few years. In addition to enhancing the pre-processing program DISPLAY, EMRC has also developed a very powerful post-processing program called DISPLAY II.

DISPLAY II is a very powerful finite element mesh generator and post processor of finite element models. DISPLAY II has outstanding color graphics capabilities for a wide variety of problems and allows graphical portrayal of model geometry and analysis results. Parallel processing into graphics, which provides a quantum leap in speed, is also available.

Analysis results which may be displayed graphically include stresses, displacements (static, dynamic mode shapes, transient dynamic snapshots, with or without animation, contours), temperatures, fatigue lives, fatigue damage, electromagnetic variables, strain energy/percentage/density, NISAOPT (optimization package) results, including boundary smoothing, and any other vector or scalar quantities the user wishes to plot via the neutral file.

■ INPUT/OUTPUT FEATURES

DISPLAY II is an interactive color graphics program that uses the latest state-of-the-art graphic techniques to create finite element models from drawings, generate mesh automatically and correct errors by viewing and listing element and node point data. DISPLAY II also has complete color graphics post-processing capabilities.

★ Model any complex geometry using an extensive library of linear and higher order beams, shells, solids, etc.,

★ Digitize elements and nodes of a model from drawings,

★ Merge two views to create a three-dimensional model and define three-dimensional elements,

★ Automatically generate a two- or three-dimensional mesh,

★ Generate mesh by dragging a defined plane along an arbitrary path,

★ Generate a symmetric mesh by reflection about a global plane or an arbitrary plane in rectangular or cylindrical coordinates,

★ Convert lower order elements into higher order elements and vice versa,

★ Allows user to create different parts of the model individually and merges all together to form the whole model,

★ Define all NISA data groups interactively,

★ List interactively a summary of the available options,

★ Interactively edit element and node point data using cursors, digitizing tablet and keyboard,

★ Locate element or node numbers from an arbitrary view,

★ Allows users to recover the original model after an inappropriate mesh generation,

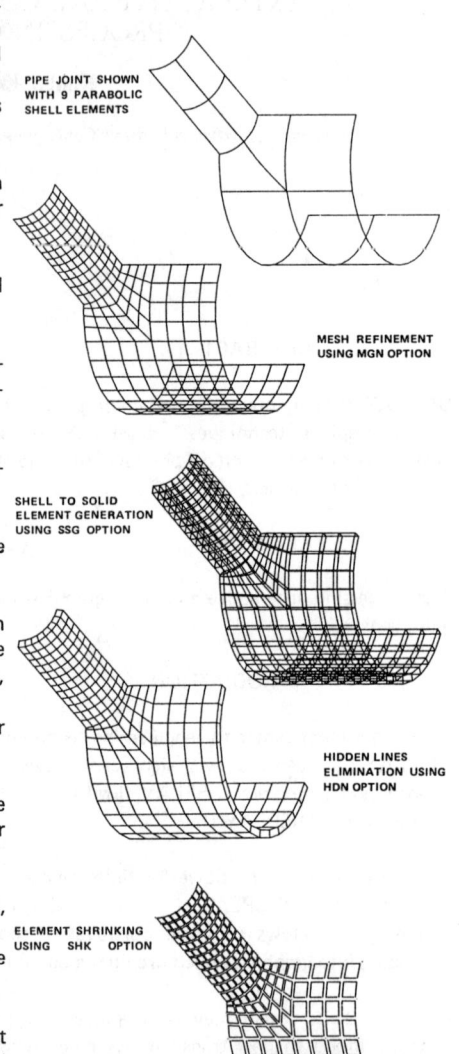

PIPE JOINT SHOWN WITH 9 PARABOLIC SHELL ELEMENTS

MESH REFINEMENT USING MGN OPTION

SHELL TO SOLID ELEMENT GENERATION USING SSG OPTION

HIDDEN LINES ELIMINATION USING HDN OPTION

ELEMENT SHRINKING USING SHK OPTION

* Select elements, nodes or element type for plotting,

* Isolate a portion, enlarge it or scale it down, rotate the view and display the model in different views,

* Display shrunk (users specified factor) elements to show element connectivity,

* Draw exact curved boundary by using shape functions,

* Display boundary faces and/or boundary of the structure with or without node numbers,

* Apply and display boundary conditions, coupled displacements, or concentrated nodal forces at any nodes,

* Save up to 10 views for later use during a session,

* Checks distortion index for 2D and 3D elements,

* Allows users to selectively calculate area and volume for 2D and 3D elements, respectively,

* Check and/or optimize wavefront,

* Captures all user's activities (history of execution) in a file called session file. This file can be resubmitted to DISPLAY to replay the whole execution,

* Allows user to generate 3D elements from 2D element mesh through the thickness

* Allows the user to have a consistent connectivity for shell elements and solid elements automatically,

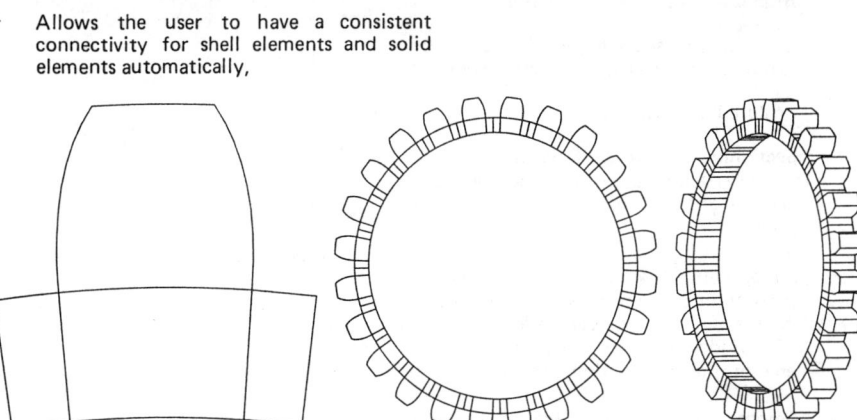

CROSS SECTION OF A CAR BUMPER. THE TRAJECTORY ON WHICH THE CROSS SECTION IS DRAGGED IS SHOWN WITH ASTERICKS AND NODE NUMBERS. HALF OF THE CAR BUMPER GENERATED BY DRAGGING THE CROSS SECTION OVER THE DEFINED TRAJECTORY.

FULL CAR BUMPER HIDDEN LINES ARE REMOVED USING HDS OPTION

A GEAR TOOTH WITH 4 PARABOLIC 2D ELEMENTS

A COMPLETE 2D REPRESENTATION OF A GEAR FROM ONE GEAR TOOTH USING SYMMETRIC MESH OPTION

HIDDEN LINES ELIMINATION USING HDN OPTION

■ OUTPUT: POST—PROCESSING

DISPLAY II has outstanding color graphics post-processing capabilities for a wide variety of problems. Some of the outstanding and frequently used capabilities are listed below:

★ User friendliness

★ Comprehensive user's manual with fast read summaries

★ Speed comparable or faster than rival existing market leaders

★ Monochrome or color

★ Static or animation

★ *Contour plotting* — Lines
                           Color fringes
- Stresses
- Displacements
- Temperatures
- Fatigue Lives
- Electromagnetic variables
- Strain energy/percentage/density
- NISA 3D fluid flow: velocity pressure and temperature distribution contours

★ Allows the user to select the color spectrum and/or equal/unequal color bands of his choice for any contour plotting. Also allows the spectrum to be reversed for real interpretation of an entity like fatigue life.

★ Boundary smoothing of shape optimized structures (see NISAOPT section)

★ Light source shading plus hidden entity removal (for realistic picture rendering)

★ Feature line plotting

★ Sectioning: Stress, displacements, pressure, velocity, temperature, etc., contour plots can be obtained on *any section through solid*.

★ *Multiple window* plots capability enables plotting of any type of plot simultaneously on the screen. One can have as many as 100 window plots on the screen exercising any of the plot options of DISPLAY II.

★ Smooth contour plots for higher order curved elements

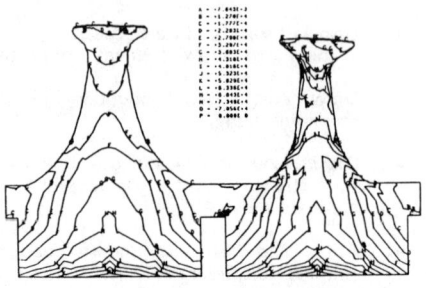

Contour plot of Von Mises equivalent stress distribution in a two-stage turbine assembly of a small jet engine.

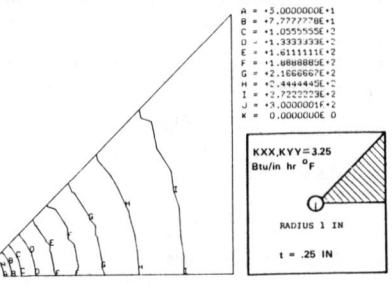

STEADY STATE HEAT CONDUCTION IN A SQUARE PLATE WITH A CIRCULAR HOLE
PLOT NO. 1
ISOTHERMAL LINES CONTOURS

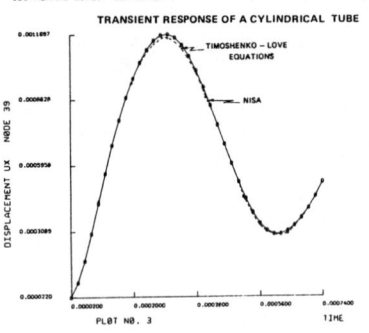

DISPLACEMENT HISTORY RESPONSE OF NODE 39

* Many other features expected in a proficient 3D graphics package are included such as: *dynamic rotation*, limiting the view to parts of the structure, *dynamic pan and zoom*, boundary line plotting, shrunken plotting, etc.

* Ultra high machine and graphics device portability. This is due to modularized software architecture, using standard FORTRAN 77 programming language. Such flexibility allows the package to take rapid advantage of the latest technological advances in hardware. This provides the user with state-of-the-art graphics, speed and bulk processing capabilities, as rapidly and economically as possible. For example, the latest graphics terminals have hardware hidden surfaces light shading, rotation and sectioning capabilities, which are much faster than their host software driven equivalents.

* *Parallel processing* into graphics, which provides a quantum leap in speed, is also available.

* Machine and graphic *device independent* — enabling rapid deployment to utilize the latest hardware technology for the user's benefit.

* Can run on almost all known graphic devices such as TEKTRONIX, RASTER TECHNOLOGY, LEXIDATA, RAMTEK, MEGATEK, HEWLETT-PACKARD, HITACHI, etc.

* Reliable and extensively tested by inhouse engineers, working on real engineering projects, before the release.

* Flexible - user requested features can be rapidly implemented.

* Displacement, velocity, acceleration, temperature vs. time plots for selected nodes

* Deformed shape, stresses, displacements, temperature and stress survey plots for composite shell at selected time intervals.

* Compatibility with analysis packages and other data bases.

DISPLAY II reads in a variety of different data/results files generated not only by NISA but by many other programs.

This capability allows translation of the data deck of programs such as NASTRAN, ANSYS and other programs to NISA. Also translation to NISA from many CAD/CAM mesh generation files such as APPLICON, AUTO-TROL, ANVIL 4000, CADAM, CALMA, COMPUTERVISION, GERBER, GRAFTEK, INTEGRAPH, CAEDS, MOVIE.BYU, PATRAN-G, SUPERTAB, and many others.

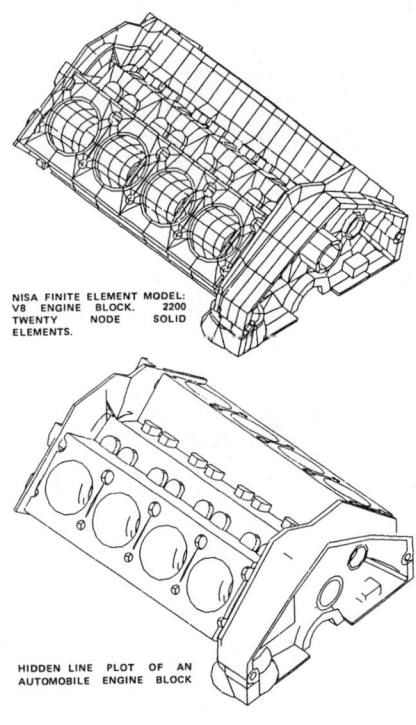

NISA FINITE ELEMENT MODEL: V8 ENGINE BLOCK. 2200 TWENTY NODE SOLID ELEMENTS.

HIDDEN LINE PLOT OF AN AUTOMOBILE ENGINE BLOCK

GRAFEM & IFAD: PREDICTIVE ANALYSIS TOOLS OF APPLICON

Darius Lahoutifard

Applicon/Schlumberger, 50 avenue Jean Jaurès, B.P. 80, 92123 Montrouge, France

ABSTRACT

APPLICON has been developing integrated and interactive solutions in CAD/CAM since 1969. BRAVO ! family of software, which contains modules of 2D and 3D design, surface and solids modeling, finite element modeling & structural analysis, kinematic and dynamic analysis of mechanisms, engineering, electric & electronic design, and finally, modules of manufacturing, works on VAX/VMS family.
GRAFEM (the pre/post-processor) and IFAD (the analysis program) are fully integrated in BRAVO ! family through the unique database. Using the part outline generated by solids modeler, surface modeler or the EDITOR (wireframe geometry), GRAFEM generates the mesh, defines and checks the finite elements model. Then IFAD (linear elastic ; static, dynamic or heat-steady) or another analysis program (like ANSYS, NASTRAN, ...) treats the model. Afterwards, the results are visualised by GRAFEM in the BRAVO ! database. The analysis can be done by IFAD (integrated) or by any other analysis code (interfaced).

SUMMARY

1) An introduction to APPLICON
2) BRAVO ! integrated CAD/CAM system
3) Structural Analysis, the Applicon approach
4) Using GRAFEM to construct finite element models
   4.1 Automatic mesh generation, MESH module
   4.2 Pre-processing facilities, MODEL module
   4.3 Checking the model, CHECK module
5) Using IFAD for FEA
6) Using external codes
7) An example of application
8) Afterword.

1.0 AN INTRODUCTION TO APPLICON

Since 1969, APPLICON, a pioneer in CAD/CAM, has been developing computer solutions for engineering applications. Initially dedicated to VLSI and PCB applications, APPLICON began to take an interest in mechanical applications in 1973.
In 1979 APPLICON set out to design a new generation CAD/CAM system that would surpass every existing system in terms of performance, reliability and ease of use.
In 1983, after four years of research and development, we see the birth of BRAVO !, APPLICON's first family of 32-bit computer-aided design, engineering, and manufacturing systems.
In 1985, MDSI, another division of SCHLUMBERGER, leader in CAM, joined APPLICON. The new enforced company proposes integrated products in CAE/CAD/CAM.

2.0 BRAVO ! INTEGRATED CAD/CAM SYSTEM FROM APPLICON

BRAVO ! is more than an advanced set of CAD/CAM features, it is a totally integrated system that links design, analysis, documentation, and manufacturing.

BRAVO ! features and array of unique capabilities, including :

> * 32-bit hardware architecture
>   -VAS-based processors provide greatly increased processing throughput for CAD/CAM applications.
>
> * advanced, high-level software
>   -all systems and applications software are written in a high-level language, making the BRAVO ! system virtually unlimited in its capacity for new applications development.
>
> * complete integration through data base management
>   -all applications work on a consistent, unified data base ; information is not duplicated, it is simply accessed when needed.
>
> * ease-of-use
>   -tutorial menus, on-line documentation, and unique shorthand input techniques help both novice and seasoned users make productive use of BRAVO !

BRAVO !'s data base facilities allow the user to create, access and format graphic and alphanumeric data to satisfy specific needs of advanced user's applications. Standard parts' libraries are accessed through the data base structure generated by the Data Base Management System.

BRAVO !'s design capabilities allow the user to create a three-dimensional wireframe, surface, or solid model. Data for all subsequent activities, such as drafting or manufacturing is derived from this geometric and textual data base.

BRAVO ! provide a large range of analysis packages that enable interactive
kinematic, mass properties, and structural analysis to reveal potential
interferences of structural deficiencies.
BRAVO !'s drafting capabilities provides an extensive range of dimensioning
and production features.
BRAVO !'s Numerical Control package automaticaly generates toolpaths using
previously designed geometry, with a complete associativity between them.

3.0 STRUCTURAL ANALYSIS, THE APPLICON APPROACH

APPLICON decided to fully integrate a structural analysis capability through
the BRAVO ! data Base Management System to eliminate the need for input files,
output files and other activities which require manual editing and user intervention. This feature is based on two products :

- GRAFEM (GRAphic Finite Element Modeling)
  for interactive generation of finitie element models and display
  of analysis result.

- IFAD (Integrated Finite Element Analysis and Design)
  companion program that performs concurrent finite element
a analysis, fully integrated with the pre/post processing capabilities
  of GRAFEM.

In the BRAVO ! system, the two packages work together in the following
manner :

The part outline is first generated at the workstation using the graphics
EDITOR (for wire frame geometry), the SURFACE MODELER (o create surface
geometry), or the SOLID MODELING II program (to build a three dimensional
model).
Via a standard menu pick, the mesh generation portion of GRAFEM is invoked
to subdivide part geometry into discrete finite elements. With the unified
data base the mesh generator simply has to read the required information
created by the graphics programs and prompt the user for parameters necessary to break the part geometry into the desired number of nodes and elements,
additional data relative to material properties, loads, boundary restraints,
etc... can be added and the completed model checked for completeness and
"goodness".
After the finite element model has been verified, the user simply chooses
another menu pick to perform analysis with IFAD, which has only to search
the unified data base to obtain all necessary information needed to perform
the finite element analysis.
Once analysis is completed, all results (displacements, stresses, strains,
etc...) are stored in the data base ready to be displayed by the postprocessor
function of GRAFEM.

Throughout the entire process, the engineer never has to leave the workstation
nor edit nor manipulate any external files.

Finite element modeling and analysis are indispensable in the modern mechanical design office. Demonstrated needs for computer aided structural analysis and design include :

* Verification of structural integrity.
* Compliance with design rules.
* Analysis of prototype structures before they are built.
* Analysis and correction of structural failures.
* Improvement of existing designs.
* Reduction of weight without impairing function.
* Performance of parametric studies.
* Reduction of costs and lead time.
* Increase of engineering productivity.

The use of GRAFEM/IFAD for analysis and design of strucural components has important benefits which include :

* The ability to interactively model and then analyse complex shaped parts that are difficult to design manually.
* Accurate and reliable results.
* More efficient component designs.
* Shortened design cycles.
* Increase productivity from engineers and designers.

4.0 USING GRAFEM TO CONSTRUCT FINITE ELEMENT MODELS

The first stage of structural analysis using the finite element method is the model building or preprocessor stage which involves several steps :

* Generation of a mesh of nodes and elements.
* Assignment of element physical and material properties.
* Definition of location and types of boundary restraints.
* Definition of location and types of structural loads.
* Verification of model validity.

GRAFEM provides the necessary capabilities to perform all of the preceding preprocessing steps in the following basic modules :

* MESH
* MODEL
* CHECK.

4.1 AUTOMATIC MESH GENERATION VIA GRAFEM, THE MESH MODULE

The MESH module is intended to provide automated methods for generating the model node and element mesh. One, two and three dimensional node and element meshes can be generated from surfaces or wireframe geometry. The geometry can be created using standard EDITOR functions, the SOLID MODELING II boundary file or the SURFACES package. All the geometric information is

easily retrievable via the Data Base Management System of BRAVO !
The mesh is generated using the definition of the model in terms of its
bounding edges and desired boundary node placement which can be used as
the basis for finite element subdivision. All the boundaries can be
composed of one or more user defined components such as lines, arcs, curves,
splines, conics, etc... Node locations are generated along an entire
boundary or a portion of it under user control which permits the specification of the spacing or the total number of nodes with the option of biasing
towards the ends or centre of the designated boundary portion.

Using the boundary definition of the geometric model, the user can generate
a lot of GRAFEM primitives to describe the finite element areas which
support the finite element mesh.
The simpliest GRAFEM primitive avalaible is the boundary which allows one
dimensional meshing to create a series of truss, beam, or spring elements.
Three types of two dimensional primitives are available : plane, shell or
surface. A plane primitive is defined by a series of boundaries implicitly
lying in a geometric plane. Shell primitives are defined with four wire
frame boundaries in geometric space, the resulting area can be either flat or
warped. Surface primitives refer to surfaces generated by the BRAVO !
SURFACE package which is directly interfaced with GRAFEM.
Three dimensional primitives (hexahedron, prism or tetrahedron) are
described using a series of boundaries (respectively 12, 9 and 6) to
define an enclosed volume. Once the GRAFEM primitives are defined the mesh
can be generated using one of the three automatic mesh generation algorithms
currently implemented in GRAFEM.
The first algorithm is based on the mapping technique. The main concept of
mapping methods are the transformation of surface and three dimensional
areas. The principle is to first define a body coordinate system, then
derive two- and three- dimensional coordinate transformations between it
and the cartesian coordinate system. This establishes the mapping of a
unit square onto a surface and a unit cube onto a volume. The mesh is
elementarily generated on the unit region and then back transformed into
the body coordinate system.
Based on this technique, GRAFEM has the following basic methods :

* Blending
  to generate
  quadrilateral
  elements on plane ;
  shell and surface
  primitives with four
  definable portions
  of exterior boundary
  and the same number
  of nodes on opposite
  sides.

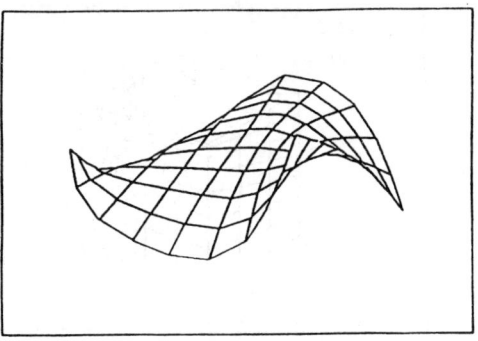

example of blending
on a warped surface

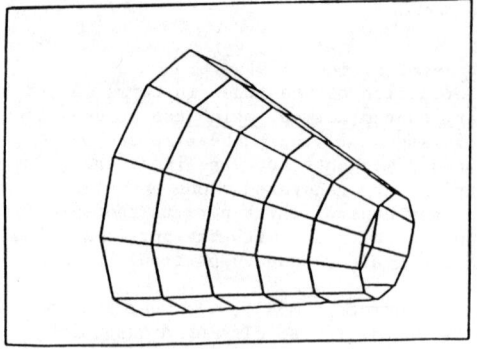

* Lofting
  Generation of quadrilateral elements on plane or surface primitives defined by two enbedded boundaries with the same number of nodes.

example of lofting
on a cone

* Trimap
  to generate triangular elements on plane primitives with three definable portions of the external boundary containing the same number of nodes.

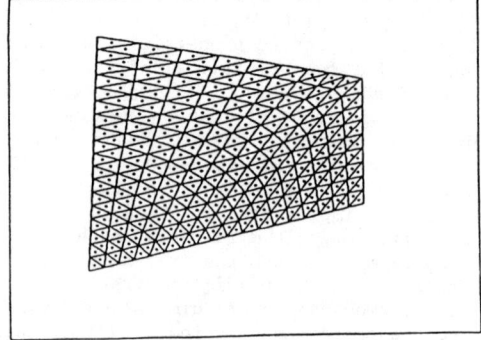

example of trimapping
inside a quadrilateral

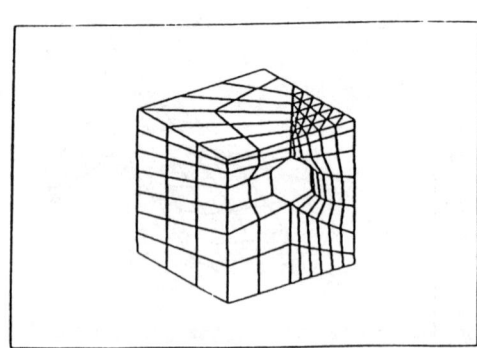

* Volume
  three dimensional generation inside a hexahedron, a prism or a tetrahedron defined volume with the same mesh gradation on the opposite faces. The element shapes result implicitly from the original volume.

example of volume
mapping on a cube

The second algorithm uses the topological searching technique for two dimensional mesh generation. This algorithm starts from the boundary polygon and step by step creates new elements by removing all particular angles (to avoid a concave region on the boundary). The resulting mesh is then smoothed by nodal averaging.
Using this technique BRAVO ! provides the following basic methods :

* Trimeshing to generate triangular elements on plane, shell and surface areas having an external boundary and one or more internal boundaries containing an arbitrary number of nodes.

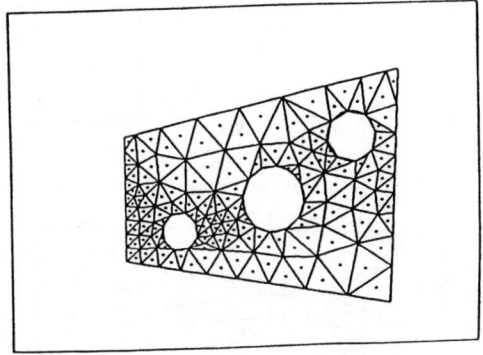

example of trimeshing

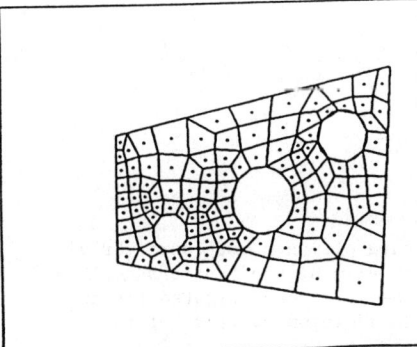

Quadmeshing :
Generation of quadrilateral elements on plane, shell and surface areas with any number of boundaries. The sum of all nodes placed on the boundaries must be an even number.

Quadmeshing example

The last mesh generation method used in GRAFEM is a drag-technique applied on a three dimensional mesh. The method starts from a two dimensional mesh defined on a plane and drags it along a specified profile.

Two methods are present in GRAFEM :

* Extrusion
  Drags the plane along a 3D-vector path, the user defines the number of element layers.

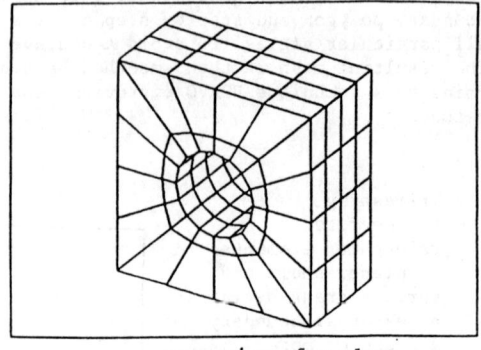

extrusion of a plane

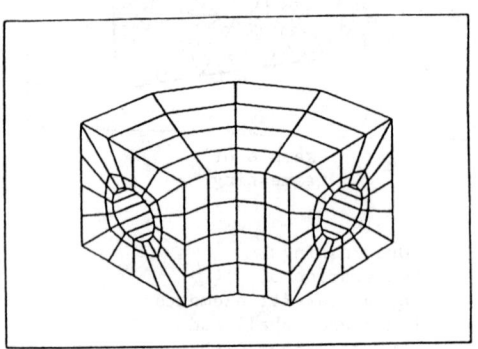

* Sweeping
  The path used during the dragging operation is a circular arc.

sweeping of a plane

The current MESH module will only generate elements with straight sides and nodes at vertices and corners of the element configurations. This is an inconvenience if the user wants to use more sophisticated finite elements having nodes along the edges in addition to those at the corners. A capability exists in the GRAFEM MODEL module, however, which allows an intermediate node to be automaticaly added at the centre of each straight edge for an element with only corner nodes. This provides an ability to use higher order elements in an analysis.

4.2 PRE-PROCESSING GRAFEM FACILITY, THE MODEL MODULE

The MODEL module of GRAFEM has two features. First is the manual generation of a finite element mesh with facilities such as copy, reflection ... of nodes and elements. Second is mesh editing which permits the individual entities or as specified groups (with all the advantages of screen selection). These capabilities supplement the automated mesh generation capability by allowing changes in the mesh to avoid badly distorted elements and permitting the modelisation of part features that are not easily generated automatically.

The specification of all element physical and material properties, boundary conditions and structural loads are also fully interactively accomplished by this module. The definition of element physical and material properties is accomplished by tabular data input. Predefined tables exists within GRAFEM for the following analysis codes :

* IFAD
* SASI/ANSYS (1)
* SDRC/SUPERB (2)
* MSC/NASTRAN (3)
* SDRC/SAGS
* MOLDFLOW
* USER-DEFINED

The final step in model preparation is frequently the resequencing of element or node numbers to minimize the time used by finite element codes to perform the analysis. MODEL provides the capability to optimize bandwidth or wavefront for the analysis phase. This procedure is not required in the case of an IFAD analysis which internally optimizes equation numbering to produce minimum solution times.

4.3 CHECKING THE MODEL WITHING GRAFEM, THE CHECK MODULE

This module is intended to help users to detect errors in finite element models before the run of the analysis. The following error checking options are available :

* Coincident node check
  Check multiple nodes at the same location with an optional merge
* Distortion check
  Locates elements in the model which have poor shapes that may produce bad results.

---

(1) ANSYS is a registred trademark of Swanson Analysis System Inc.
(2) SUPERB is a trademark of Structural Dynamic Research Laboratory
(3) NASTRAN is a trademark of the National Aeronautics and Space Administration.

loads by creating temperature loads in GRAFEM for a structural analysis.
That is another benefit of an integrated system.

6.0 USING EXTERNAL CODES TO PERFORM ANALYSIS

GRAFEM can also be used as a pre/post processor with larger sized codes
(SASI/ANSYS, MSC/NASTRAN, SDRC/SUPERB, and many others) to perform more
complex and non-linear calculations.
When the user wants to activate another analysis code, APPLICON provides
direct interfaces to the third-party analysis program, such as SASI/ANSYS
MSC/NASTRAN, SDRC/SUPERB .. SDRC/SAGS, MOLDFLOW or a user defined program,
via data input/output files.

7.0 AN EXAMPLE OF APPLICATION

A thin shell model

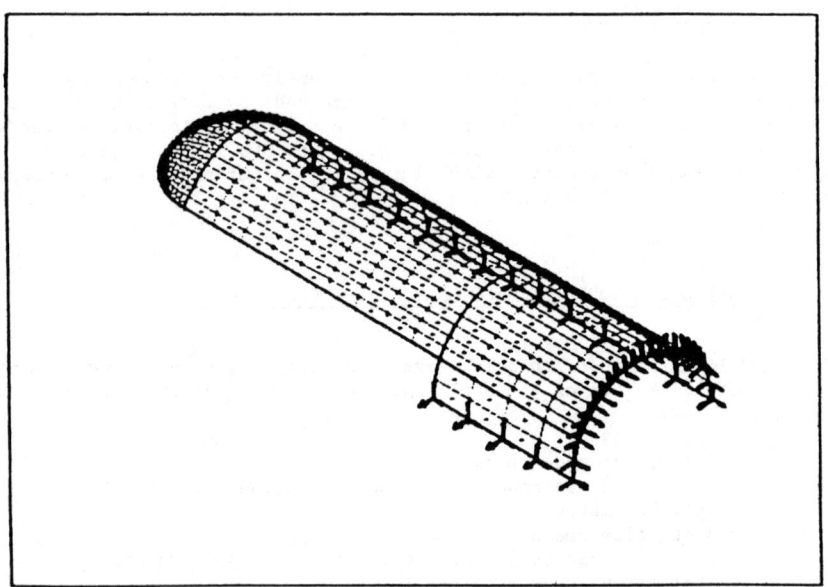

The restraints on the nodes are represented by arrows ;
A simple arrow for a translation restraint,
A double arrow for a rotation restraint.

* Free edge check
  Locates and displays all free edges of the model to visually check for holes or cracks inadvertantly caused by missing or incorrectly connected elements.
* Warping check
  Determines warping factors for shell elements when all nodes do not lie in a plane which can produce invalid results.

4.4 POST PROCESSING FACILITIES OF GRAFEM, THE RESULT MODULE

The RESULT module provides, to the user, an integrated tool for processing the enormous quantities of data generated by finite element analysis. This is a convenient, time saving procedure that helps the user understand the behaviour of complex structures. The module is able to visualize the following results :

* Deformations
  The deformation is visualized with a user-specified scale factor and an optional "animation" which permits the control of the deformation during the growth of loads. The animation is very useful for visualizing mode shapes after a dynamic analysis.
* Stresses
  The contour stress calculation of principal, principal bending, shear and Von Mises stresses could be displayed with an optional number of either coloured or labelled contour lines.
* Isotherms
  With the same display options as contour stresses.

5.0 USING IFAD FOR FINITE ELEMENT ANALYSIS

IFAD provides an integrated capability for performing certain types of finitie element analysis on the BRAVO ! system. The program efficiently analyzes a specific class of structural problems that involve linear, elastic behaviour and small structural displacements in static or dynamic mode. This class of problem, where stresses, strains and deformations are directly proportional to applied loads, constitues about 80 percent of finite element analysis performed by mechanical design engineers. The remaining small percentage of analyses, in which stresses, strains, deformations, etc, are not proportional to loading can be analyzed by other programs which are interfaced to GRAFEM.

IFAD provides a linear steady-state heat transfer analysis, as well. The same elements generated by GRAFEM may be used either for a thermal analysis or structural analysis.
It is important to note that after a thermal analysis is done, the resulting computed temperatures can be used automatically to induce thermal stress

Contour stress (VON-MISES) in 8 colors :

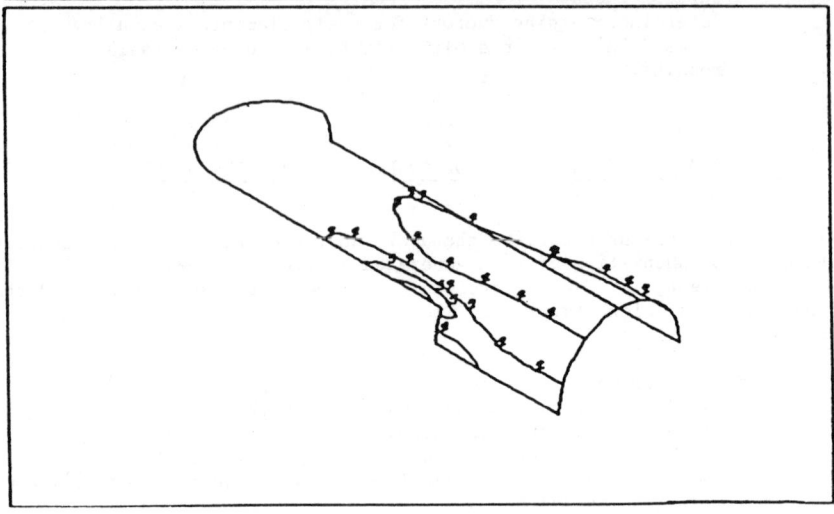

First mode shape of vibration in animation :

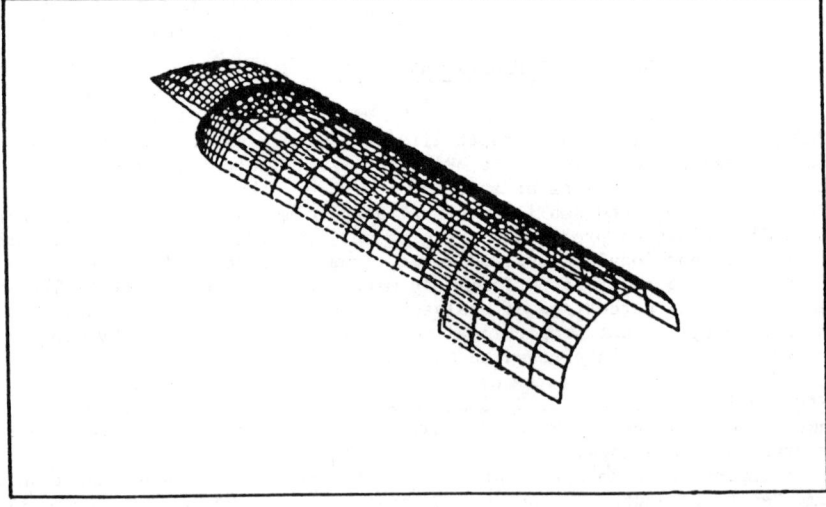

8.0 AFTERWORD

APPLICON is committed to providing computer aided design tools for the mechanical engineering market. Finite element analysis has an important place in overall design of mechanical components and constitutes one of the key components in a CAE package. APPLICON's intention is not to replace NASTRAN, ANSYS or other popular general purpose finite element analysis codes with its GRAFEM/IFAD products but rather to supplement the capabilities of the general purpose codes with an integrated FEA capability.

It is important to note the difference between interfaced and integrated in the context of finite element analysis. Interfaced means that the analysis codes communicate with the pre/post processor through the use of external data files that must be monitored and maintained by the user. Integrated means that finite element modelling, analysis and postprocessing functions use a common data base for communication. At first glance, this may not be an important distinction since the basic objective of predicting structural behavior can be achieved in either case. However, the use of an integrated FEA capability has some significant advantages for design engineers and many have already been discussed. In particular one of the real advantages that can be emphasized is the shortened turn-around time to produce analysis results since the user does not have to manipulate external data files. This is especially important when interactive changes are being made to optimize a design since many analysis runs are needed. It is difficult to really appreciate the amount of time that can be saved using an integrated analysis program in this instance until it is personally experienced.

APPLICON is committed to the continued development of its integrated FEA products. As time goes on, capabilities such as computer assisted design optimization, interactive query and report generation and comparative results' plots that take advantages of the finite element data base will be added to further differentiate the products as tools for design engineers.

Chapter 2
INDUSTRIAL APPLICATIONS OF STRUCTURAL ANALYSIS SYSTEMS

INDUSTRIAL APPLICATIONS OF THE FINITE ELEMENTS AND BOUNDARY ELEMENTS ANALYSIS SYSTEM "CA.ST.OR"

M. Afzali and M. Cristescu

CETIM, 52 Avenue Félix Louat, 60300 Senlis, France

INTRODUCTION

CA.ST.OR is general purpose Finite Elements and Boundary Elements system covering a wide range of applications and Computer capabilities.
The developments of this software are based on the extensive experience of CETIM in solving the engineering problems and its position in the industrial environment. This allows the software to be well-suited to problems encountered in mechanical engineering.

Two kinds of software are proposed to the users :

- CA.ST.OR software running on work-stations, mini and main frame computers covering a large number of industrial applications with interactive input data and graphique display.

- CA.ST.OR BE software, running on micro-computers with interactive procedure and graphique display suitable for design offices.

This paper describes CA.ST.OR softwares running on work-stations, mini and main frame computers.

This software allows to perform two-dimensional and three-dimensional thermal and stress analysis with linear and non-linear behaviour. Seismic analysis, fluid structure interaction and also dynamic analysis of rotating machinery can be performed. For three dimensional thermal and elastic analysis, Boundary Method is used.

FIELD OF APPLICATION

The system is composed of four parts :

- CA.ST.OR 2D performs thermal and linear and non-linear static analysis of plane or axisymmetrical stuctures with symmetric or non-symmetric loadings.

- CA.ST.OR 3D performs thermal and linear elastic analysis of three dimensional structures using Boundary Elements method.

- CA.ST.OR SD performs static and dynamic mechanical analysis of 3D bolted and welded structures (plates, shells, beams, ...) and of 3D continuous media with linear elastic behaviour.

- CA.ST.OR MT performs dynamic bending and torsional analysis (natural frequencies and mode shapes) of interconnected shafts.
  All programs are written in Fortran 77 with interactive data input and free formatted input for batch and are running on CRAY XMP, and VAX 11/780, IBM 43** and work-stations Micro-VAX, Appolo.

In two dimensional analyses material non linearities as plasticity or viscoplasticity and cyclic thermo-plasticity are included. The contact problems (geometry non-linear) can be also analysed. Steady state and transient thermal analyses can be performed in two and three-dimensional modelizations.

The temperature file is used for thermal loading in elastic or plasticity analyses. Other loadings may be concentrated forces, pressure and shear forces, rotational and gravitational forces or prescribed displacements. Some specific application like fracture mechanics in two and three-dimensional structures can be also performed. Generally speaking CA.S.T.OR software are suitable for the following applications :

Engine components, mechanical transmission components, pressure vessels, compressors, gas turbines, mechanical components in nuclear industry, welded and bolted structures in buildings, offshore platforms, nuclear plant and general mechanical components, reservoirs and immerged structures, etc...

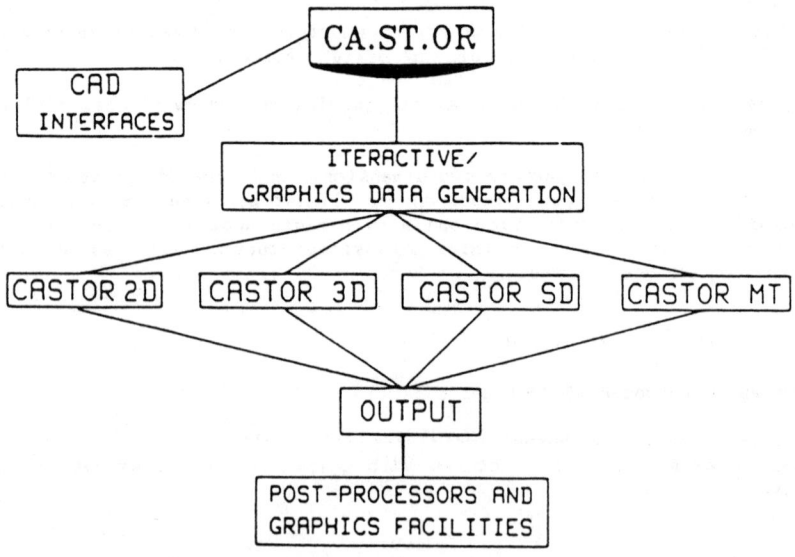

CA.ST.OR Software

PROGRAM DESCRIPTION

CA.ST.OR 2D

Based on Finite Element Method allows to perform 2D thermo-elasticity or thermo-elasto-visco-plasticity analysis of plane or axisymmetrical structures [1-3]. The size of CA.ST.OR 2D is about 60.000 statements but the memory size needed for an analysis depends on the size of the problem and because the memory is dynamically allocated, the size limitation depends on computer capability.

Main features :

- Interactive and graphic display input data
- Mechanical analysis
  . plane strain, plane stress, axisymmetric (with non axisymmetric loading)
- Material behaviour
  . elastic, plastic, visco-plastic
- Thermal analysis
  . steady-state, transient
- Contact problems
- Graphic post-processor
- Post-processor (Analysis)
  . fracture mechanics, fatigue analysis, ...

Options :

. PREED, M2D

This option performs an interactive-graphics input data for CA.ST.OR 2D. In all steps of the analysis the user is guided by the menus and graphic display. At any stage it is possible to modify the contour, the mesh refinement or introduce a filet in a sharp edge. After geometry input the stucture is discretized into 6-node elements by an automatic mesh generator.
The node renumbering reducing computation time in FEM analyses is included. Special contact elements can be used by this option. After meshing boundary conditions and differents load cases are introduced with graphique symbols.

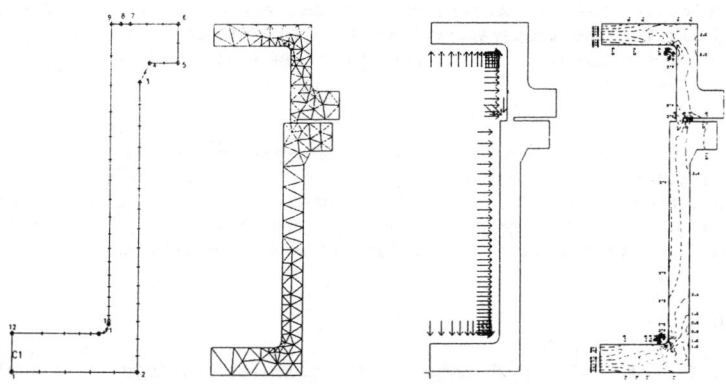

Figure 1 : Example of graphic display

F E2D

This option performs elastic stress analysis of 2-D plane or axisymmetric structure. The structure may be composed of one or several isotropic materials. The interpolation functions are quadratic.

The necessary data are :
- description of geometry using the corresponding file generated by M2D
- material properties
- boundary conditions (given displacements, elastic supports perfect contact, perfect sliding or contact with friction between the structure's components). For the contact problems with unknown contact a special contact element (fig. 1(c)) is used. The algorithm for perfect sliding or perfect contact is incremental type, but in case of friction an iterative procedure is used.
- loadings may be concentrated forces, pressure and shear forces, rotational and gravitational forces, thermal loadings (temperature file generated by TH2D).

The results are the displacements, strain and stress tensors principal stresses and Von Mises and Tresca equivalent stresses at each node. The displacements and stresses files are generated for graphic interpretation of results.

. TH2D

This option performs steady state and transient thermal analyses of 2D plane and axisymmetrical structures. The analyzed structure may be composed of one or several isotropic materials.

The data are similar to those in E2D :

- description of geometry (geometry file generated by M2D or by the user),
- material properties (it can be dependent on temperature)
- boundary conditions (given temperature, given flux, convection, internal power),
- evolution of the boundary conditions with respect to time, and the time-step in transient analysis. The evolution of boundary condition is considered to be linear with respect to time.

The results are the temperature at each node and for each time-step in transient analysis. The temperature file is also generated for isothermal plotting and/or for thermal loading for stress analysis (E2D).

. EF 2D

Elastic stress analysis of 2D plane or axisymmetric bodies under non axisymmetric loading can be performed by this option. For loading a Fast Fourier Transformation is used. The data and results are the same as in option E2D except that the boundary conditions are restricted to given displacements and elastic supports. The angles for which the results must be printed are needed.

. EVP2D

This option of CA.ST.OR 2D performs thermal-elasto-viscoplastic analysis of 2D plane or axisymmetrical structures in the frame work of small strains and large displacements for isotropic and anisotropic materials. The paractical

problems as creep, plasticity and visco-plasticity may be analysed by this option.
Mechanical and Thermal loadings may vary with respect to time. The program takes into account the variation of material properties with respect to temperature.
Following behaviour laws may be considered :

- elastic behaviour (fig. 2a)
- elasto-plastic behaviour with and without work hardening (Fig. 2b)
- elasto-viscoplastic behaviour (Fig. 2c).

The input data for description of geometry M2D and boundary conditions are similar to EF2D. The loadings (similar to E2D) and their evolution with respect to time are needed.
The algorithm in EVP2D is incremental and iterative. At each step the displacements, strains, stresses and plastic or visco-plastic strains increments are calculated ; the material non linearities (plasticity or viscoplasticity) appear in the second member.

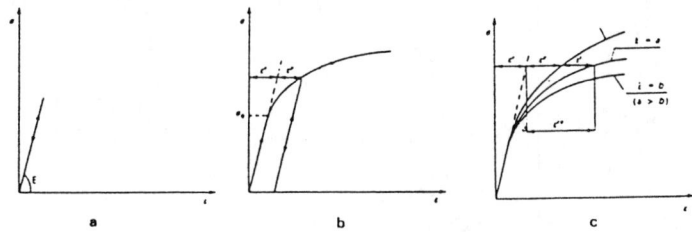

Figure 2 : behaviour laws in CA.ST.OR 2D
a) elastic,
b) elasto-plastic
c) elasto-viscoplastic

Iteration procedures are adopted for system resolution. The results are the same as those given by E2D for each computation step prescribed by the user. The plastic or viscoplastic strains are also given.

. NX2D

This option performs elastic analysis of axisymmetrical shells composed by isotropic or anisotropic materials. The elements are 2-node with 4 DOF per node (radial, axial, circonferential displacements and one rotation), gene rated by automatic mesh generator.
The results are the displacements rotations, stresses (in elements local base) and forces at each node of mesh. The stresses at the shell surfaces are given.

. PC2D

This option performs the cyclic thermo-plasticity based on a simplified approach [4] of the 2D plane or axisymmetrical stuctures in small strains and small displacements. The materials are considered elasto-plastic with linear kinematic work hardening. The initial residual plastic strains may be considered in the structure.
PC2D gives some information about the structure behaviour after a great number of cycles (adaptations or accomodations) without computations at each cycle usual in fatigue simulations.

The necessary data for this option are similar to those in EVP2D. The results are the plastic strains, elastic or inelastic stresses, work hardening parameter field, and inelastic strains.

. PP2D

This option is composed of several post-processors for fracture mechanics application, selective impression of results etc...

. D2D

This option allows to visualize interactively the geometry generated by the above options before and after loading on a graphic terminal or by a plotter with zoom possibility. The results (displacements, strains, stresses and temperatures) may be displayed or plotted as isovalue curves, colour fill area or printing of results values at each node.

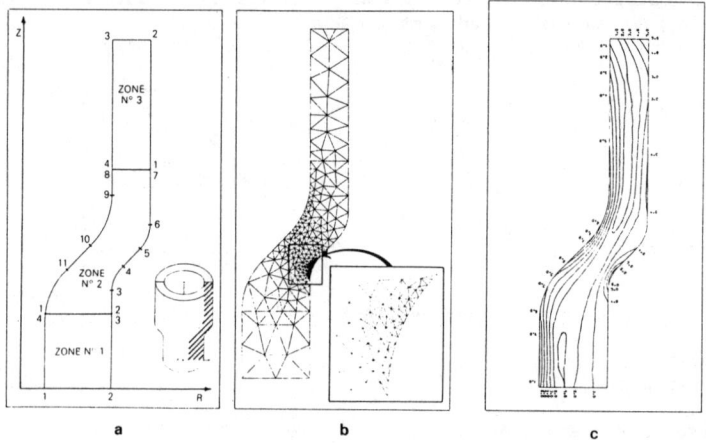

Figure 3 - Transient thermo-elastic analysis of a tube

(a) geometry
(b) mesh,
(c) iso-value of Von Mises of stresses

CA.ST.OR 3D

Based on Boundary Element Method performs thermo-elasticity analysis of 3D structures [1-5-9].

Main features :

- 3-D surface discretization
- 3-D elastic analysis
- 3-D thermal analysis (steady-state and transient)
- thermo-elastic analysis
- fracture mechanics applications
- visualisation of results on a intersecting plane
- graphic pre and post-processors

Options

. PRE3D, M3D

Semi-automatic mesh generator for discritization of 3D surfaces into subregions and elements. The surface elements are 6-node triangle and 8-node quadrangular elements (figure 4). Node coordinates may be in cartesian, cylindrical or spherical basis. PRE3D is an interactive-graphique program for input data. It offers several possibilities of visualisation and anable to introduce the data by means of menus.

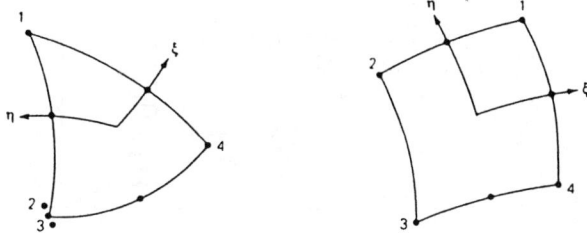

Figure 4 - Elements in CA.ST.OR 3D

. E3D

This option performs the elastic analysis of the 3D structures in small strains and displacements. The structure may be constituted by 10 isotropic materials.

The necessary data are :

- general informations : interpolation functions (linear or quadratic), plane or cyclic symmetries,
- geometry description (M3D)
- material properties (PRE3D)
- boundary conditions (given displacements on nodes, lines or elements, sliding on subregions interfaces, elastic support) (PRE3D)
- loadings (concentrated forces, distribution tractions on line or element, rotational and gravitational forces ,thermal loading) (PRE3D).

The results are the displacements, stresses, principle stresses, equivalent Tresca and Von Mises stresses at each node and at any other point on the surface or inside the structure prescribed by the user.

. TH3D

This option performs the steady state and transient heat transfert in the 3D structures.
The necessary data are :

- general information (same as E3D)
- geometry description (same as E3D)
- material properties,
- boundary conditions given temperature on nodes distributed temperature or flux on elements, heat transfer with exterior domains. In case of transient heat transfer, the evolution of boundary conditions with respect to time should be given.

- output are the temperature, flux, temperature gradient for the nodes and requested points. The temperature file for thermal loading in E3D or plotting the isotherm is generated.

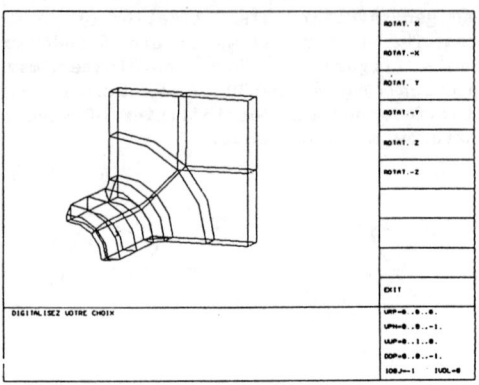

Figure 5 - PRE3D Menus

. PP3D

This option is composed of several post-processors :

PP3D-POST : calculates the solutions for the points on the surface and inside the structure.

PP3D-COMB : performs the linear combination of elementary load cases;

PP3D-SPECF : allows a selective impression of results

PP3D-MODIF : performs the same analysis as in E3D or TH3D for a structure with local modification compared with the reference structure.

PP3D-JRICE : calculates the J. integral of Rice with applications in fracture mechanics

PP3D-COUPE : generates the solutions files in order to plot the iso-value curve of stresses or temperatures on a plane intersecting the structure [7] (figure 6).

PP3D-RECUP : restart of E3D or TH3D

PP3D-SIGMA : calculates the stress tensor components with best precision for a node on a sharp edge or on a corner [7].

PP3D-RESTR : generates the solution file of a limited number of subregions.

. D3D

This option allows to visualize the geometry generated by M3D, E3D or TH3D before and after loading on a graphic terminal or by a plotter with zoom possiblity. It allows also to plot the iso-value curves of results on 3D surface with hidden lines.

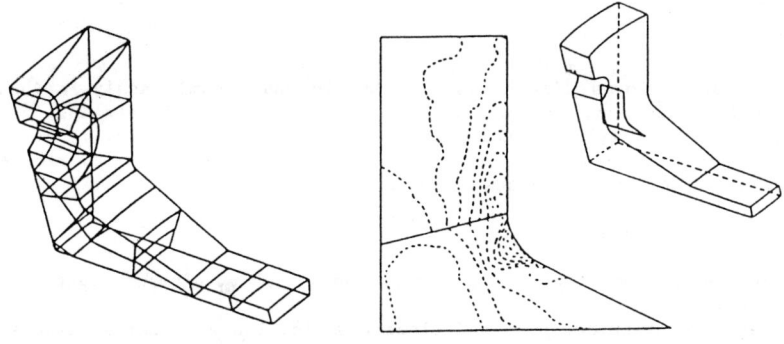

Figure 6 - Iso-value Von Mises stresses on an intersecting plane with zoom possibility

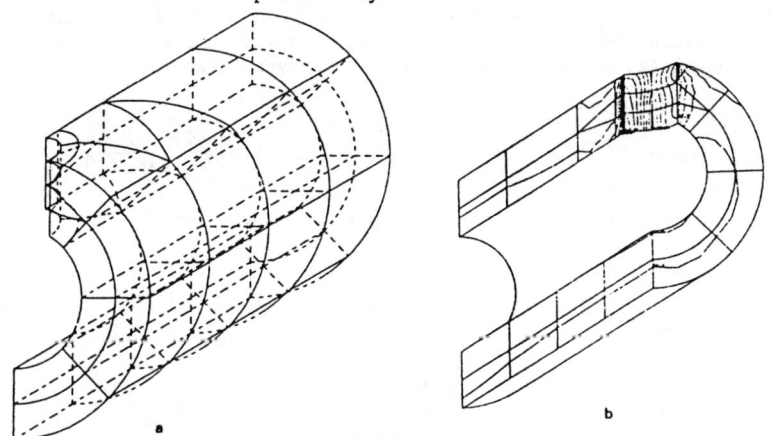

Figure 7 - Thermoelastic analysis of a heat exchanger

a) mesh,
b) iso-value of stresses

CA.ST.OR SD

CA.ST.OR SD performs static and dynamic analysis of 3D structure by Finite Element Method [1, 10-12]. The pre-processors and several post-processors are included. The size of the analysed structures may be very important because of the dynamically allocated memory.

Main features :

- static and dynamic of 3-D structures
- dynamic response
- seismic qualification
- random wind loading
- fluid-structure coupling
- graphic pre and post-processor

Options

. PASD

This option performs linear elastic, static and dynamic analysis (natural frequencies, and mode shapes) of 3D structures with small strains. Several types of elements (plate, shell, transition, brick, beam, etc...) are shown in the element library. Automatic node renumbering in order to reduce the bandwith and computation costs is included.

The necessary data are :

- general parameters (type of analysis, nodes number, element groups number,...)
- geometry description, node and element definition and element groups with corresponding material properties and distributed loadings,
- boundary conditions,
- nodal loads (static) or nodal masses (dynamic)

The results are the generalized forces and displacements in case of static analysis, critical loadings and mode shape in case of buckling analysis, and natural frequencies and mode shapes in case of dynamic analysis.

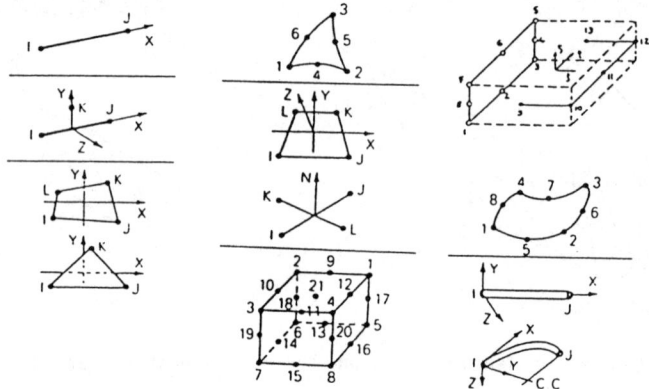

Figure 8 - CA.ST.OR SD : Element library

. STRSD

Performs the computation of stresses in beam, plate and pipe elements from the generalized forces. For other elements this option gives the equivalent stress (Tresca or Von Mises) and principal stress tensor.

. BASSD

This option allows to compute dynamic response (using mode superposition) of a structure submitted to a transient excitation.

. CMCSD

Performs the linear combinations of elementary load cases.

. SRSSD

Computes the response of a structure to earthquake excitations using the method of the sum of the modal maximum responses (response spectrum analysis).

. VENT

This option performs the structure analyses under random wind loadings with computation of fatigue life time.

. REASD

This option computes the generalized nodal forces (reaction forces).

. MASSD

This option performs fluid-structure coupling using Boundary Element Method for fluid and FEM for the structure [11]. Two kinds of problems may be analysed :

- immerged structures in infinite fluid
- reservoirs containing the free surface fluid

. EDISD

Selective edition of results

. D3D

Like in CA.ST.OR 3D, this option allows to visualize the geometry before and after loading or stress distribution on a graphic terminal or by a plotter.

CA.ST.OR.MT

Based on Finite Element Method performs dynamic analysis of rotating machineries [1,13]. The size of this program is about 10.000 instructions.

Mains features :

- dynamic analysis of torsional natural frequencies of shafts
- critical speed
- stability threshold, unbalance response of rotating shafts.

Options

. TORMT

Performs computation of torsional natural frequencies and associated mode shapes for interconnected shafts.
The necessary data are :

- material properties
- description of geometry (diameter and length or torsional stiffness and inertia)
- rotational speed ratio between the different shafts.
The results are the natural frequencies and associated mode shapes.

. DYNMT

This option allows to calculate the critical speeds, stability threshold, unbalance response of rotating shafts upon many bearings.

The necessary data are :

- material properties,
- description of geometry
- mass, diametral and polar inertia of added rigid disks,
- evolution of stiffness and damping coefficients of bearings with rotational speed.

The results are :

- evolution of natural frequencies and modal damping with rotational speed of the rotor,
- mode shapes and critical speeds,
- amplitude and plane of the shaft with unbalanced masses.

CA.ST.OR - CAD INTERFACE

An interface between CA.ST.OR 2D, 3D and CAD software EUCLID has been developed. By this interface user introduce only the mesh refinement, boundary conditions and loadings with full interactive input data procedure.

HARDWARE COMPATIBLITIES AND CA.ST.OR AVAILABILITY

CA.ST.OR software are commercialized by CETIM over the world. The english versions of CA.ST.OR 2D, 3D are available. Those who wish to use CA.ST.OR on their own comuters may obtain information regarding detailed capabilities and prices from CETIM. CA.ST.OR is available on the following computers :

- VAX, Micro-VAX
- Apollo
- IBM 43**
- PRIME
- CRAY XMP

For using the CA.ST.OR software different possibilities are adpated :

- CETIM's Engineers may performs your stucture analysis using CA.ST.OR software. A detailed report will be supplied.
- CA.ST.OR software may be used by your staff on CETIM's computers.
- CA.ST.OR software are available on the CISI, CGG and INVECTOR Networks
- CA.ST.OR software may be implemented on your own equipment.

Documentation

A complete documentation of CA.ST.OR which is regularly updated is available :

- user's manual
- theoretical manual
- tests manual
- documentation of the programs.

INDUSTRIAL APPLICATIONS

CA.ST.OR 2D Applications

Notch (shape optimization)

Study of a notch under mechanical loading and shape optimization in order to decrease the stresses.
This problem has been carried out by using CA.ST.OR 2D with an automatic shape optimization algorithm which is under investigation. For discretization 6-node elements are used. Following figures show, stress and iso static-stress distribution before and after optimization.

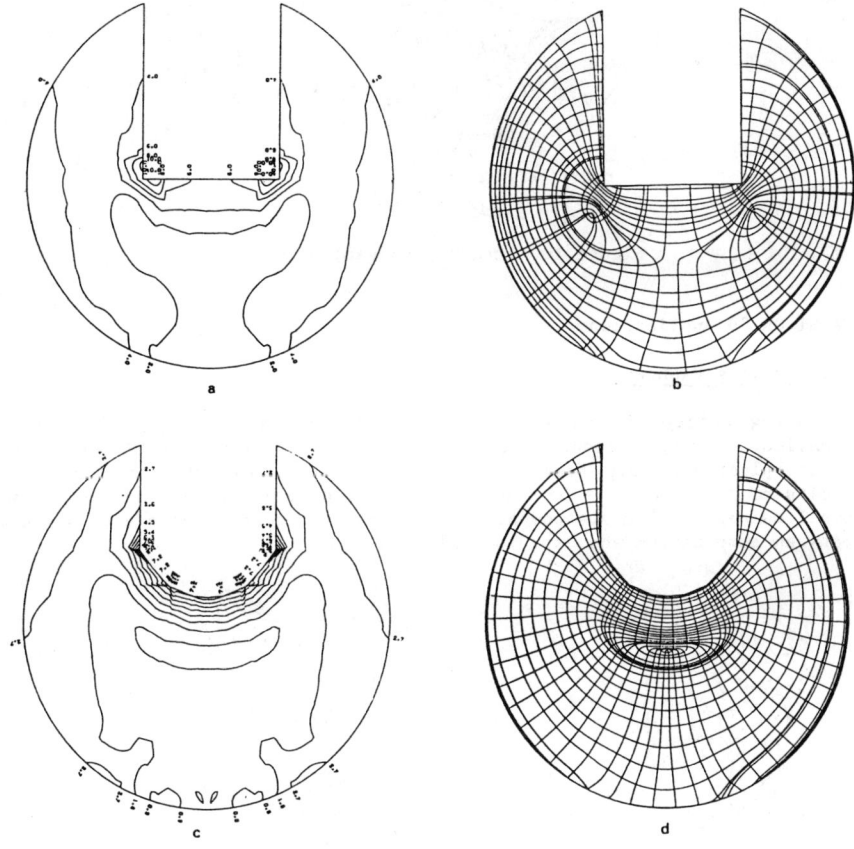

Figure 9 - Notch

a,b) stresses and iso-static stresses before optimization
c,d) stresses and iso-static stresses after optimization

. Crack propagation

Study of crack propagation, evaluation of Stress Intensity Factor of a plate. The plate has been discretized by 6 node elements with refined elements around crack front by using automatic mesh generator (M2D).

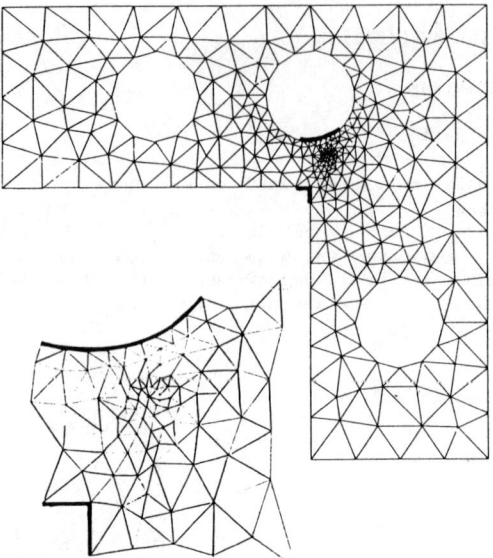

Figure 10 - crack propagation in a plate

CA.ST.OR 3D Application

. Connecting Flanged

Operating safety of equipment such as pressure vessels depends upon the behaviour of their connecting flanges. A 2 D finite element analysis in elasto-plasticity has been carried out in order to estimate the working limits of the flange. A 3D elastic analysis by Boundary Element method with small number of elements comparing with Finite Element gave a good agreement between computation and experimental results.

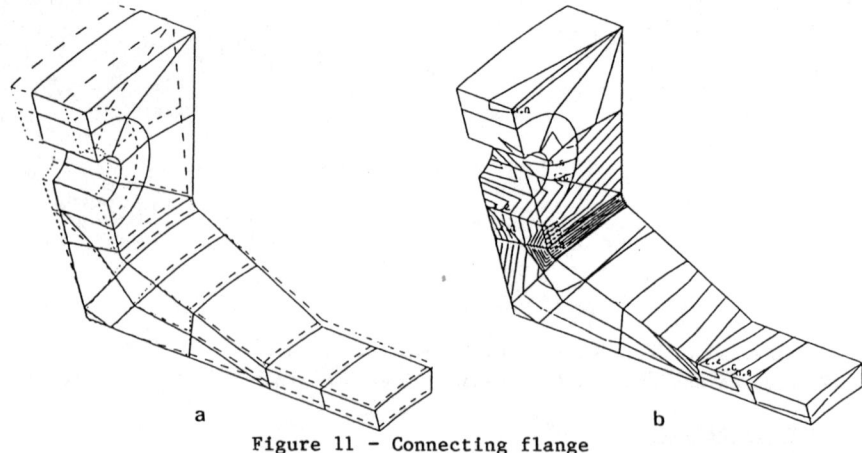

Figure 11 - Connecting flange

(a) mesh before and after loading and (b) sress distribution on the 3-D surface

. Acceptability of defects in Turbine disks

This problem was to study the 3-D carck propagation inside a disk of a high power turbine. Boundary Element technique is very well adapted to fracture mechanics and CA.ST.OR 3D was used for this problem. This work has been carried out under the heading of safety in nuclear and the critical size of the defects has been determined.

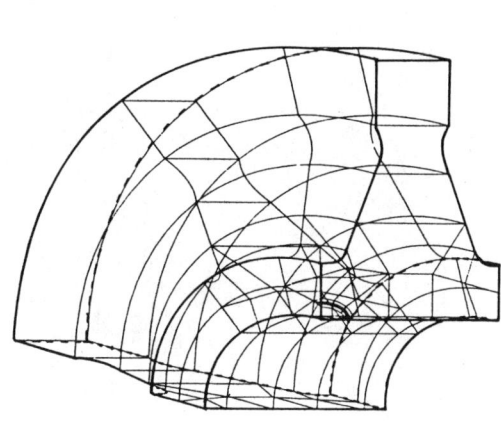

Figure 12 - Study of 3-D crack propagation in turbine disks
by Boundary Element Method

. Crank-arm

CA.ST.OR 3D has been used for stress analysis of crak-arm on diesel engine. The problem was to study the behaviour of the crank-arm under mechanical loadings specially the bolting forces. Influence of a fillet radius near bolt has been also studied in order to decrease the stress level. The 6-node and 8-node boundary elements are used for the modelization. Stress distribution and deformed structure have been displayend on a graphic terminal with zoom possibility.

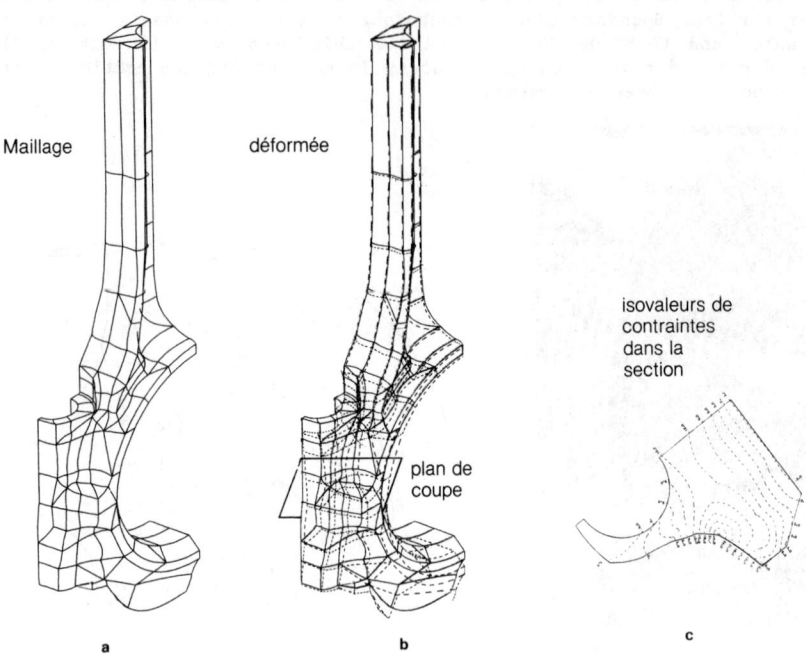

Figure 13 - Crank-arm

(a) mesh before and after loading
(b) iso-value curve of stresses
(c) iso-value stresses in a intersection plane.

CA.ST.OR SD Applications

. Statue of Liberty

For the 100th anniversary of the Statue of Liberty CETIM has carried out the analysis of the structure using CA.ST.OR SD. The aim of the study was to investigate life time of the structure under random wind loading more than 120 km/h.

The statue was modelized by the beam and plate elements with 12.000 degrees of freedom. The stresses in static and dynamic analyses have been evaluated and are used for estimation of life time by fatigue analysis.

Figure 14 - Statue of Liberty

a) inside structure
b) skin

. Water tank

Static, dynamic and seismic analysis of a water tank has been carried out by CA.ST.OR. SD.
The discretization has been done by shell elements. The following figures show mesh, first to 4th mode shapes.

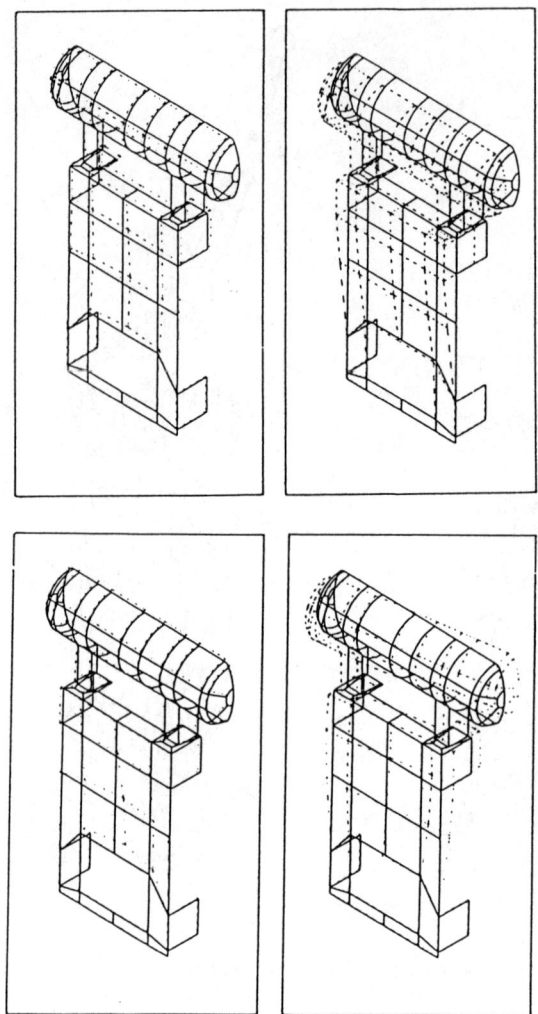

Figure 15 - Seismic qualification of a chassis supported water tank.
(Ste Damois et Cie) - Doël III nuclear plant (Belgium)

. Valve casing

In this problem stresses and displacement of a value casing under mechanical loading have been calculated. For discretization shell, 3D solid and 3D solid - shell transition elements have been used. The loading cases are pressure, applied bending and torsional forces.

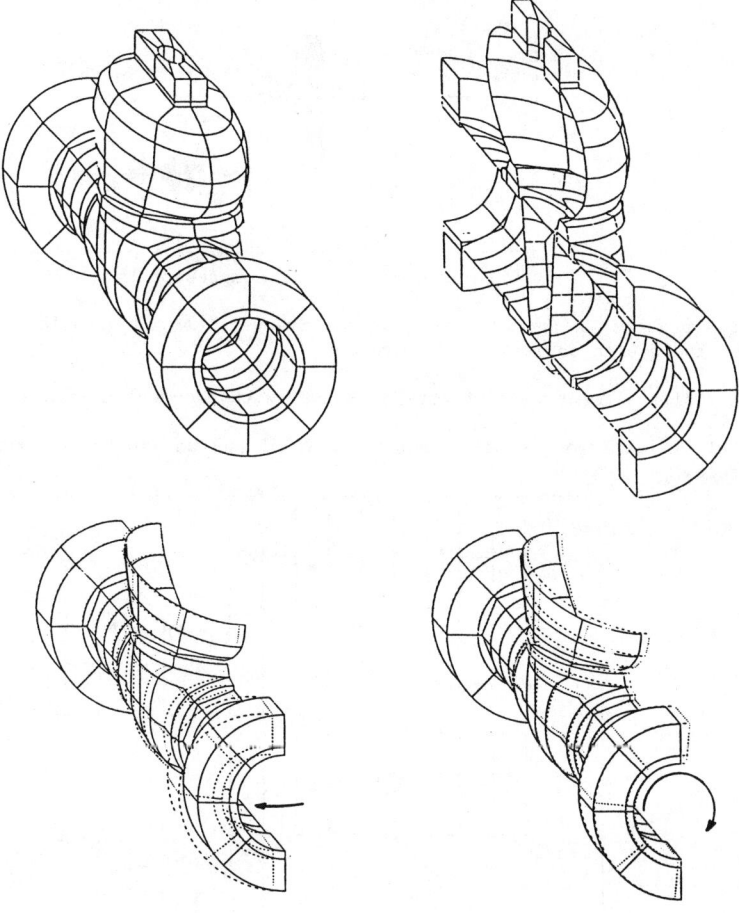

Figure 16 - Modelization of valve casing by finite elements before and after loading.

CA.ST.OR MT Application

. <u>Air-compressor</u>

The gear branched system as shown, consists of :

- an air-compressor (driven machine)
- a fly wheel
- two couplings (flexible)
- gear wheels (reduction)
- a turbine

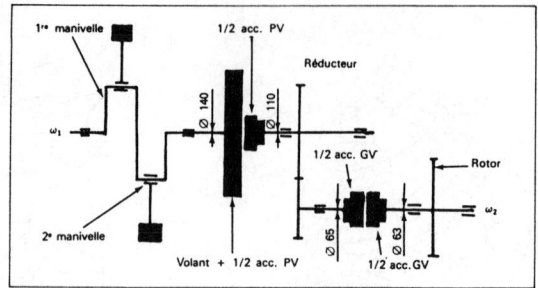

Figure 17 - Air compressor

The problem is to calculate natural frequencies and associated mode shapes of the system in torsional vibration.

A finite element discretization is used with two-node elements (8 elements)

This calculation is performed usign TORMT and an exemple of output is shown below.

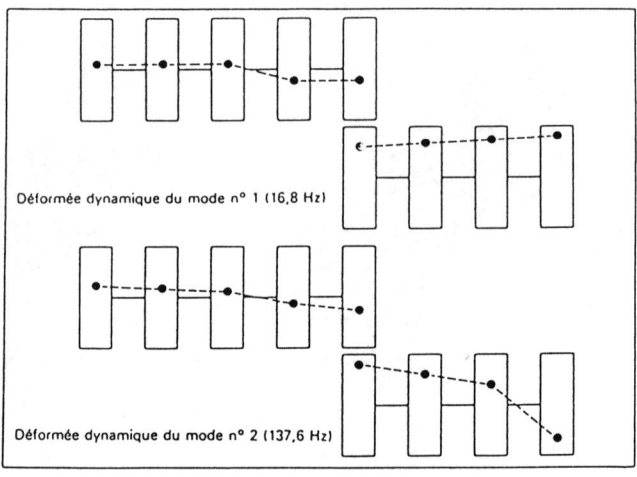

Figure 18 - Mode shapes

. <u>Air ventilator</u>

This rotor, as shown in Fig. 19, consists of a shaft with a rigid disk, hinged on two flexible bearings.

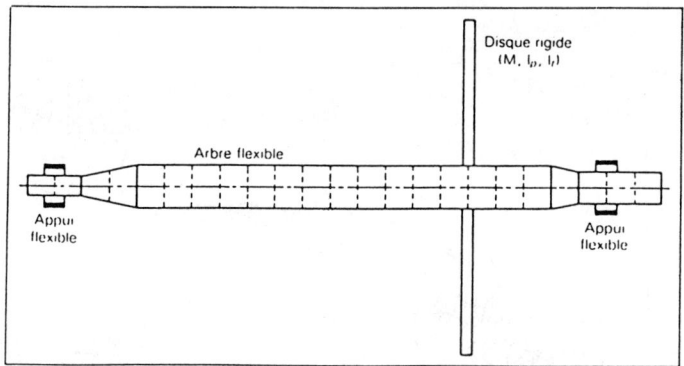

Figure 19 - Modelization of air ventilator

We want to calculate

- the critical speeds
- the unbalance response

of the complete system in bending vibrations.

A finite element discretization, using a special "rotor element" (2 nodes beam element with shear and gyroscopic effects) is applied.

The calculations are performed with the option DYNMT of CA.ST.OR-MT.

Different levels of output are available :

- influence of rotational speed on the natural frequencies of the rotor-bearing system and calculation of critical speeds.

- The mode shape evaluation for each critical speed (backward and forward whirl).

- Evolution of amplitude and phase with rotational speed at different nodes.

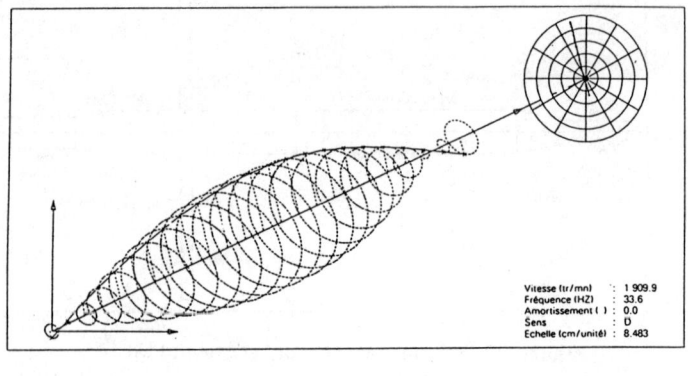
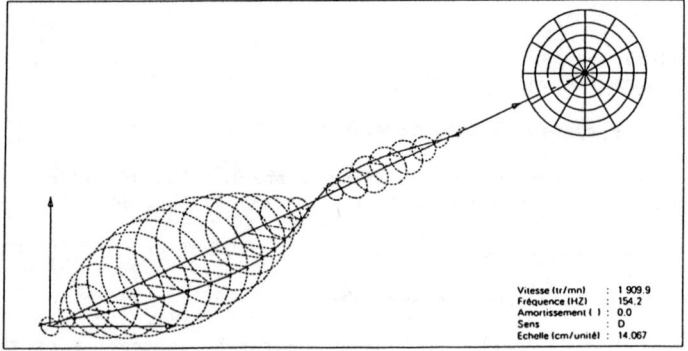

Figure 20 - Computation of critical speed

REFERENCES

[1] "CASTOR Software", CETIM Documentation (1982)

[2] M. Dubois, M. Cristescu, A. Turbat
"Non linéarités physiques et géométriques par la Méthode Eléments finis". CETIM - Report (1983)

[3] A. Turbat, F. Convert, N. Skalli
"Prediction of Thermal residual stresses by the finite element method. Effect of a phase", proceeding of the 3rd Int. Conf. on Num. Methods in Thermal problems (1983).

[4] J. Zarka and J. Csier
"Elastic-plastic response of a structure to cyclic loading : practical rules "Mechanics Today, Edit Nemat-Nasser, Vol.6 ; P.93 (1979)

[5] J.C. Lachat and J.O Watson
"Effective numerical treatment of boundary integral equation", Int. J. Num. Meth. Engng, (1976)

[6] J.C Lachat and J.O Watson
"Progress in the use of boundary integral equations illustrated by examples"
Comp. Meth. Appl. Mech. Enging. (1977)

[7] M. Afzali and A. Chaudouet
"A plane intersection of a three dimensional boundary elements mesh and stress : displacement contour plotting", Bound. Elem.Meth. Engng., Springer Verlag, pp. 594-606 (1982)

[8] J.M. Boissenot et al
"Application de la méthode des équations intégrales à la mécanique" - CETIM report (1978)

[9] A. Chaudouet, M. Afzali
"CA.ST.OR 3D : Three dimensional Boundary Element analysis Computer Code".
Proceeding of 5th Int. COnf. on BEM, Japan (1983)

[10] A. Bonnefoy, P. D'Anthouard, J.F Billaud
"Seismic analysis of Equipment subjected to multiple support Response spectra input",
7th sysm. on Earthouak Eng. Roorkee, India (1982)

[11] Y. Ousset and M.N. Sayhi
"Added Mass computations by Integral Equations Methods"
Int. J. Num. Meth. Engn. Vol. 19, 1355- 1373 (1983)

[12] P. d'Anthouard
"About Seismic Qualification of Equipments by Multi-spectra Method" Transactions of the 7th Int. COnf. on SMIRT, Chicago (1983)

[13] J. Peigney
"Prediction of Dynamic properties of rotor supported by Hydrodynamic Bearings using FEM"
Int. J. of Computers and Structure, Vol. 12, n°4 (1980)

[14] A. Bonnefoy, T. Belbin, M. Accoley
"Statue of Liberty Wind loading Analysis" CETIM, report 8 442.00/8214 (1984)

[15] M. Afzali, P. Devalan
"Structure analysis software on Mega-Mini and Micro-Computer" 5th Finite Element Systems Seminar, Southampton, England (1984)

ON THE AUTOMATIC SIMULATION OF TWO-DIMENSIONAL METAL FORMING PROCESSES BY THE FINITE-ELEMENT METHOD

J. C. Gelin and P. Picart

Université de Valenciennes, 59326 Valenciennes, France

ABSTRACT

Since the need for non-linear analysis of structures has significantly increased during the recent years and will continue to do so, and since ever more complex problems are being tackled, much emphasis is currently being placed on the development of more general and automatic solution schemes.

The objective in this presentation is to describe various algorithms for more automatic solutions in the simulation of two-dimensional metal forming processes by the finite element method.

For the simulation of deformation where an high accuracy is required, we use an updated stiffness matrix which is based on generalized consistent operators. An incremental objective integration scheme is employed for the integration of constitutive equations, which is based on the choice of an intermediate integration configuration.

Then, an algorithm for the automatic load stepping is presented, which is based on a relaxation method, in conjunction with the use of BFGS method and line searches in the overall solution strategy.

In order to facilitate the definition of the industrial problems, the user can defines one or more contactors, and the variable boundary conditions are automatically take into account, including the effects of friction between the dies and workpiece. Futhermore the program can calculate the pressure distribution on the dies and the elastic residual stresses in the workpiece.

The research developped represents some efforts towards more effective automatic incremental solution schemes for general non-linear analysis.

KEYWORDS

Non-linear analysis, automatic solution, metal forming processes, implicit scheme, tangent stiffness, automatic load stepping, elastic-plastic material, contact, friction.

INTRODUCTION

Metal forming problems arise quite naturally in many manufacturing processes such as extrusion of square or axisymmetric shapes, deep drawing, forging and upsetting.

These processes have all have two characteristic in common. First, they involve large deformations in which the strains are dominated by large plastic flow. Second, the deformations are strongly dependent upon contact conditions, and friction between dies and workpiece can play an important role in the overall deformation process.

The designer who develops a metal forming for manufacturing some metal product must know, first the power required by the process, which presupposes the knowledge of the load deflection curve. Next, he needs to be sure that the desired shape can be achieved for a given die configuration. And finally, he needs to know an accurate estimate of the stress and strain distribution in the produce, in order to be sure that the formability limits are not attained for example. Futhermore he can need some estimates of the residual stresses in his finished product.

Early work in the field of large deformation plasticity using rigid-plastic constitutive equations to develop matrix or finite element solutions to many steady or unsteady metal forming processes have been proposed by Lee and Kobayashi (1973), Kobayashi (1982). Another approach is to assume that the material is a rigid-strain hardening material and treat the problem as one of flow problem. Zienkiewicz and Godbole (1974), Zienkiewicz, Jain and Onate (1978), Zienkiewicz, Onate and Heinrich (1981) follow this approach, in treating the material as essentially a non-Newtonian fluid. Such above recalled treatments can give good solutions to both steady state and transient problems, but the lack of knowledge concerning the stress distribution, the residual stresses in the workpiece, and the fact that the displacements are not known directly from the solution but must be determined from an integration of the volocities limits the possibilities of these solutions.

Another and more widely used approach is to treat the material as an elastic-plastic strain hardening material performing an incremental analysis. The first elasto-plastic formulation suitable for large strain and large displacement was presented by Hibbit, Marcal and Rice (1970). They used an incremental Lagrangian approach and pointed out than an additional initial stress in stiffness matrix, being dependent on current loads, was missed in ordinary small strain formulations. Later Mc Meeking and Rice (1975) derived an Eulerian type of finite element formulation which is the basis of the most commonly used updated Lagrangian formulation. Alternative formulations and implementations, using directly the principle of wirtual work on the configuration after deformation are due to Nagtegaal (1982), and more recently a consistent tangent operator have been proposed by Simo and Taylor (1984).

A consise survey of the litterature related to large deformation elastic-plastic problems including unilateral and friction have been recently presented by Cheng and Kikuchi (1985).

In the present paper, starting from the principle of virtual work, the boundary value problem of arbitrary amount of deformation is formulated in the deformed configuration. By choosing the reference configuration coincident at time t with the current configuration we obtain a suitable finite element formulation of the problem. To allow for the effect of finite rotation and to satisfy the requirement of objectivity in the material constitutive equations, an implicit integration shceme is proposed.

The formulation of the principle of virtual work is completed with a friction law deduced from an isotropic sliding rule, based on the work of Taylor (1981), Taylor and Becker (1983).

For the incremental solution of the problem, we propose in conjunction with the tangent stiffness matrix a quasi-Newton method based on the BFGS approximation. Then an automatic load stepping algorithm is proposed, which is based on the well known Riks method (1979). Some classical bench mark problems are choosen to examine the numerical solution obtained from the computer code 'ASTRID' developped by the authors.

Several delicate problems such as the importance in selecting the finite element discretization and the size of increment are carefully investigated and discussed. The industrial examples concern the upsetting of a cylinder, a two-heads forming problem, and the axisymmetric extrusion problem of a billet.

INCREMENTAL FORM OF THE PRINCIPLE OF VIRTUAL WORK

For a deformed body in equilibrium, once the constitutive equation is choosen (stress-strain relation or incremental stress-strain relation), the stress field can be solved in using the following governing equations, given by Hill (1959) :

$$\text{div } T + \rho^\circ b = 0 \quad \text{in } \Omega \tag{1.a}$$

satisfying the boundary conditions

$$u = \bar{u} \quad \text{on } \Gamma_u \tag{1.b}$$

and

$$Tn^\circ = \bar{t}^\circ \quad \text{on } \Gamma_\sigma \tag{1.c}$$

where T is the first Piola-Kirchhoff stress tensor defined in the deformed configuration Ω, b is the specific body force vector, and u is the displacement vector which is specified by a given vector function $\bar{u}$ on the portion Γ_u of the boundary Γ of the solid under consideration.

The weak form associated with the equations (1.a, b, c) is the principle of virtual work

$$\int_{\Omega^\circ} T : \dot{F}^* dV - \int_{\Gamma^\circ_\sigma} \bar{t} \dot{x}^* dS = 0 \tag{2}$$

where x^* is an admissible position field such that $x^* = x^\circ + u^*$ and F^* is the gradient of position, $(F^*)_{ij} = \dfrac{\partial x^*_j}{\partial x^\circ_i}$, the dot indicate the time derivative.

Equation (2) can be rewritten by making the following choice. Instantaneously, choose the current configuration to coincide with the reference configuration. Then the deformation gradient is simply the identity tensor, all stress tensors are the same and equation (2) can be written as :

$$\int_{\Omega} T : F^* dV - \int_{\Gamma_\sigma} \bar{t} \, v^* dS = 0 \tag{3}$$

We can take the time derivative of equation (2) relatively to the new reference configuration and we obtain immediatly :

$$\int_\Omega \dot{T} : L^* dV - \int_{\Gamma_\sigma} \dot{t}\, v^*\, dS = 0 \tag{4}$$

In replacing $\dot{T}$ by the value obtained in derivating the relation $\tau = TF^T$ we obtain

$$\dot{T} = \dot{\tau} - \tau L^T \tag{5}$$

If the incremental constitutive equations are expressed in term of the Jaumann or corotationnal rate of Kirchhoff tress tensor, relation (5) can be transform like as :

$$\dot{T} = \overset{\nabla}{\tau} + L\tau - 2D\tau \tag{6}$$

where $\overset{\nabla}{\tau}$ is the Jaumann rate of Kirchhoff stress tensor.

Taking into account equation (6), and replacing $\dot{T}$ in equation (4), we obtain immediatly :

$$\int_\Omega (\overset{\nabla}{\tau} + L\tau - 2D\tau) : L^* dV - \int \dot{t}\, v^* dS = 0 \tag{7}$$

It is easy to remark that the variationnal form generated by equation (7) is symmetric and can be written as :

$$\int_\Omega (A^{ep}:D):D^* dV - \int \dot{t}\, v^* dS = 0 \tag{8}$$

where A^{ep} is the elastic-plastic operator that takes into account the terms which are function of stress tensor :

$$A^{ep}: D = \overset{\nabla}{\tau} + L\tau - 2D\tau = C^{ep}: D + L\tau - 2D\tau \tag{9}$$

where A^{ep} is a function of material behaviour and stresses at time t.

Equation (8) is solved between t_n and t_{n+1} and we obtain :

$$\int_\Omega (A^{ep}:D\Delta t) : D^* dV = \int_{\Gamma_\sigma} (\bar{t}+\Delta \bar{t})v^* dS - \int_{\Gamma_\sigma} \bar{t}v^* dS \tag{10}$$

equation (10) is the equation to solve to find the incremental displacement field $\Delta u = v\Delta t$ between t and $t+\Delta t$

FINITE ELEMENT DISCRETIZATION OF EQUILIBRIUM EQUATIONS

The equilibrium equations for the continuum have been derived in a previous section. Here, these equations are reduced to a discrete set of equations by the introduction of the finite element method, which consists of dividing the body into subregions, or elements. Within a given element, the value of the incremental displacement field can be interpolated from nodal point values by

$$u = \underline{N}\underline{u}$$

where the vector $\underline{u}$ represents the vector of incremental nodal point displacements, and $\underline{N}$ the matrix of shape functions at time t.

The classical operator giving the strain rate is

$$D = \frac{\partial v}{\partial x} = \underline{B} \, \underline{u}$$

where $\underline{B}$ is the strain interpolation matrix, like as in small strain theory.

Without the terms associated with the contact friction boundary conditions, equation (10) for a single element can be written as :

$$\underline{v}^{*T} \int_{\Omega^e} (\underline{K}^{ep})^e dV^e \cdot \underline{u} = -\underline{v}^{*T} \int_{\Omega^e} \underline{B}^{e^T} \underline{\sigma} \, dV^e + \underline{v}^{*T} \int_{\Gamma^e_u} \underline{N}^{e^T} \underline{t} \, dS^e \qquad (11)$$

where the superscript $(.)^e$ means for one element.

Summing all the element contributions results instantaneously in a system of linear equations

$$\underline{v}^{*T}(\underline{K}^{ep} \cdot \underline{u} + F_{int} - F_{ext}) = 0 \text{ for } \underline{v}^* \neq 0 \qquad (12)$$

Equation (12) represents the tangent stiffness equation for a fully Newton iteration. Due to material and geometrical nonlinearly, equation (12) is solved iteratively, for a given time step $t_{n+1} - t_n = \Delta t$

$$(\underline{K}^{ep})^{n+1 \, (i-1)} \Delta \underline{u}^{(i)} = F_{ext}^{n+1} - F_{int}^{n+1(i-1)} \qquad (13.a)$$

$$u^{n+1(i)} = u^{n+1(i-1)} + \Delta u^{(i)} \qquad (13.b)$$

with the initial conditions

$$(K^{ep})^{n+1} (o) = (K^{ep})^n$$

$$u^{n+1(o)} = u^n$$

where $(K^{ep})^n$ and u^n are respectively the stiffness matrix and the displacement at the increment n after convergence.

INCREMENTAL OF INCREMENTAL CONSTITUTIVE EQUATIONS

Knowing the displacement field at time $t_{n+1} = t_n + \Delta t$, the problem here is to compute the stress field corresponding to this time, starting from the stresses known at time t_n. For simplicity and brievety we shall note σ^n the Cauchy stress tensor at time t_n and σ^{n+1} the Cauchy stress tensor at time $t_n + \Delta t = t_{n+1}$. In classical large strain plasticity problems three conditions must be satisfied :

i) if the body is subjected to a rigid body motion between t_n and t_{n+1}, the stress increment is equal to zero, the stresses tensor is transformed like as a tensor $\sigma^{n+1} = Q\sigma^n Q$ where Q is an orthogonal tensor (rotation tensor).

ii) if the body is subjected to a pure deformation, the spin induced by the motion is equal to zero.

iii) if the stress state at the time t is such that $f(\sigma)=0$, where f is elastic-plastic yield function and if plastic loading occurs during the time step, we have to satisfy $f(\sigma^{n+1})=0$.

Following the work of Hughes and Winget (1980), Pinsky, Ortiz and Pister (1983), Gelin (1985), we can choose an intermediate configuration defined

by
$$x^{n+\alpha} = (1-\alpha)x^n + \alpha x^{n+1} \tag{14}$$

where α is an integration parameter selected in the range $0 \leq \alpha \leq 1$, $x^{n+\alpha}$ represents the position of a point M in the body for a time $t_{n+\alpha}$.

Introducing the corotationnal transformation, which is consistent with the definition of the Jaumann stress rate, we can write

$$\sigma^{n+1} = Q^n \sigma^n Q^{n^T} + Q^{n+\alpha} (\Delta\sigma)^{n+\alpha} Q^{n+\alpha^T} \tag{15}$$

where Q^n and $Q^{n+\alpha}$ are orthogonal tensors given by the following relations :

$$Q^n = ((1-\alpha)\omega^{n+\alpha} + I)^{-1}(I - \alpha\omega^{n+\alpha}) \tag{16}$$

$$Q^{n+\alpha} = (1-\alpha)Q^n + \alpha Q^{n+1} \tag{17}$$

where $\omega^{n+\alpha}$ is the spin rate increment mesured on the intermediate configuration.

It is easy to see that if the body is subjected to a rigid body motion the increment of strain rate between t_n and t_{n+1} is equal to zero, such that the second term in the r.h.s of equation (15) is equal to zero, also the contition (i) is satisfied.

It can be shown that condition (ii) is satisfied only if $\alpha = 1/2$, it results from some calculations to identify $\omega^{n+\alpha}$ with 0 when $F_n^{n+1} = S$, where S is a symmetric definite positive tensor.

At this point it can be seen that equation (15) cannot be solved directly if we have no subsidiary condition.

This subsidiary condition is furnished by the fact that in elastic-plastic calculations, the increment of plastic effective strain is uniquely determined by a scalar equation of the following type, see Simo and Taylor (1985), Gelin (1985) :

$$\Delta\bar{\varepsilon}^p = \gamma(s^{n+1})^e / \|(s^{n+1})^e\| \tag{18}$$

where $(s^{n+1})^e = (\sigma^{n+1})^e - \frac{1}{3} tr (\sigma^{n+1})^e .1$ is the deviatoric elastic prediction given by :

$$(\sigma^{n+1})^e = Q^n \sigma^n Q^{n^T} + Q^{n+\alpha} (C^e : D^{n+\alpha}) Q^{n+\alpha^T}$$

and γ is given by the following scalar equation

$$h(\gamma) = -g(\bar{\varepsilon}^{p^n} + \gamma) + \sqrt{\frac{3}{2}} \|(s^{n+1})^e\| - 2G\gamma = 0 \tag{19}$$

which can be solved by a simple local Newton procedure.

The incremental gradient of deformation between t_n and t_{n+1} is easily obtained with the relation

$$x^{n+1} = x^n + \Delta u$$

$$\frac{\partial x^{n+1}}{\partial x^n} = I + \frac{\partial \Delta u}{\partial x^n} \tag{20}$$

where I is the second order identity tensor.

The increment of strain rate tensor $D^{n+\alpha}\Delta t$ is given by the following relation

$$D^{n+\alpha}\Delta t = \{[(1-\alpha)I + \alpha F_n^{n+1}]^{-1}[F_n^{n+1} - I]\}^S, \qquad (21)$$

and the increment of spin tensor is given by

$$\omega^{n+\alpha}\Delta t = \{[(1-\alpha)I + \alpha F_n^{n+1}]^{-1}[F_n^{n+1} - I]\}^A \qquad (22)$$

The numerical form of the tensors Q^n and $Q^{n+\alpha}$ are easily obtained from equation (16) and equation (17).

The stress computational procedure presented here satisfy incremental objectivity and consistency with the elastic-plastic constitutive equations, or elastic-viscoplastic constitutive equations.

ITERATIVE SOLUTION PROCEDURES

In a previous section, we seens that the elastic-plastic large strain problem is equivalent to the solution of a system with the following type

$$K(u)\Delta u = F_{ext} - F_{int}(u) = R(u) \qquad (23)$$

where Δu is the displacement increment to calculate, F_{ext} is the nodal external traction vector applied an the structure and $F_{int}(u)$ is the vector of internal nodal force, $R(u)$ is the residual of nodal forces.

At time t_n, the stiffness matrix K is constant and independent of u. The modified quasi-Newton methods (m.Q.N.) consists to find a matrix G which satisfy the quasi-Newton equation

$$G(u) \cdot (u - \tilde{u}) = R(u) - R(\tilde{u}) = y \quad (d = \tilde{u} - u). \qquad (24.a)$$

and we can apply the standard BFGS correction to obtain an approximation of G matrix

$$G_c = \frac{y\,y^T}{y^T d} - \frac{Gd \cdot d^T \cdot G}{d^T G d} \qquad (24.b)$$

For next iteration, matrix G is replaced by $G + G_c$

The application of this correction to equation (23) is performed as following, during a time step Δt corresponding to $\Delta t = t_{n+1} - t_n$

$$K_{n+1}^{(i-1)}(u_{n+1}^{(i-1)}) \cdot u^{(i)} = R(u_{n+1}^{(i-1)}) = R_{n+1}^{(i-1)}$$

where subscripts indicate the increments and superscripts the iterations in the increments. With the notations above introduced, we have

$$d^{(i)} = u^{(i)} = u_{n+1}^{(i)} - u_{n+1}^{(i-1)}$$
$$y^{(i)} = R(u)^{(i)} - R(u)^{(i-1)}$$

and then we can compute a corrected stiffness matrix :

$$K_c^{(i)} = \frac{y^{(i)} y^{(i)T}}{y^{(i)T} d^{(i)}} - \frac{K_{n+1}^{(i-1)} d^{(i)} \cdot (K_{n+1}^{(i-1)} d^{(i)})^T}{d^{(i)T} y^{(i)}} \qquad (25)$$

so that

$$K_{n+1}^{(i)} = K_{n+1}^{(i-1)} + K_c^{(i)} \qquad (26)$$

The previous iterative solution method will be used in conjonction with an incremental "loading procedure" so as to trace the complete load path. As a consequence, the increment size should be automatically selected in relation with the severity of the non-linearities encountered. Maximum increment sizes should also be specified. Here, we adopt a very simple approach for regulation of the increment sizes following the work of Riks (1979), Crisfield (1982).

Riks (1979) notes that the gradient or out-of-balance force vector can be written as :

$$R = \lambda F_{ext} - F_{int} \qquad (27)$$

where F_{int} is a function of the stresses and displacements, λ is the load level parameter, and F_{ext} is some fixed applied load vector.

If an iteration is performed in the standard manner for a given load level λ_i and a given gradient $G(\lambda_i)$ the gradient for same adjusted load level $\lambda_i + \Delta\lambda_i$ is

$$G(\lambda_i + \Delta\lambda_i) = G(\lambda_i) - \delta\lambda_i R \qquad (28)$$

With the addition of the load level λ, there are N+1 variables and N+1 equations that are required, N equations are associated with the N degrees of freedom, while the N+1 th equation is a constraint on the increment length $\Delta\ell$:

$$\Delta u^T \Delta u = \Delta\ell^2 \qquad (29)$$

Applying equation (28) to the standard equation (24), and after some calculations gives :

$$a_1 \delta\lambda_i^2 + a_2 \delta\lambda_i + a_3 = 0 \qquad (30)$$

For the scalar unknown $\delta\lambda_i$, the coefficients a_1, a_2 and a_3 are given by

$$a_1 = \Delta u_t^T \Delta u_t$$
$$a_2 = 2(\Delta u + g_t)^T \Delta u_t$$
$$a_3 = (\Delta u + g_t)^T \cdot (\Delta u + g_t) - \Delta\ell^2$$

where $\Delta u_t = (K_{n+1}^{(i-1)})^{-1} R$ is the displacement vector associated with $K_{n+1}^{(i-1)}$ and $g_t = -[\text{diag}(K_{n+1}^{(i-1)})]^{-1} R$ is a tangent displacement vector associated with $K_{n+1}^{(i-1)}$.

The method discribed above provides a powerful tool for choosing and cutting the increment sizes. It is implemented in the program 'ASTRID'.

CONTACT AND FRICTION

The effects of friction can be very important in many metal forming problems and many manufacturing processes use lubricants to try to reduce the friction between the die and the workpiece. The mechanics of lubrication are very complicated and numerical models for these problems are severely lacking. Oden and Martins (1985) in an important review paper present an excellent discussion of friction and lubrication. They identify three different lubrication regimes :

   Type I   - Quasi-static dry friction
   Type II - Dynamic, sliding friction
   Type III - Wear and plowing

This paper is essentially concerned with quasi-static dry friction which is the most adequate for our present purpose. It supposes that metallic surfaces in contact are pressed slowly together and are in static equilibrium or are slowly displaced relative one to another.

Only the contact between one deformable body and a rigid surface is considered as it is shown in figure 1. The rigid bodies, which are named contactors are assumed to be flat, and constitued of a sequence of surfaces inclined at an angle θ to the x coordinates axis.

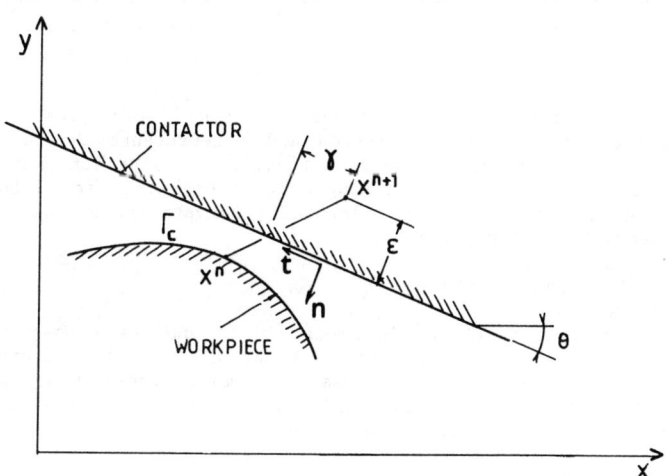

Fig. 1 - Geometry and notation used in contact problem with dry friction.

We shall note Γ_c the candidate surface contact and we suppose that the body may come in contact with the flat surface of the contactor. The position of a point on the surface of the body at the time t_n is denoted by x^n and x^{n+1} is the position of the same point at time $t_n + \Delta t = t_{n+1}$. As indicated on figure 1 contact has occured for the point and x^c is the position of the point on the rigid surface at which contact first occurs.

The incremental displacement for the time step is :

$$\Delta u = x^{n+1} - x^n \qquad (31)$$

Denote by η the portion of the displacement increment which gives first contact. Then :

$$x^c = x^n + \eta \Delta u \qquad (32)$$

and the generalized contact strains are defined by

$$\varepsilon = -(1-\eta)\Delta u \cdot n \qquad (33)$$

$$\gamma = -(1-\eta)\Delta u \cdot t \qquad (34)$$

where n is unit normal and t the unit tangent to the contactor oriented as shown in figure 1, ε is the normal strain and γ is the sliding strain.

The contact constraint requires that inequality

$$\varepsilon \leq 0 \qquad (35)$$

be satisfied for all points on the surface of the body.

For simplicity only a Coulomb (dry friction) model is considered and we use a Lagrange multiplier method to enforce the contact condition (Coulomb condition) :

$$S \leq \mu N \qquad (36)$$

where N is the resultant of the normal traction vector over some area on Γ_c μ is the coefficient of friction and S represents the resultant of the tangential component of the surface traction t_c. The constraint, equation (36), is accomplished by assuming a functional form for S that gives qualitative agreement with the experimental observations, as Taylor (1981), Taylor and Becker (1983) reported :

$$S = \frac{2\mu N}{\pi} \tan^{-1}(\gamma/\gamma^*) \qquad (37)$$

The parameter γ^* is a weighting parameter which can be choose equals to 0.1mm in most of the applications. If the value of γ^* is too important the details to the frictional stresses at small displacements are smoothed, but for a problem with very large sliding motions these small displacements are probably not of much importance.

NUMERICAL EXAMPLES

The following example problems are intended to verify the formulations given in this paper and to show the capability of the computer code 'ASTRID' developped.

Upsetting of a cylindrical bloch

This problem is the upsetting of a cylindrical block shown in figure 2. The block has an initial diameter of 10 mm and an height of 15 mm. The mechanical properties and the hardening effect of the material are specified as follows : Young's modulus E=210000 MPa, Poisson's ratio ν=0.3 initial yield strengh σ_y =342,2 MPa, strain hardening law of the following type : $\sigma_o = K\bar{\varepsilon}^n$ with K=1032.21 MPa and n=0.147. Due to the symmetry a quarter of the block is analyzed and a special arrangerment of quadrilateral and triangular elements permit the upper coin of the specimen to fold under the platens.

Figure 3 illustrates the computed results for the upsetting load as a function of the upper displacement of the block, in the case of sticking friction and in the case where the coefficient of friction μ_F is taken equal to 0.3

Three deformed meshes at 25 %, 50% and 70% of height reduction are shown in figure 3 where we can see the importance of folding effect near the upper corner of the specimen. The folding is automatically takes into account with the contact and friction algorithm.

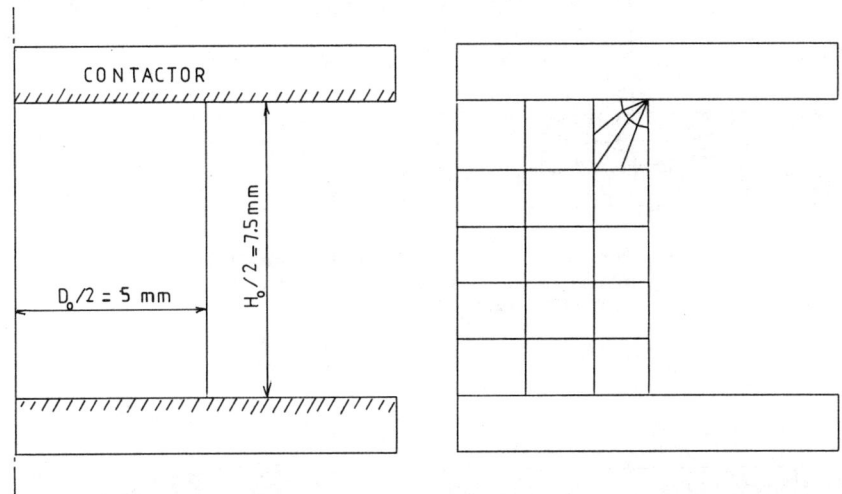

Fig. 2 - Geometry and initial finite element mesh for an upsetting analysis

Figure 4 shown the distribution of equivalent plastic strain in the deformed shape for a reduction in height equals to 70 %, in the case of sticking friction conditions. It is noteworthy to see that the most important deformation are concentraded in the center of the specimen, and in the corner which folds under the dies. Some experimental results based on hardness and indentation measures are in good agreement with this observation, see Gelin (1985) :

Axisymmetric extrusion problem

Figure 5 illustrates the axisymmetric extrusion problem where a driven piston forces the billet through the die to produce the extrudate. Plastic flow is confined to vicinity of the die, the material which has not yet entered in the die region is elastic, it is loaded beyond the plastic yield in the conical part of the die, and unloaded as it emerges from the die.

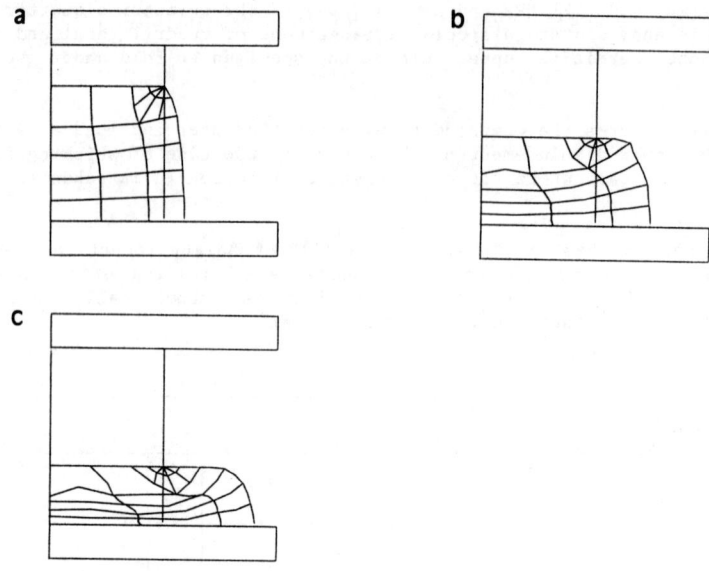

Fig. 3 - Deformed meshes at 25% reduction of height (a), 50% reduction of height (b), and 70% (c) reduction of height.

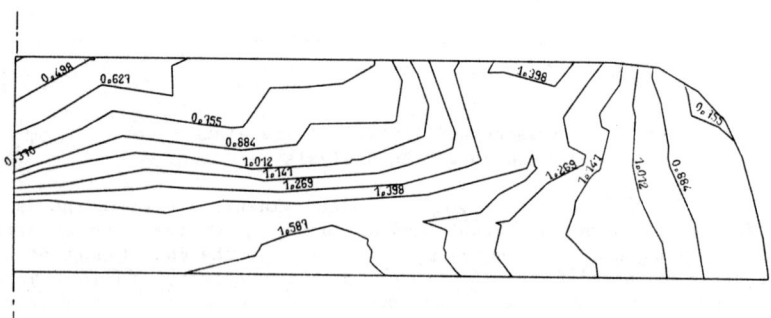

Fig. 4 - Distribution of equivalent plastic strain in the upsetting of a cylindrical block

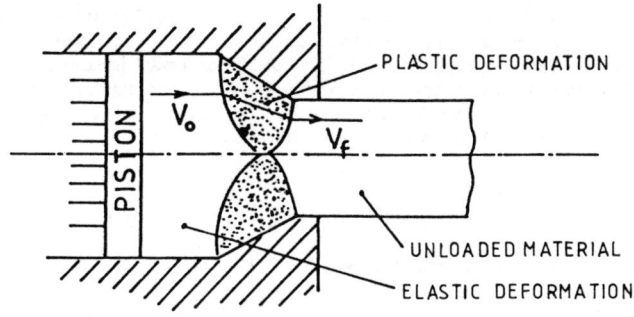

Fig. 5 - Axisymmetric extrusion problem through conical dies.

The mechanical properties are specified as follows : Young's modulus E=210000 MPa, Poisson's ratio ν =0.3, initial yield strengh σ_y =507 MPa, strain hardening law $\sigma_o = K\epsilon^n$ where K=1238.3 MPa and n=0.18. For such a problem, two computations have been realized. First, frictionless axisymmetric conditions are imposed and a prescribed piston displacement of 0.05mm per increment is used. Figure 6a shows the undeformed configuration and figure 6b shows the distorted mesh after 30 loading increments with a total displacement of 0.75 times the initial diameter.

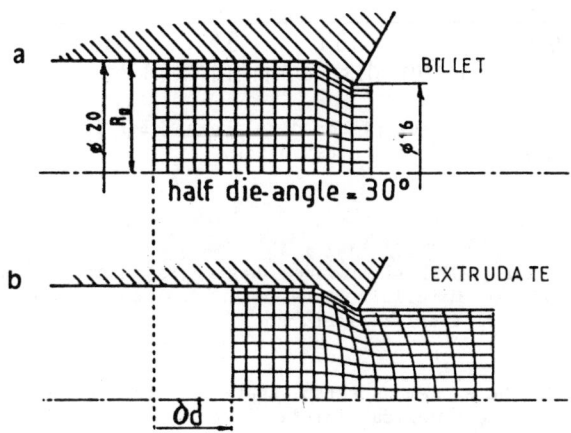

Fig. 6 - Undeformed mesh and deformed finite element mesh after 30 increments.

The loading curve versus piston displacement reveals the initiation and the appearence of a steady state flow where the load applied on the piston is nearly constant. The oscillation denoted in figure 7 are due to the fact that a discrete model is used to simulate the flow through the conical die, and during steady state the number of nodes in contact with the dies is variable. The peaks and valleys correspond respectively to the maximum and minimum number of contact points between the workpiece and the die. A computation have been carried out with a coefficient of friction between workpiece and die μ_F=0.3. The material properties, loading steps and initial mesh are the same as above and after a piston displacement equals to 0.75 times the initial radius the deformed mesh is about the same as in previous case. The most interesting remark is on the loading curve where we can see the influence of friction. The curve corresponding to the dry friction (μ_F=0.3) is over the curve corresponding to the frictionless case (μ_F=0), this fact is commonly observed in experiments.

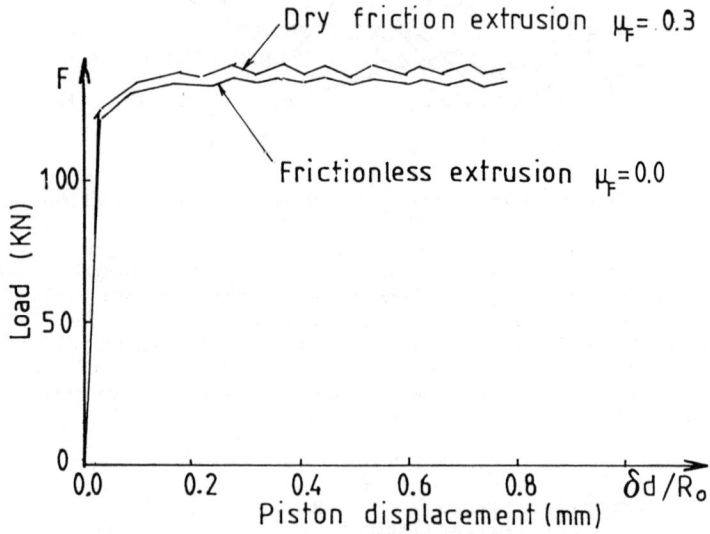

FIg. 7 - Extrusion force versus piston displacement for frictionless extrusion and dry friction extrusion.

CONCLUSION

A finite element program based on updated Lagrangian formulations for a large class of non-linear materials have been realized, including the treatment of contact and friction problems, and automatic iterative procedures.

The results presented here demonstrated that the formulations provide a satisfactory basis for the numerical solutions of this class of problems.

The contact and friction algorithm is an efficient tool that allow for the pulling away or removing of the dies in the forming processes.

As the natural coarse of development, an extension of the present work would be to take account of friction to calculate the stress distribution in the dies, and to take account of temperature effects in both material constants and surface properties.

REFERENCES

Cheng, J.H., and N. Kikuchi (1985). Comput. Meth. Appl. Mech. Enging, 49, 71-108

Crisfield, M.A. (1982). Incremental/iterative solution procedures for non-linear structural analysis. Proceedings 1st Num. Meth. Nonlinear Problems, Ed. by D.R.J. Owen, Pineridge Press

Gelin, J.C. (1985). Modèles numériques et expérimentaux en grandes déformations plastiques. Thèse de Doctorat d'Etat - Université P. et M. Curie, Paris VI.

Hibbit, H.D., P.V. Marcal and J.R. Rice (1970). Int. J. Solids Structures, 6, 1069-1089.

Hill, R. (1959). J. Mech. Phys. Solids, 7, 209-225.

Hughes, T.R.J., and J. WInget (1980). Int. J. Num. Meth. Eng., 15, 1862-1867.

Kobayashi, S. (1982) Thermoviscoplastic analysis of metal forming problems by the finite element method. In Num. Meth. Industrial Forming Processes. Ed. by J.F.T. Pittman and al. Pineridge Press, 17-22.

Lee, C.H., and S. Kobayashi (1973). J. Eng. Ind., 7, 865-873.

Mc Meecking, R.M., and J.R. Rice (1975). Int. J. Solids Structures, 11, 601-616.

Nagtegaal, J.C. (1982). Comput. Meth. Appl. Mech. Enging., 33, 469-484.

Oden, J.T., and J.A.C. Martins (1985). Comput. Meth. Appl. Mech. Enging., 52, 527-634.

Pinsky, P.M., M. Ortiz and K.S. Pister (1983). Comput. Meth. Appl. Mech. Enging, 40, 137-158.

Riks, E. (1979). Int. J. Solids Structures, 15, 529-551.

Simo, J.C., and R.L. Taylor (1985). Comput. Meth. Appl. Mech. Enging., 48, 101-118.

Taylor, L.M. (1981). A finite element analysis for large deformation metal forming problems involving contact and friction. TICOM Report 81-15. The Texas Institute for Computational Mechanics.

Taylor, L.M., and E.B. Becker (1983). Comput. Meth. Appl. Mech. Enging., 41, 251-277.

Zienkiewcz, O.C., and P.N. Godbole (1974). Int. J. Num. Meth. Eng., 8, 3-16.

Zienkiewcz, O.C., P.C. Jain and E. Onate (1978). Int. J. Solids Structures, 14, 15-38.

Zienkiewcz, O.C., E. Onate and J.C. Heinrich (1981). Int. J. Num. Meth. Eng., 17, 1497-1514.

FORGE2: PROGRAM FOR SIMULATING THE HOT-FORGING OF METALS BY FINITE ELEMENTS

Y. Germain, E. Wey and J. L. Chenot

Ecole Nationale Supérieure des Mines de Paris, Sophia-Antipolis, Valbonne 06560, France

SUMMARY : FORGE2 is a computer program for simulating the hot forming of metals by forging. It can be used to predict the variation in the filling of the contours of the die by the metal, the distortion of the material and the forces applied to the tools throughout the process. We detail here all the modules which make up FORGE2 : the finite element calculation module, and the operating modules for the data input and the analysis of the results. Industrial examples are given, demonstrating the capabilities of the program as an aid to the design of the optimum shapes of blanks and dies.

1. DESCRIPTION OF THE MODEL
1.1 Basic law

The rheological behaviour of hot metal alloys (*) is, in the great majority of cases, characterised by a relationship between the flow stress σ_0 and the strain rate $\dot{\varepsilon}$. A model of the material can be suitably produced by means of a relationship or law of behaviour expressing σ_0 in terms of $\dot{\varepsilon}$ in the form of a power law :

$$\sigma_0 = K\sqrt{3}\,(\sqrt{3}\,\dot{\varepsilon})^m \quad (1)$$

σ_0 et ε are the invariants of the deviatoric parts of the stress tensor S and the strain rate tensor $\dot{e}$ respectively, with $\sigma_0^2 = 3/2\ S:S$ and $\dot{\bar{\varepsilon}}^2 = 2/3\ \dot{e}:\dot{e}$ (: represents the tensorial contracted product). K and m are coefficients, which may not be constant, designated the consistence and the coefficient of sensitivity to the velocity (0<m<1 for the usual materials). They are measured by means of a standard test (torsion, compression, etc).

The law used in our model for the generalised three-dimensional space is close to the completely plastic rigid model of Von Mises, with the tensorial relationship :

$$S = \frac{2}{3}\,\frac{\sigma_0}{\dot{\bar{\varepsilon}}}\,\dot{e} \quad (2)$$

where σ_0 is given by (1). To this equation is added the incompressibility relationship tr $\dot{\varepsilon}$ = 0, verified everywhere in the material.

1.2. Friction law.

The second aspect of the model is the friction, a controlling phenomenon in forging for the study of the filling of the contours of the dies.

The model consists of the imposition of a shear stress τ on the metal-tool interface. We used here a relationship which gives τ as a function of the sliding velocity of the material over the tool v_g.
It is of the general form :

$$\tau = -\alpha \frac{v_g}{|v_g|^{1-p}} \qquad (3)$$

α et p are coefficients which may not be constant with time and which vary over the frictional interface. With p = 0, the expression reproduces the model of Tresca. For p ≠ 0, the friction can be treated as identical to the behaviour of a layer of lubricant which has a rheology of the same type as the material itself (ref (2)). This case is called a viscoplastic frictional model.

The experimental identification of the frictional coefficients can be achieved by the traditional ring test.

1.3 Formulation by means of finite elements.

The time having been split up into steps of length δt, we shall make an assumption of a quasi-stationary condition (**). For each element δt, the problem consists of calculating the velocity field, by solving the equilibrium equation and equations (2) et (3). This set of relationships is condensed into a variable principle which allows the speed v to be extracted from a family of fields, confirming the boundary conditions of the velocities imposed. The incompressibility relationship is eliminated by a penalisation technique. Resulting from this variable principle is an equation in the form of an integral, non-linear with v (the problem is linear for m = p = 1, a condition which is never met for the usual metal alloys).

Once it is split up by finite elements, this equation is put into a matrix form G = 0, where G is a dimensional vector to the total number of degrees of freedom (i.e., of the order of 2 x n if n is the number of nodes in the finite element mesh). The cancellation of G is obtained by the Newton-Raphson method.

The full calculation of the variation with respect to time is carried out incrementally. The shape of the part at t+δt is determined as a function of its shape at the instant t and of the velocity field (assumed constant with δt), integrated between t and t+δt.

1.4 Problems of contact at the part-die interface.

There are two types of problems : the creation of a new contact and the separation of a zone previously in contact. The first problem is treated by projecting on to the surface which is closest to the die all the nodes of the mesh which are within a die after displacement through the time element δt. The disturbance of the displacements is very localised and the error introduced is of a lower order than that applied by the approximate integration of the finite elements equations.

The second case (separation) is provided for ; it requires a computer interpretation of the notion of contact (unilateral conditions). An algorithm in FORGE2 controls the separation of the nodes, from an evaluation of the state of the forces exerted by the medium on the tool.

(*) the hot range is, in general, defined by temperatures T>1/2 T_f, where T_f is the melting point in degrees Kelvin.

(**) The inertia forces are neglected. These forces (and also gravitational forces) are, for low-velocity forging, considerably less than the forces required to deform the metal. It is permissible to neglect them.
The reader could find further information in GERMAIN Y. - Engineering Doctorate thesis - Ecole des Mines de Paris - France -

2. Range of application.

FORGE2 is applicable to the study of geometries which can be reduced to a two-dimensional representation. Such is the case for :
- long products, where a transverse section is examined ; example of such a part : a turbine blade.
- parts with a revolutionary symmetry ; a radial section is considered , example : rotating parts in a motor car or an aircarft.
  FORGE2 is applicable to models of materials which reveal flow stresses which are sensitive to the rate of distortion (visco-plasticity). The elasticity is neglected because of its minor share in the final distortion. Friction is represented by a model, allowing all cases of forging with lubrication to be studied. All sorts of lubricant can be simulated , oils or glass-base lubricants, for example.
  The program has been developed for isothermal superplastic forging. The present version does not take into account any thermal interaction. FORGE2 will be used for the traditional hot forging, where thermal effects are present, to obtain an initial idea of the flows and the forces. The version with a thermal calculation will supplement this first approximate simulation.
  The program FORGE2 has been designed to be as simple as possible to use : the procedure for the initiation of the program is as similar as possible to the true procedure for the development of a forging case. The definition of a set of upper and lower dies and of the initial shape of the part to be forged is done on a graphical background. The shapes can be altered very rapidly, if the user considers it worthwhile in view of the results of a previous calculation. The calculation time (several hours CPU on a mini-computer) makes it possible to use FORGE2 for determining the optimum design of parts and dies.

3. Description of the program.

FORGE2 is a computer program based on a method of finite elements. The program can be used for arbitrary shapes of dies and blanks. It is an effective tool for predicting, in the course of the process :

- external shapes of the part (prediction of the correct filling of the dies).

- distortions at all points in the part. These are represented in three ways :
1) - by the scalar field $\dot{\bar{\varepsilon}}$ rate of distortion,
2) - by the scalar field $\bar{\varepsilon}$ total distortion (this is the sum of the values of $\dot{\bar{\varepsilon}}$),
3) - by the state of marked points, displaced by the material.

- overall and local forces on the material contours.

Principal characteristics :

- Control by means of the program of the complex boundary conditions : metal-tool contacts, free edges.

- Display of the position of the nodes of the mesh with respect to the velocity field (Lagrange expression). The calculation is continued until the generation of the mesh ceases, detected automatically by an alogrithm. The calculation is continued after an operation to reconstitute the mesh, performed by the operator using sub-routines supplied with the calculation program.

- Possibility of mixing triangular and quadrilateral elements of two types : linear or quadratic (Langrange elements).

- No limitation on the definition of the dies or on the shapes of the blanks.

- Access by the user to the modification of special sub-routines. These concern :

   . the press control velocity,
   . the definition of the coefficients for the laws of behaviour for a particular problem.

Library of elements.

The plane field is divided up into a mesh of 2D elements which are available in the FORGE2 library. We have quadrilaterals (9 and 4 nodes) and triangles (6 and 3 nodes). Further information is given in the table below :

Number of nodes	type of interpolation	Gaussian integration formula	name
4	linear	4 points 1 point	Q04P04A Q04P01A
9	quadratic	9 points 4 points	Q09P09A Q09P04A
3	linear	1 point	T03P01A
6	quadratic	7 points 4 points	T06P04A T06P07A

NB : Only elements which have the same type of interpolation may be mixed together in the same mesh.

Operational :

FORGE2 is accompanied by pre- and post-processor programs for the preparation of data in an intercommunication form (division of parts into meshes, splitting up of the dies, definition of parameters), and for analysing the results.

- MESHING module : this generates a mesh for the part and displays it for checking. The numbering and the band width are provided by the program automatically.

- DIE module : this defines the shapes of the dies, with a graphical display. The upper and lower dies are defined by broken lines in any position (the finished part position can, for example, be chosen). The coordinates of the points are stored in a file. With an operational program, points can be added to or deleted from the dies, or the coordinates altered, in an intercommunication form. These dies are defined with a vertical displacement, so as to be applicable, when necessary, to different sizes of blank.

- DATA module : this defines the necessary data for the model :
    . material and lubrication data,
    . blocking and movement of the dies,
    . total travel of the moving die,
    . convergence threshold,
    . parameters on files for print-out of results.

- VISUAL module : at various stages of the forging operation, this displays the external shapes and the distortion of the initial mesh.

- ISO module : this displays the distortions, rates of distortion and hydrostatic pressures in the form of contour diagrams.

- FORCE module : this displays the variation in the forging force with respect to time.

- REMESHING module : this performs the necessary operation to restart the calculation after the degeneration of the mesh. See paragraph 5, example 1.

Structure of the program :

The program is written in standard FORTRAN 77. The modular structure of FORGE2 allows sub-routines to be modified an introduced, without alteration to the general arrangements. This is important for future developments of the program (improvements to the algorithms, etc).
  The user can, as the need arises, define certain modules :
- press control module. In order to be able to simulate all types of press (hydraulic press, steam hammer, cam press, etc), or particular operating modes such as constant nominal velocity or pre-set forging, a module is accessible to the user to program the case he is concerned with.
- "material behaviour" module : Rheological measurements reveal, as applicable, either that the coefficients of the law of behaviour are dependent on certain variables (e.g. dependent on $\bar{\varepsilon}$), or a law defined by steps in $\dot{\bar{\varepsilon}}$. With this module, the coefficients in each element can be updated at each step in time (at the Gaussian integration points).

- "variable friction" module. With this module, the characteristics of a lubricant can be taken into account (variation of the coefficients of a friction with time, etc). FORGE2 provides for the updating of the coefficients on each of the sides of the finite elements in contact with the dies.

These "USER-SUBROUTINE" modules confer on FORGE2 the capability of a research and development tool.

4. Computer system.

The minimum configuration for dealing with a realistic industrial case is a computer which has a memory of 1 Moctets, with a disc of 20 Moctets. It should be noted, however, that the size of the memory is directly related to the mesh sizes dealt with by program, so that it is possible to use FORGE2 with a configuration having a smaller memory, if the meshing is limited to a maximum dimension.
The type of computer proposed is in the series :
- VAX series with VMS operating system (from the µVAX 2 to the 8800).
- APOLLO terminal with AEGIS operating system.
- IBM, with VM operating system and GKS plotter or 5080 station and CAEDS program.

The programs may be stored either on floppy disc or on magnetic tape.

5. Examples of applications.

5.1. Example 1 : Indentation of a cylinder (detailed case).

5.1.1. Description.

- Geometries

The definition of the dies and the initial position of the part are shown on figure 1. The dies are constituted by a moving punch and a fixed base. The part is in the form of a circular cylinder with a diameter of 100 mm and a height of 40 mm, simply placed on the base. The contact with the tool consists of sliding with friction.
The calculation was taken as far as a punch displacement corresponding to 50% of the initial height of the part. Hereafter, we shall call this displacement relative to the punch, the rate of indentation.

- Meshing

Because it was axially symmetrical, we meshed half the disc. The size of the finite elements in the region of the radius on the upper die was made slimmer by comparison with the remainder of the mesh. At this point the mesh dimensions must be chosen with respect to the order of magnitude of the radius of curvature of the radius (a square whose side is equal to a quarter of this radius).
The major reason is to avoid the mesh too soon becoming unsuitable for continuing the calculation, once there is contact with the radius. On figure 2, we have illustrated this point, taking a mesh length of the same order as the radius of curvature.

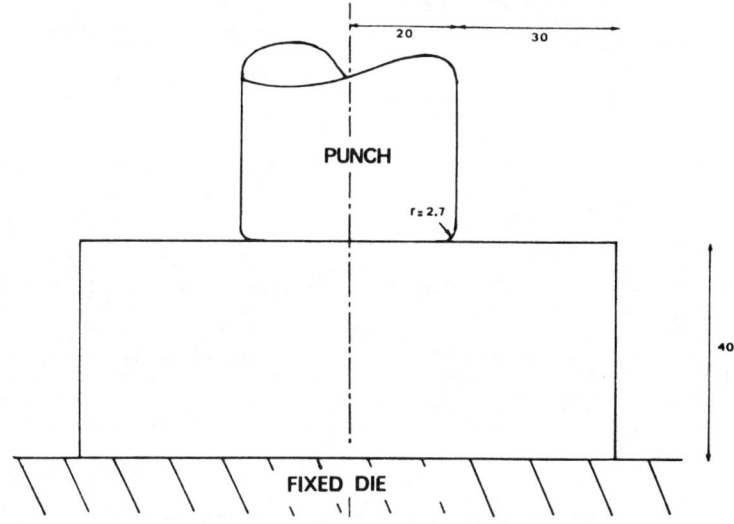

Figure 1 : definition of the geometry in millimetres.

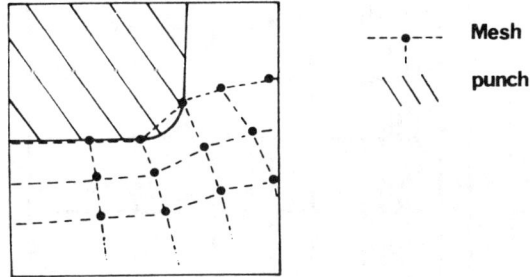

Figure 2 : example of a mesh unsuitable for the satisfactory development of the calculations.

The calculations cannot be continued for two major reasons :
- too high a volumetric proportion enters the tool,
- The determination of the distortions around the radius is rendered impossible - the curvature of the radius, for example, plays no role in the flow.

In general, the initial meshing of the part is an operation of primary importance, It is necessary, in fact, to locate elements to a high density in zones where the geometry varies greatly, and in zones where it is suspected that there will be large distortions. Here, the experience of the user will play its part (through, possibly, a previous calculation). A good meshing will thus allow a correct solution to be obtained, and will minimise the number of remeshing operations during the calculation steps. On the other hand, in order to reduce the calculation time, it is worthwnile to reduce the density of the mesh in zones where it is presumed there will be little distortion.

It snould be noted that, in carrying out this operation, we arrrive at elements of diverse sizes. This diversification may also be necessary to render a part of complex shape into a series of simpler pieces. Each zone is defined topologically as a "rectangle", each side of which is constituted by an assembly of segments of straight lines and circular arcs. For each of the parts of the side, the number of nodes required and their spacing is determined (constant, or arithmetical progression, starting from one of the two ends or from both ends). To make the automatic meshing of the zone work, it is necessary for two "opposing sides" of the "rectangle" to have the same number of nodes. The definition of a zone (sides and nodes along the sides) is obtained by means of an operating program, the result of which is stored in a file (modifiable if necessary). A second operating program performs the meshing of each zone and the assembly of the zones. It optimises the numbering of the nodes to reduce the calculation time for the problem, and the size of the memory required.

On figure 3, we have plotted the mesh for the different divisions.

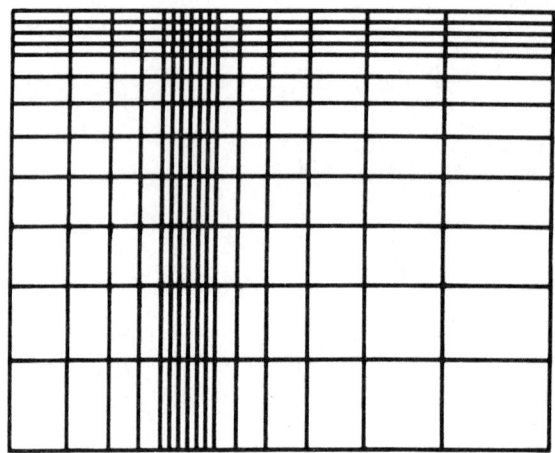

Figure 3 : Meshing of the part. The complete mesh contains 221 nodes and 192 elements, and the band width is 21.

The dies are defined by segments of straight lines. Figure 4 shows the meshing described previously fixed between the two dies. The latter is produced by the VISUAL display module of FORGE2.

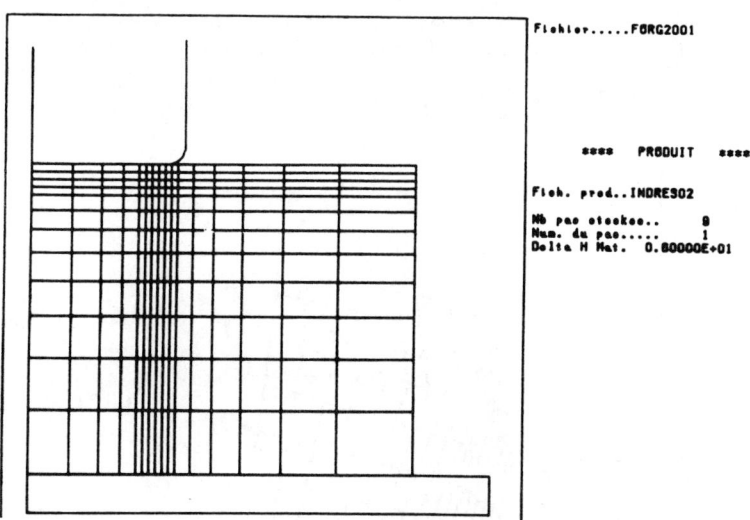

Figure 4 : mesh and dies for the study of the indentation of a disc.

5.1.2 Initiation of the calculation.

The data for the case to be dealt with are :
m = 0,2 (hot steel) ; K is defined as 1 ; p = 0,2 et α = 0,05 (low friction).
Time interval : this is defined by a descent of the punch at each time interval equal to 1% of the current height of the part.

5.1.3 Results.

Necessary stage : remeshing of the distorted part

As we foresaw during the definition of the mesh, the zone situated in the region of the radius is the seat of major distortions. The consequence of this is that the mesh becomes unsuitable for the continuation of the calculation, for the reasons given in the preceding paragraph. From the information acquired at this stage, it is a case of generating a new mesh. This operation consists of :
1/ maintening the positions of the nodes which constitute the boundary of the part,
2/ maintaining the values of $\bar{\varepsilon}$ calculated from the start of the compressive deformation up to that instant. They are defined at very precise points, which here are the positions of the integration points.

From a knowledge of the contour of the part, a mesh can be defined, using the special program for this task. The criteria for defining this new mesh are those which preceded the design of the initial mesh. The second task consists of allocating to the integration points the values of $\bar{\varepsilon}$ from those known values on the abandoned mesh. This operation is performed in 3 stages :

1/ Calculation of the values of $\bar{\varepsilon}$ at the nodes of the previous mesh.
2/ The obtaining of a field of nodal values of $\bar{\varepsilon}$ on the new mesh.
3/ The allocation of a value of $\bar{\varepsilon}$ to each integration point on the new mesh.

These operations are performed by the operating program REMESHING.

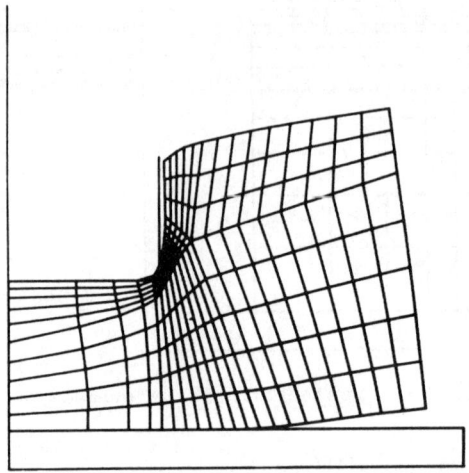

Figure 5 : Distorted mesh at 50% of the degree of indentation and after 4 resmeshings. Note the separation of the lower side portion of the disc, forecast by FORGE2 and observed experimentally.

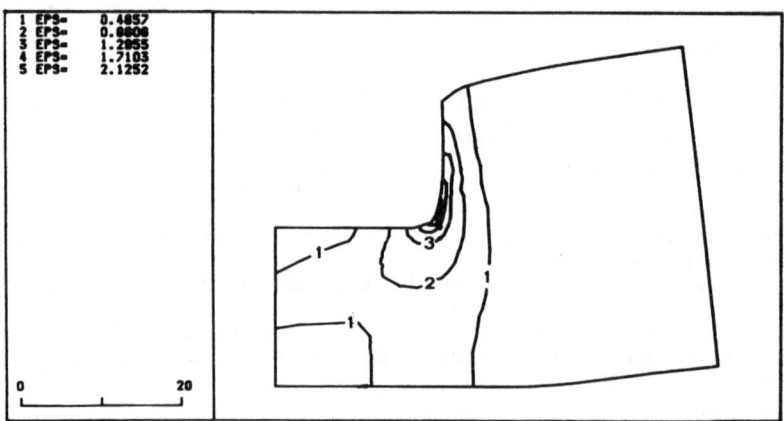

Figure 6 : Contour diagram of the cumulative distortion $\bar{\varepsilon}$. This variable allows the distortion condition in the part to be located and quantified (maximum values around the punch and unaffected zone in the periphery).

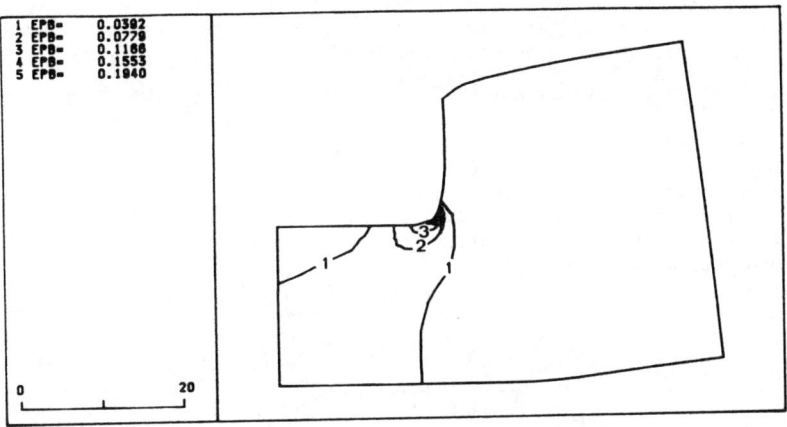

Figure 7 : Contour diagram of the rate of distortion $\dot{\bar{\varepsilon}}$. This variable allows the zones in the part where the distortion is changing at a given instant to be located and quantified (the maximum is situated on the punch radius).

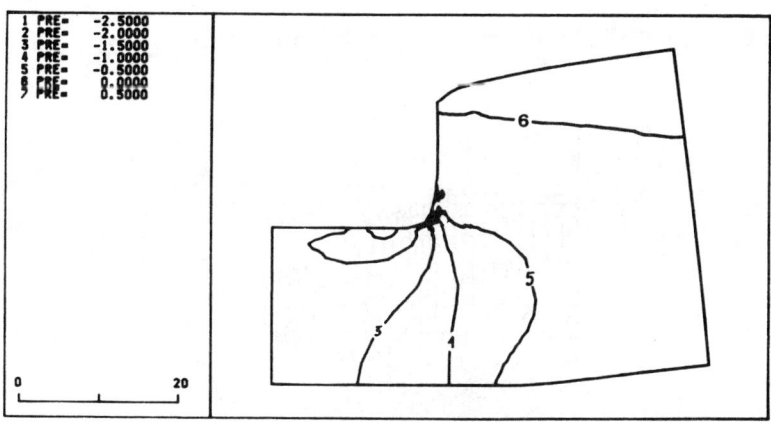

Figure 8 : Contour diagram of the hydrostatic pressures. This variable represents a mean stress condition (the negative values (positive resp.) correspond to a compressive condition (tensile resp.)).

5.2. Example 2 : stamping of a rear axle crown wheel.

This is an axially symmetrical motor car part. The geometry of the blank and the shape of the dies are given on figure 9.

The true forging characteristics are :

- travel of the die 36.6 millimetres (mm)
- duration of the operation 0,162 seconds
- mean forging velocity 226 mm/sec
- material : steel 33CD4, AFNOR Standard
- temperature of the material : 1150°C (Cold dies)
- lubrication : graphite and water.

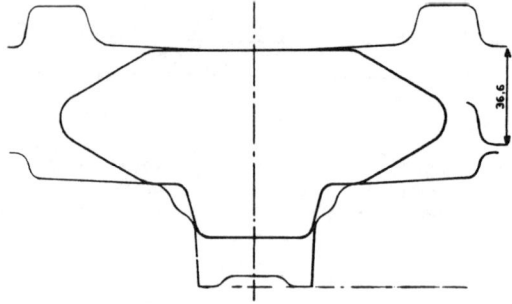

Figure 9 : Geometry of the blank and the dies studied.

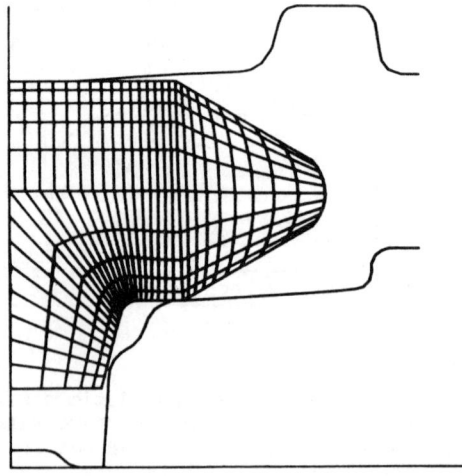

Figure 10 : Illustration of the mesh after compression between the dies.

The data for the simulation program :

Given the mechanical properties of this steel, we chose a value for m of 0,2. The consistence was defined as 1. For the friction, we chose the values of p = 0,2 et α = 0,15.
For this example, we simplified the data for the control of the die ; the velocity was assumed constant at 226 mm/s. The time interval corresponds to 1% of the descent of the die.

Results :

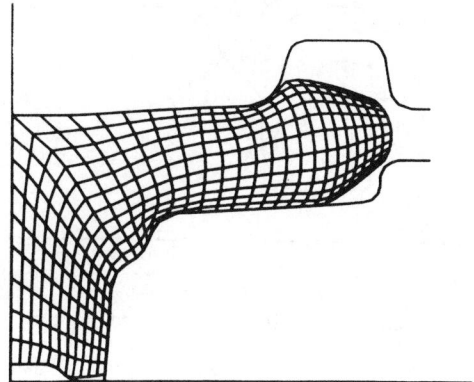

Figure 11 : State of filling of the dies for 70% compression. The part was remeshed once.

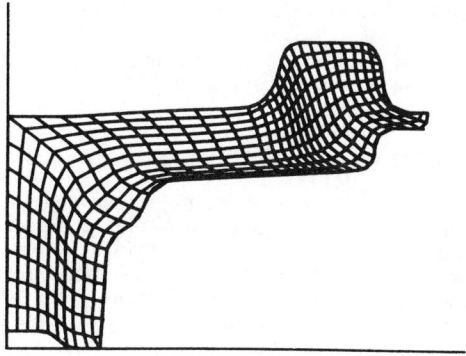

Figure 13 : End of the simulation, with the dies completely filled.

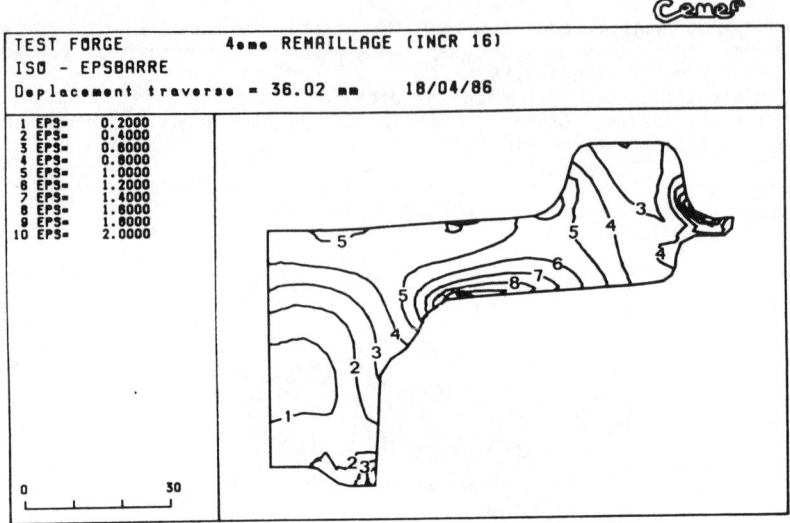

Figure 13 : Contour diagram of $\bar{\varepsilon}$ in the finished part.

With this example, we show that the FORGE2 program allows us to study the filling of a complex die with a reasonable degree of approximation, at relatively low cost. On a VAX 11/750 from Digital Equipment this work took :

- description of the die   } 1/2 day
- initial meshing
- various data and initiation of the first calculation : 1 hour
- remeshing and initiation of the calculation (4 times) : 2 hours
- analysis (various plots)   : 1 day

The calculations required approximately 10 hours on the computer. The whole of the work thus required approximately 2 days.

5.3. Example 3 : Forging of a turbine disc.

This disc is a rotating part in an aircraft jet engine. The geometry of the dies is given on figure 14. This example provides a comparison between the results of FORGE2 and experimental ones. For this, the part was made from a Lead-Tin eutectic alloy (Pb 38% - Sn 62%). The rheology of this material was determined by compression tests on cylindrical pins, while the friction was evaluated by ring tests. The meshing of the cylindrical blank is shown on figure 15.

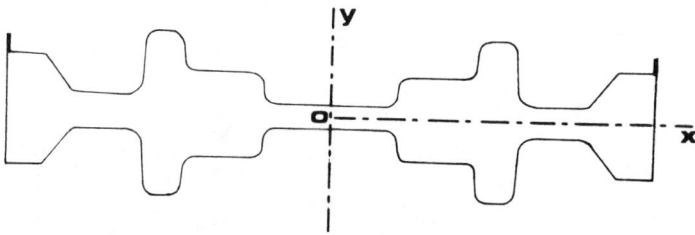

Figure 14 : Geometry of the dies : Oy is the axis of revolution and Ox is a plane of symmetry.

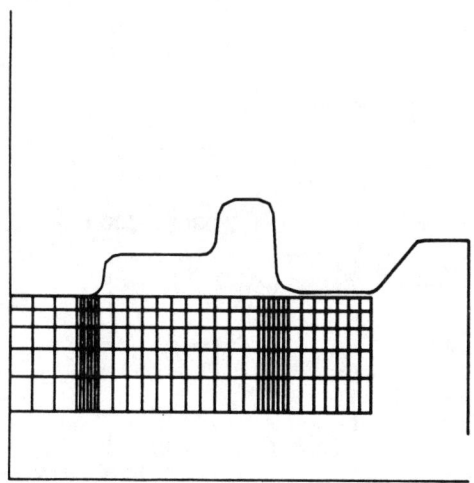

Figure 15 : Meshing of the cylindrical blank with compression between the dies (VISUAL program). Due to symmetry, only a quarter of the geometry is studied.

Results :

Comparisons between the results of the model and the experimental measurements are shown on figures 16 and 17.

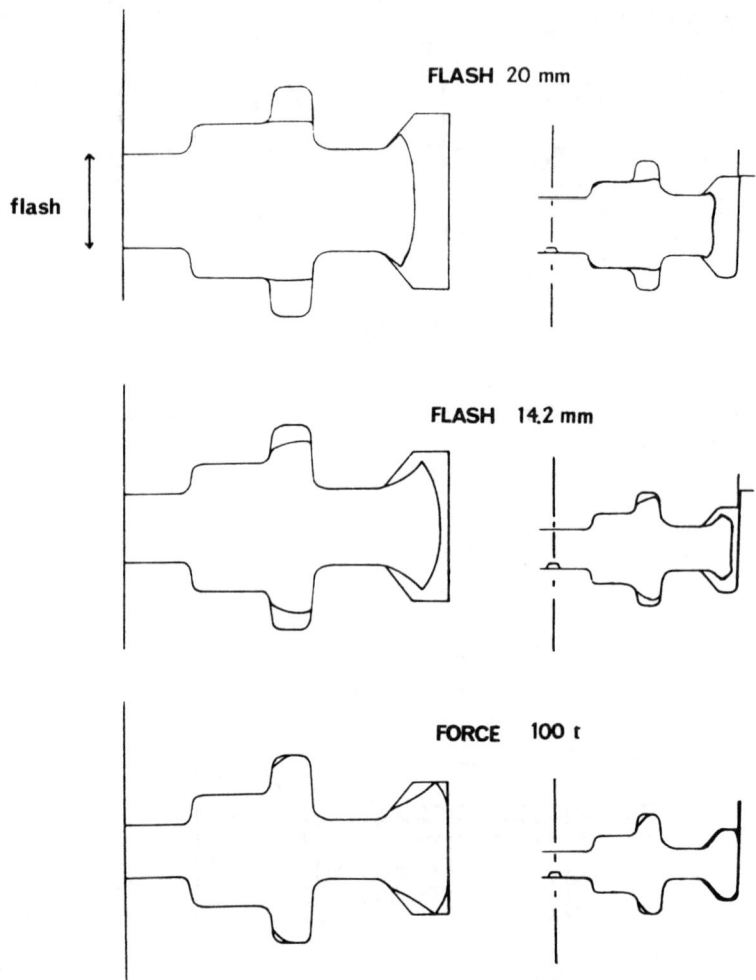

Figure 16 : Comparison of the filling of the dies. On the right the experimental measurements, on the left the results of FORGE2, at three stages :
1) 20 mm flash, 2) 14.2 mm flash, 3) forging force of 100 tonnes.
(NB : the calculation required 6 remeshings and 10 hrs on the VAX 11/750).

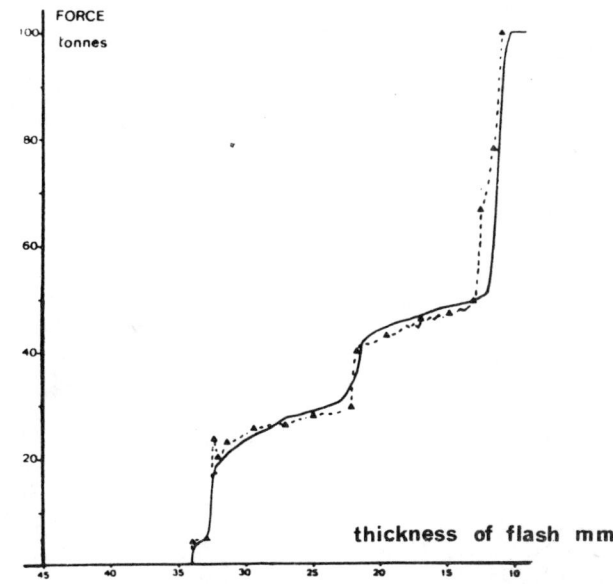

Figure 17 : Forging force with respect to the thickness of the central flash - full line : experimental curve - broken line : FORGE2 results.

Conclusion :

This example gives an idea of the level of accuracy which the user of FORGE2 can expect. Agreement between experimental results and those of the model is very good, for the filling of the dies and for the force curve, essential points in the study of a forging process.
To conclude, we give the last result provided by FORGE2.

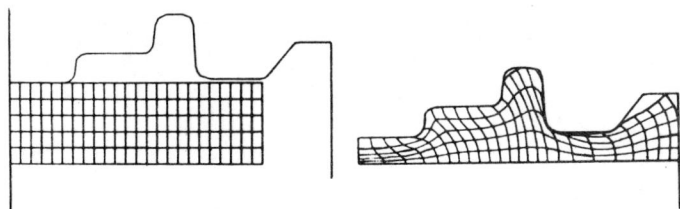

Figure 18 : On the left, definition of the marking of points on the initial blank - on the right, the deformed condition. These points were made on the material (this mesh was not used for the calculations). The distortion modes can thus be seen (shear or elongation), and this result can be correlated with the morphology or the grain flow.

Reference :

"A finite element analysis of shaped lead-tin disk forgings".
GERMAIN, MOSSER, J.L. CHENOT.
Paper presented to the NUMIFORM International Congress, August 1986.

DYNAMIC DESIGN OPTIMIZATION OF THE BASEPLATE OF A NUCLEAR INSTRUMENTATION VERTICAL CABINET

R. Filidoro and N. Pezzella

Nuovo Pignone, Divisione Valvole e Strumente, Bari, Italy

C. Pappalettere

University of Bari, Italy

ABSTRACT

This paper explains the optimization criteria used for the baseplate design of a modular cabinet which had already been qualified for nuclear uses. The aim here was to assure the qualification for the cabinet-baseplate structure by not altering the vibration modes and, therefore, the seismic dynamic response. The possibility of connecting several cabinet by means of their baseplates was also analyzed, obtaining similar dynamic behaviours. The analysis of the stresses due to the seisma shows the baseplate is suitably designed if it has a stiffness which, in practice is infinite.

KEYWORDS

Nuclear qualification; instrumentation cabinet; baseplate; modal analysis; response spectrum analisys.

INTRODUCTION

The vertical cabinet discussed here is a modular system of electronic instruments for nuclear applications (Fig. 1a). These cabinets come in a standard-size units and so the system can be adapted to the size and needs of the nuclear power plant. Each single cabinet contains:
- a power supply which makes it self-sufficient;
- interconnection matrixes for all the instruments making up the system;
- galvanic separation terminal boards or barriers for the connection of the cables coming from the field;
- all the rack mounted instruments making up the system.

The above components are housed in a cabinet-structure made of a welded steel frame covered by sheet metal panels. The set is assembled on a foundation, by means of a baseplate in between which is needed to raise the surface it rests on up to the level of the false floor of the control room (Fig. 1b).

On the cabinet, numerical and experimental seismic studies had previously been carried out in order to qualify it for nuclear uses.
To extend this qualification to cases where it is to be installed with a baseplate, this baseplate was designed so that it

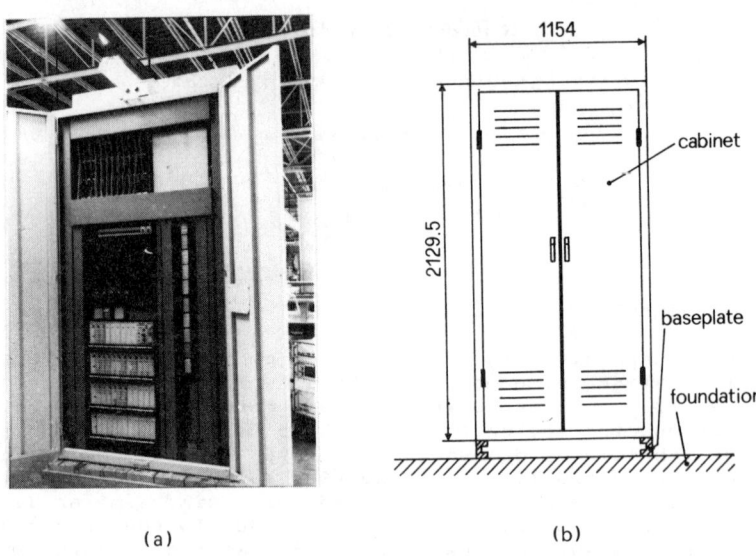

Fig. 1. Structure analyzed: a) photo of the cabinet; b) outline drawing.

would not considerably affect the vibration modes nor, foreseeably, the seismic response.
Starting from the already-available first values of the cabinet's natural vibration frequencies, several baseplate configurations were analyzed which led to the optimization of the dynamic response.
The analyses were performed using the finite element method of the SAP V, version 2, program, qualified by Nuovo Pignone for nuclear uses.
Since the first natural vibration frequencies of the optimized complete structure (cabinet and baseplate) turned out to be lower than the imposed acceptability levels, using the same numerical technique, a Response Spectrum analysis was used to check that the stress values in the baseplate were lower than the allowable ones.
The combination of the responses of the different vibration modes, in the range of the first 100 Hz, was carried out in accordance with the NRC reg. guide 1.92.
The cabinet was then idealized as a vertical beam with its mass concentrated at its centre of gravity and rigidly connected to the baseplate which, in turn, was schematized with beams.

For this structure, the first three natural vibration modes were
calculated, in order to demonstrate its equivalence, from the
point of view of vibration, with the above complete structure.
Finally, this equivalent module was used to verify that the
vibrating behaviour of a group of 5 cabinet is not negatively
affected by the bolting connection of the relative baseplates.
Also this analysis was done with the same finite element program

MODELS ANALYZED

Complete Single Structure

The final mesh used for the seismic analysis of the complete
structure, made up of cabinet plus baseplate, is given in
Fig. 2.

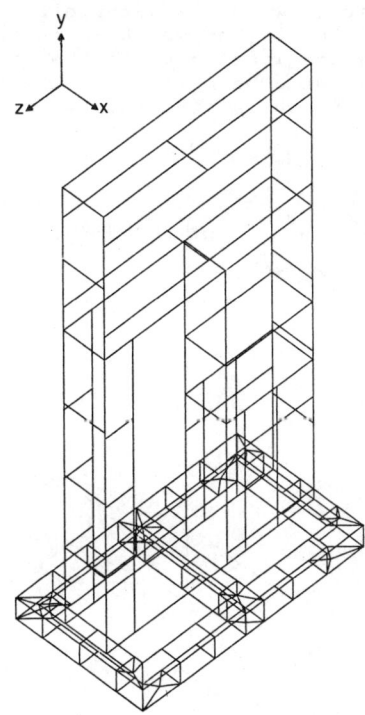

Fig. 2. Complete single model: undeformed shape.

The upper part represents the cabinet and consists of 141 beam
elements and 112 joints, of which 91 concern the structure and
21 define the local axes of the beam sections. Their geometric
properties were obtained from the manufacturing drawing of the
cabinet, made with commercial standard-shape beams.
The lower part concerns the baseplate and is made up of C-shape
beams, discretized with 112 joints, of which 6 are for the rigid
connection with the cabinet structure and 118 are plate elements, 66 being quadrangular and 52 triangular.
To obtain the support reactions, 18 joints and 18 boundary ele-

ments were added to the mesh. These joints were assumed to be perfectly fixed, since this support condition was taken to be the most realistic one.
The plate elements forming the baseplate were considered with their self weight. The masses of the beam elements of the cabinet structure and the instruments contained in it were added as masses concentrated at the joints corresponding to their centres of gravity.
30% of the overall weight of 540 Kg is made up of electronic instruments. This implies that the cabinet is completely filled.

Simplified Single Structure

Fig. 3 gives the mesh used for this analysis. It represents the single cabinet together with its baseplate and is made up of 31 beam elements and 25 joints, of which 23 represent the structure itself and 2 define the local axes of the beam sections. The cabinet was idealized as a beam fixed to the baseplate. The mass and the inertia of the whole structure were concentrated in its centre of gravity.

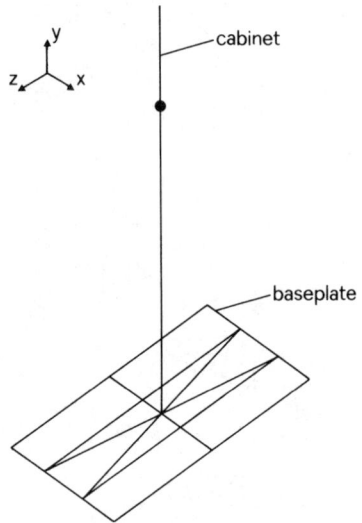

Fig. 3. Simplified single model: undeformed shape.

The geometric characteristics of the baseplate beams and the "cabinet" beam, the values of their masses and their inertia and the co-ordinates of their centre of gravity were derived from the results of the previous model optimization.

Quintupled Simplified Structure

The last mesh (Fig. 4) is made up of a group of 5 simplified model modules, in which the baseplates, spaced 30mm apart, are connected with beams representing the bolts. It is therefore made up of 125 joints and of 163 beam elements corresponding to 5 times the single structure and 8 bolts connecting the baseplates.

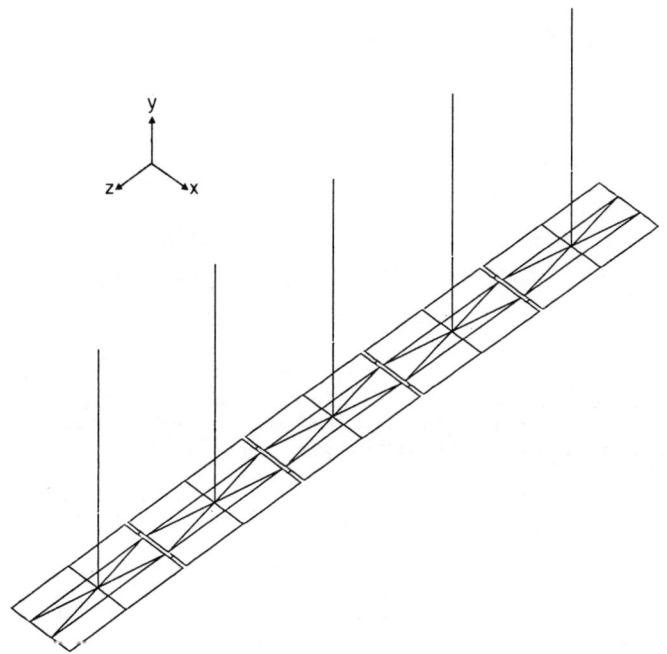

Fig. 4. Quintupled simplified model: undeformed shape.

MODAL ANALYSIS RESULTS

The complete single structure model proved to be the best one after various design attempts.
Different analyses were carried out for it as the thickness of the plates of the baseplate was varied, discretizing the structure achieved by full penetration butt-welded C-shape beams. This was done in order to obtain first natural frequencies very close to those of the cabinet without baseplate, recorded in previous numerical and experimental studies.
The results of this optimization is shown in the graph of Fig. 5, which gives the variation in value of the 1st natural vibration frequency of the complete structure against the thickness of the C-shape beam plates of the baseplate.
This graph confirms the expected results that only an infinitely stiff baseplate could mantain unvaried the natural vibration frequencies of the single cabinet.
Therefore, to minimize the foreseeable reduction in the complete structure's natural frequency values, it was decided to use, for the baseplate, 20mm thick C-shape beams, which proved to be most compatible with manufacturing requirements.
The choise gives, in terms of vibration modes, the results shown

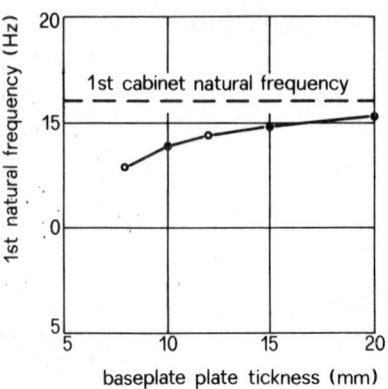

Fig. 5. Effect of the plate thickness of the baseplate C-shape beams on the 1st natural vibration frequency of the complete single structure (see Fig. 2).

in Table 1. This table also compares the analysis results, concerning the simplified single structure and the quintupled one.

Table 1 Modal analysis results

	complete single structure		simplified single structure		quintupled structure	
mode	freq.(Hz)	direct.	freq.(Hz)	direct.	freq.(Hz)	direct.
1	15.2	x	15.0	x	15.0	x
2	16.8	z	16.7	z	15.0	x
3	24.8	x & z	24.8	x & z	15.0	x
4	60.8	x	--	---	15.0	x
5	65.7	z	--	---	15.0	x
6	71.0	x	--	---	16.7	z
7	79.3	y & z	--	---	16.7	z
8	86.2	x	--	---	16.7	z
9	94.9	x & z	--	---	16.7	z
10	108.9	y	--	---	16.7	z
11	---	---	--	---	24.8	x & z
12	---	---	--	---	24.8	x & z

Figures 6, 7 and 8 show the deformed shapes of the vibration modes of the single complete structure, the simplified single structure and the quintupled one, respectively.
Fig. 5, the deformed shapes and Table 1 permit one to establish that:
- by adding a baseplate made of 20mm thich C-shape beams, the

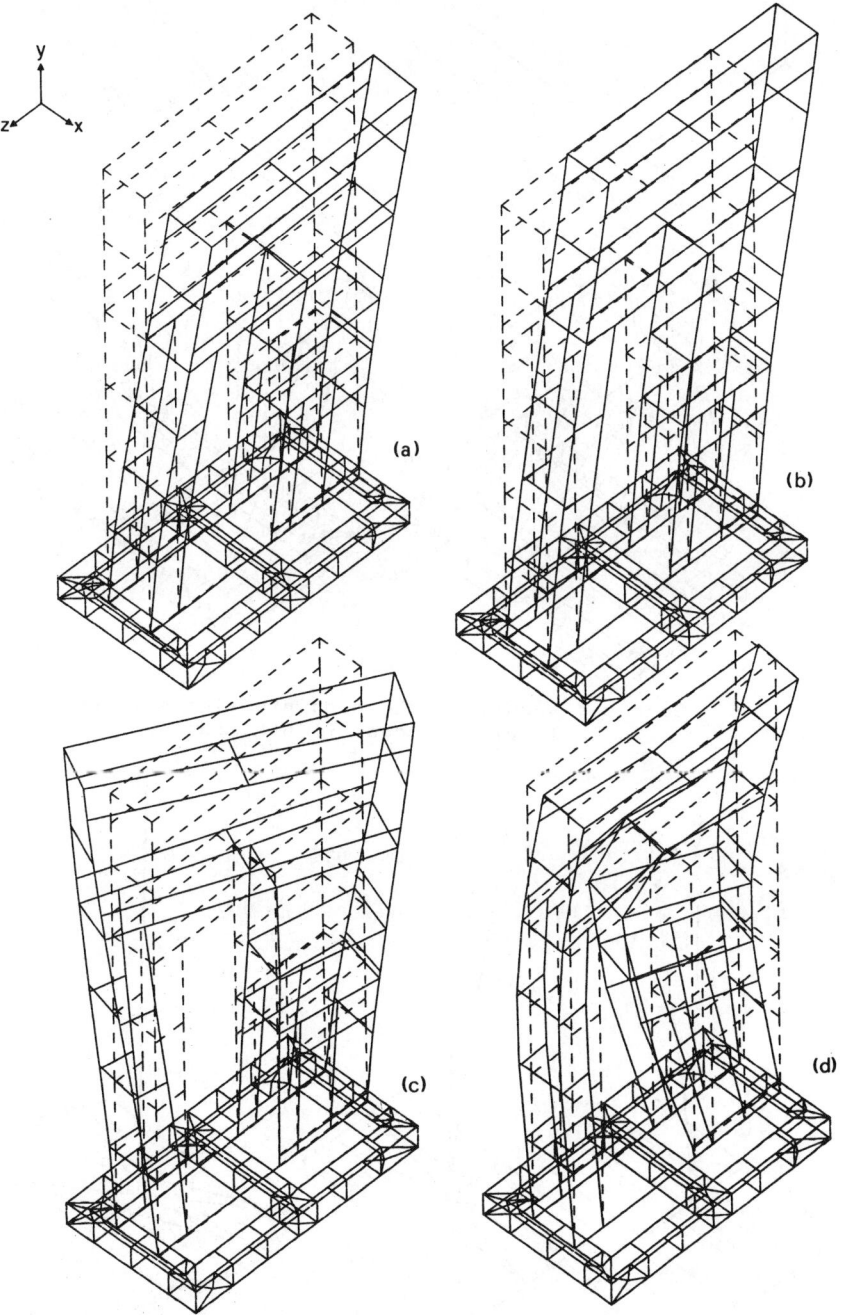

Fig. 6. Deformed shapes of the complete single structure:
a) 1st mode; b) 2nd mode; c) 3rd mode; d) 4th mode.

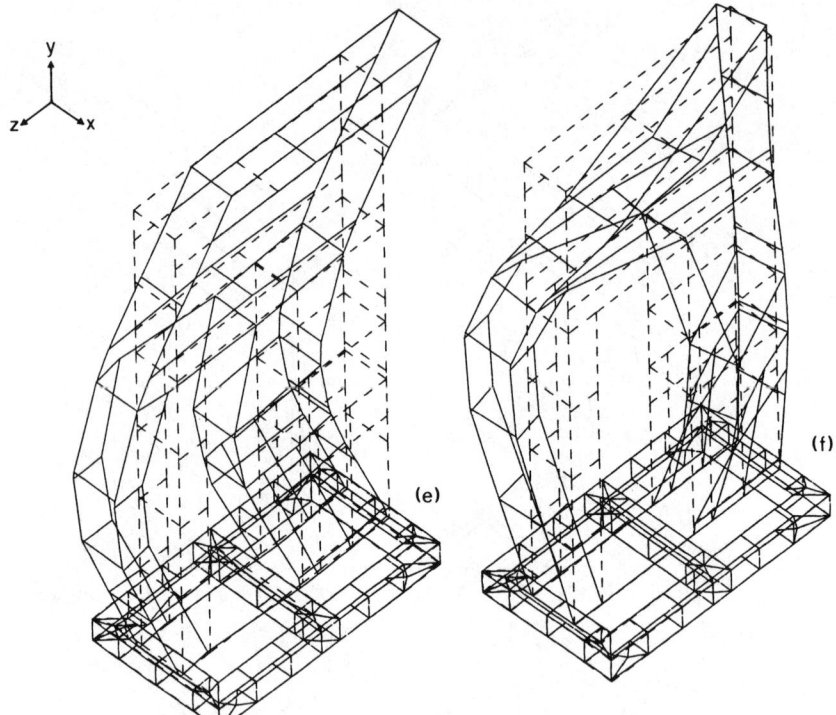

Fig. 6. Deformed shapes of the complete single structure: e) 5th mode; f) 6th mode.

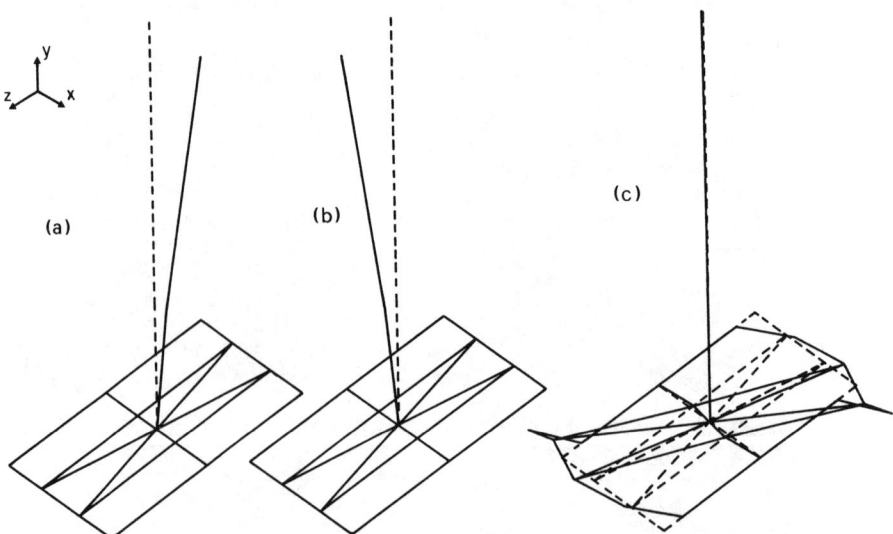

Fig. 7. Deformed shapes of the simplified single structure: a) 1st mode; b) 2nd mode; c) 3rd mode.

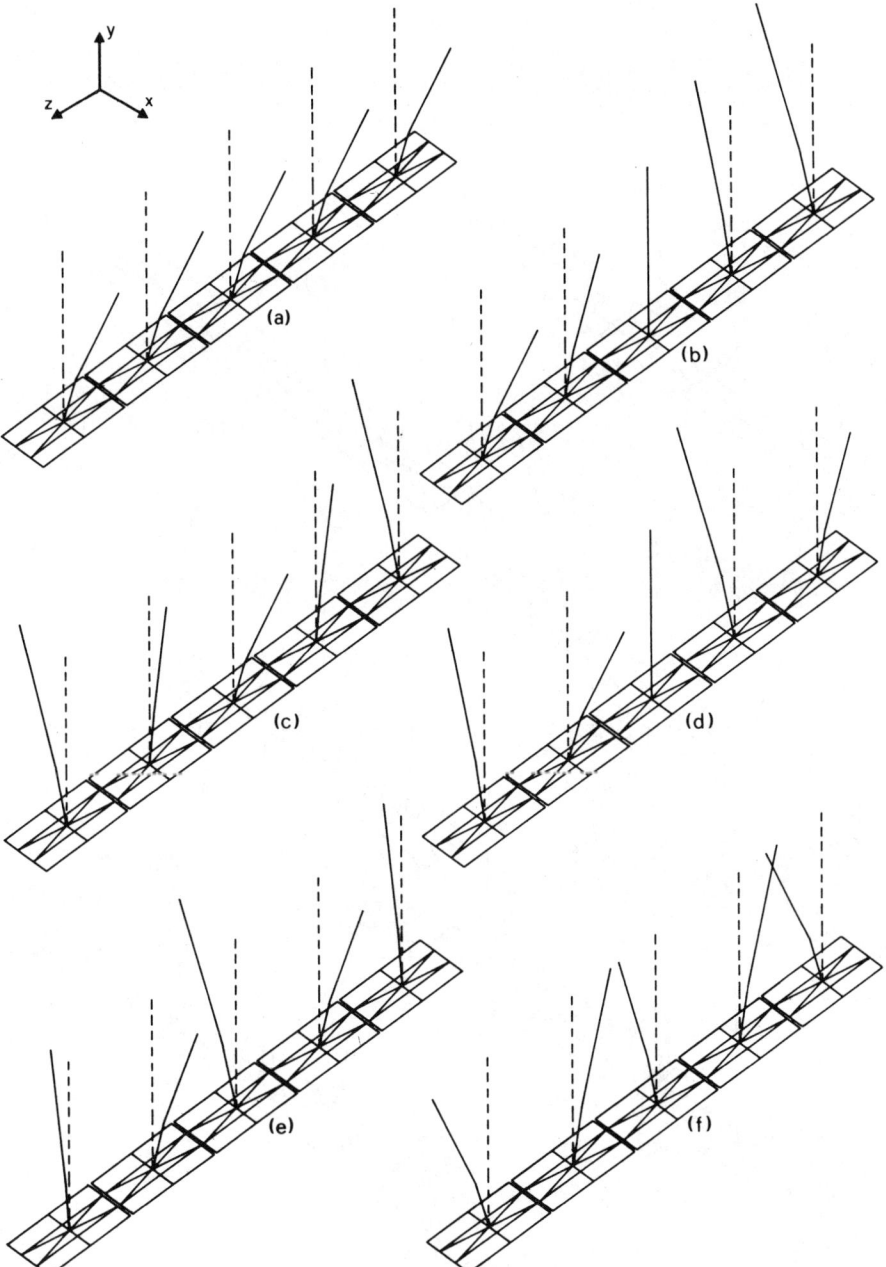

Fig. 8. Deformed shapes of the quintupled simplified structure:
a) 1st mode; b) 2nd mode; c) 3rd mode;
d) 4th mode; e) 5th mode; f) 6th mode.

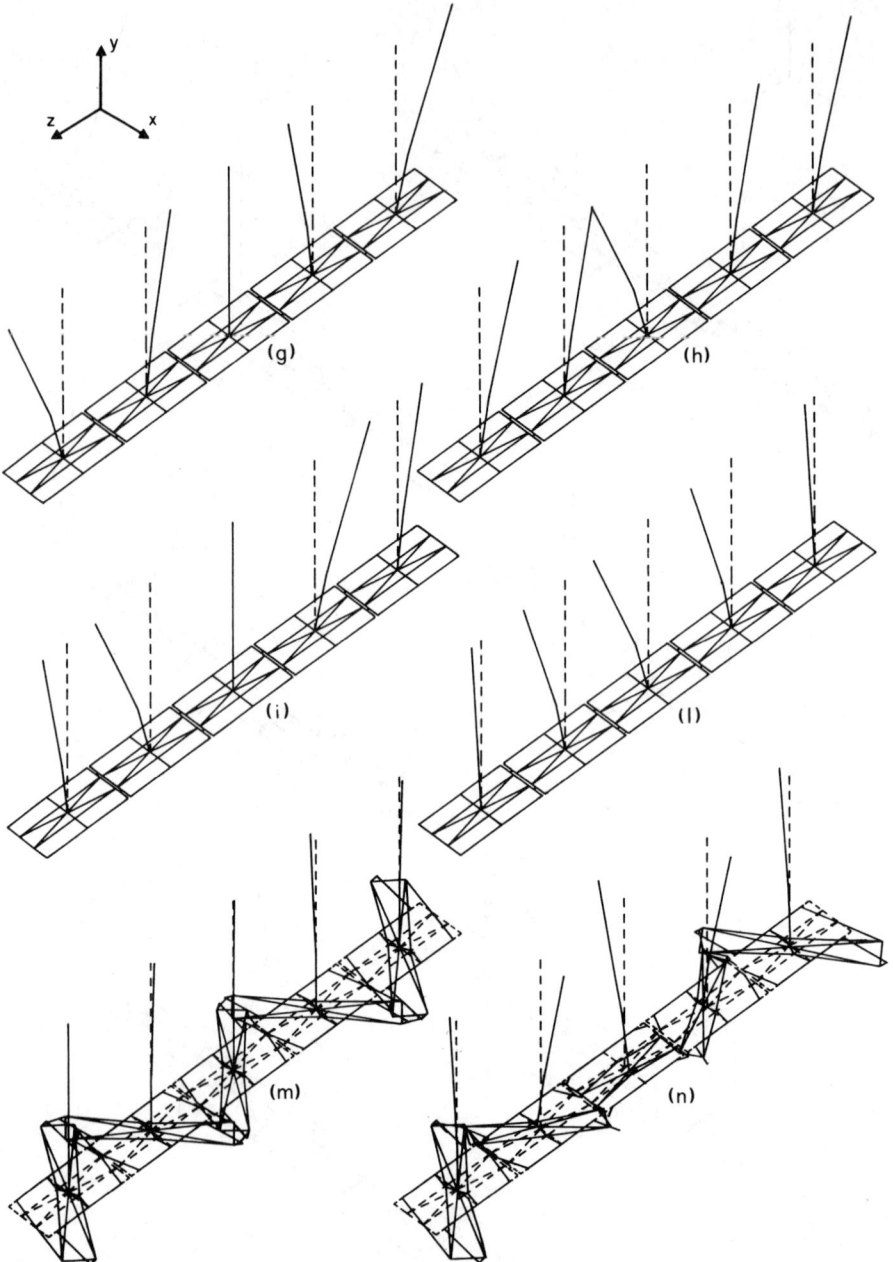

Fig. 8. Deformed shapes of the quintupled simplified structure:
g) 7th mode; h) 8th mode; i) 9th mode;
l) 10th mode; m) 11th mode; n) 12th mode.

first natural vibration frequency of the cabinet alone is slightly reduced (approx. 4%); consequently, the next natural frequencies are similarly reduced and, the expected dynamic seismic response will be almost the same as for the cabinet alone;
- if suitable geometric characteristics, masses and inertias are used as input data, even a complex structure can be analyzed with simplified models, thus obtaining congruent responses;
- as foreseeable, assembling several single structures, does not alter the natural vibration frequencies values, even if multiplying the vibration modes with very close frequency values.

RESPONSE SPECTRUM ANALYSIS RESULTS

Since the first natural vibration frequencies fall below the acceptable value, a Response Spectrum Analysis was done on the complete single structure to check the acceptability of the base plate stress values.
Fig. 9 gives the load spectra applied horizontally (directions x and y) and vertically (direction z).

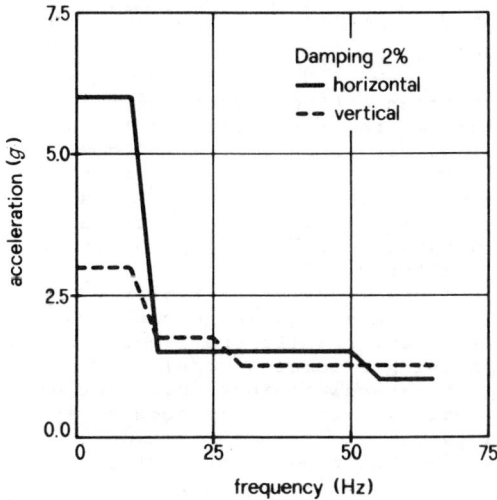

Fig. 9. Safe Shutdown Earthquake load spectra.

The combination of the various vibration mode responses (from 0 to 100 Hz) was performed in accordance with the NRC reg. guide 1.92, as shown in Table 2.
The most stressed part of the baseplate proved to be one of the elements near its joints connecting it to the cabinet. The element stress was 24.5 N/mm², which is the sum of membrane plus bending stresses in the two directions of the plate plane.
The analysis gave a maximum shear stress of 3.3 N/mm².
The maximum tensile and shear stresses in the bolts connecting the baseplate to the foundation were 29.4 and 23.5 N/mm², respectively.
The maximum deflections were found at the top of the cabinet and were: 2.3, 0.16 and 1.83 mm, for the transversal, vertical and

longitudinal directions (x, y and z) respectively.

Table 2 Response Combination Method

U=response (force, moment, translation etc.)
U_{1xx}=resp. in ith mode, x earthquake direct., x spectrum input
U_{1yy}=   "   "   "   " , x   "   " , y   "   "
.   .   .   .   "   " . .   "   "
.   .   .   .   "   " . .   "   "
U_{1zz}=   "   "   "   " , z   "   " , z   "   "

$$U_{xx} = \sqrt{U_{1xx}^2 + U_{2xx}^2 + \ldots + (U_{jxx} + U_{kxx})^2 + \ldots + U_{nxx}^2}$$

U_{yy}, U_{zz} found similarly and assuming that modes j and k are within cluster factor distance and

$$U = \sqrt{U_{xx}^2 + U_{YY}^2 + U_{zz}^2}.$$

All sums in the above equations are sum of absolute values.

CONCLUSIONS

The first and most important conclusion of this numerical analysis is that the cabinet remains qualified for nuclear uses even when it is installed with a baseplate which makes the centre of gravity of the distributed masses move upwards.
By optimizing the baseplate configuration in such a way that it is comparable to an infinitely stiff structure, though feasible in practice, the natural vibration modes of the original cabinet remain virtually unaltered.
The analysis of the behaviour of a simplified cabinet-baseplate structure proves that, when the geometries, masses and inertias are known exactly, the results are almost the same as those which are obtained using a complex model.
The connecting up of several cabinets does not alter the response of the single cabinet, if done in such a way as to avoid any dynamic interferences.
Finally, this study has shown that a structure which can be defined as infinitely stiff is also structurally stable.
The finite element method used proved the above conclusions which could not be demonstrated using simplified calculations, even when they could be expected.
The plotting of the undeformed and deformed shapes confirmed the correctness of the meshes used and enabled an easy-understanding of the phenomena involved in the analysis.

STATIC ANALYSIS OF LARGE FRAMEWORKS

C. T. F. Ross

Portsmouth Polytechnic, UK

ABSTRACT

Four microcomputer programs are described and applications are made of these programs to a number of large structures, including pin-jointed and rigid-jointed space frames, grillages, the transverse frame of a supertanker and the transverse section of a gravity dam.

In all cases, the finite element method was used, with the aid of an expanded Sinclair QL microcomputer.

Two different screen dumps were used, which enabled the figure on the screen to be dumped, both before and after processing.

KEYWORDS

Microcomputer programs; finite elements; frameworks; grillages; in-plane plates.

INTRODUCTION

The four computer programs, which were written in Sinclair Super Basic, covered the following types of structure:-

(a) Three-dimensional pin-jointed trusses.

(b) Grillages.

(c) Three dimensional rigid-jointed frames.

(d) In-plane plate problems.

The present author discovered that when a 256 k bytes RAM pack was attached to the expansion port of a 128 k bytes Sinclair QL, the largest matrix that could be accepted by this machine in Super Basic was of order 237 x 237, and when this RAM pack was replaced by a 512 k bytes RAM pack, a matrix of order 312 x 312 was accepted. Thus, with such a relatively large RAM space available, it was possible to analyse large structures via the finite element method. In all cases, advantage was taken of the possibility of any sparsity of the matrix by storing only the upper half of the band of the stiffness matrix that contained non-zero elements, shown by equations (1) and (2).

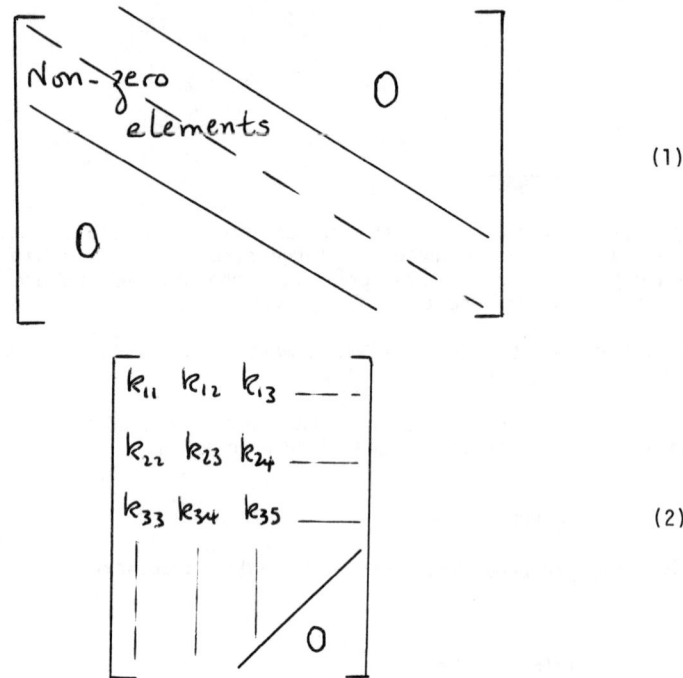

Solution of the simultaneous equations was carried out by triangulation, (Ross, 1985). A description of the capabilities of each of the four computer programs will now be given, together with applications of them to some realistic problems.

(1) Microcomputer program for a three dimensional pin-jointed truss. This program uses a three dimensional skeletal element with two end nodes and three translational degrees of freedom per node. Prior to computational processing, the computer program draws a three dimensional view of the framework onto the screen, which can then be dumped onto an inexpensive dot matrix printer.

The computational processing includes the calculations for the nodal displacements and element forces, and the post processing, includes a three dimensional view of the deflected form of the framework onto the screen, which can then be dumped. Figure 1 shows the plan view and front elevation of a Schwedler dome, which was subjected to a wind load acting from left to right, together with a snow load, and Figs. 2 and 3 show screen dumps of the plan view of the truss, both before and after processing. The dome had 24 nodes, with a total of 72 degrees of freedom.

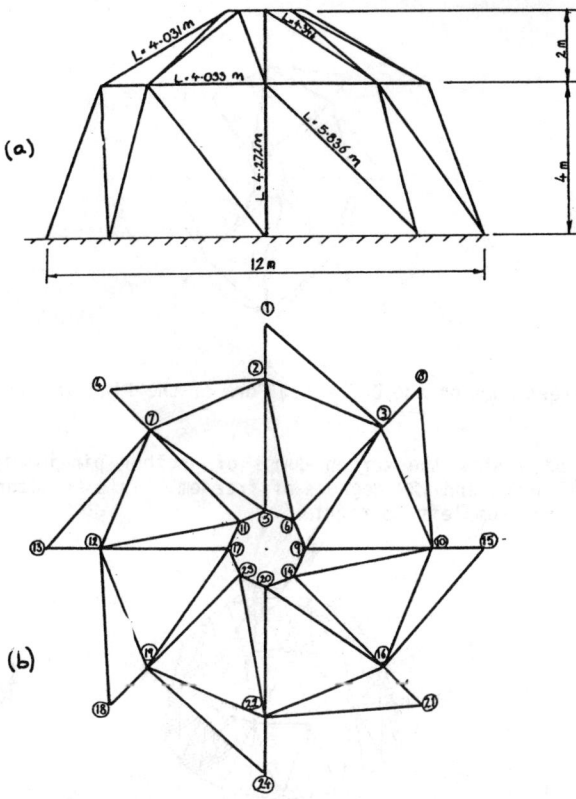

Fig. 1. Two-Tiered Schwedler Dome, (a) Front Elevation, (b) Plan.

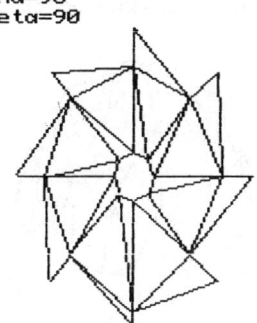

Fig. 2. Screen Dump of the Plan of the Schwedler Dome.

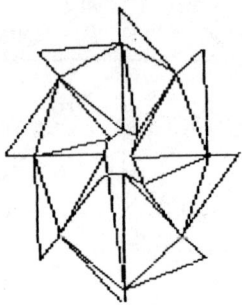

Fig. 3. Screen Dump of the Deflected Form of the Plan of the Schwedler Dome.

Figures 4 and 5 show the screen dumps of another pin-jointed space truss, which had 43 nodes and 129 degrees of freedom. This structure was subjected to a wind load from left to right.

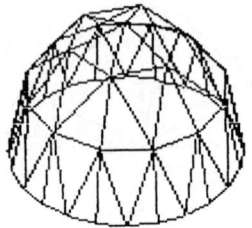

Fig. 4. Screen Dump of a Pin-Jointed Space Truss Before Processing.

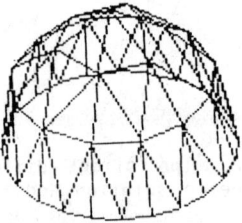

Fig. 5. Screen Dump of the Deflected Form of a Pin-Jointed Space Truss.

(2) <u>Microcomputer program for grillages.</u> This program can calculate rotations, deflections, moments and torques in skew or orthogonal grillages of complex shape and with complex boundary conditions. The loading can be a complex combination of distributed and point loading, and the geometrical properties of the grillage can be different, if required.

Each element was of one dimensional form, with two end nodes and three degrees of freedom per node; one being an out-of-plane translational deflection and the other two being in-plane rotational displacements.

The example chosen to demonstrate the capabilities of this program, is the orthogonal grillage of Fig. 6, which was simply-supported around its boundary. The grillage had 73 nodes, with 219 degrees of freedom, and it was subjected to a distributed load of 2792 N/m in both the x° and y° directions.

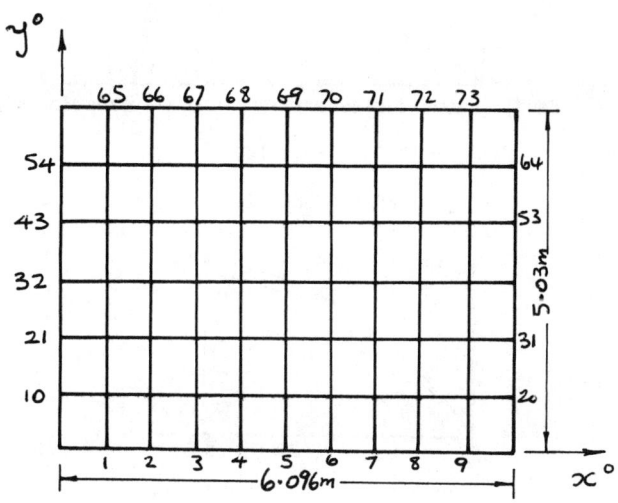

Fig. 6. Orthogonal Grid, Subjected to Out-Of-Plane Loading.

Bending moment diagrams for some of the members of the grid are given in Figs. 7 and 8, where it can be seen that they compare favourably with the solution of Vedeler, (1947). The slight differences in bending moment predictions, between the Vedeler solution and the microcomputer solution, is due to the fact that as the Vedeler solution is based on orthotropic plate theory, which assumes that some of the applied load is transmitted directly to the boundary, via the plating near the edge of the grid. This assumption is not the case for the matrix solution.

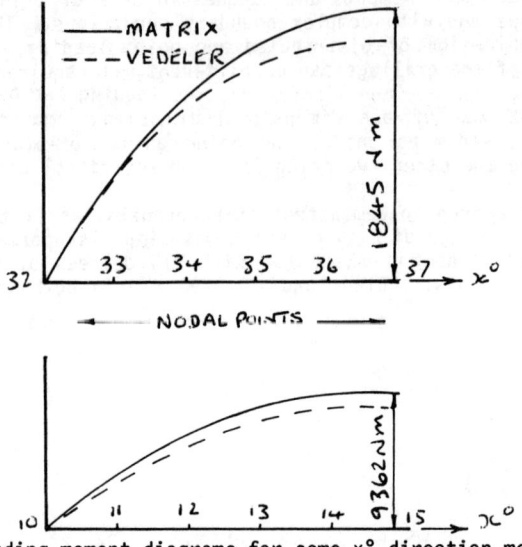

Fig. 7. Bending moment diagrams for some x° direction members.

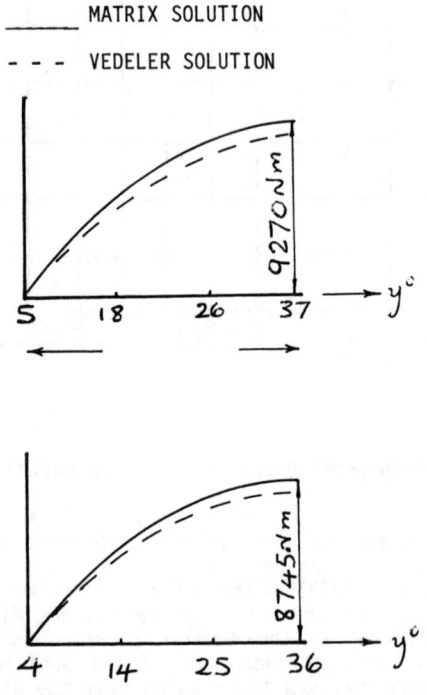

Fig. 8. Bending Moment Diagrams for Some y° Direction Members.

(3) **Microcomputer program for a rigid-jointed space frame.** This program uses a three dimensional skeletal element with two end nodes and six degrees of freedom per node. The six degrees of freedom consist of three translational displacements and three rotational displacements, so that there are 12 degrees of freedom per element. The frameworks can be of complex shape, with complex boundary conditions, and the loading can be a complex combination of distributed and point loads and couples. The cross-sections of the elements of the framework can be unsymmetrical, and their geometrical and material properties can be different, if required.

To demonstrate the capabilities of the program, the rigid-jointed tower of Spiller's, (1972), was used, as shown in Fig. 9. This tower had 28 nodes and a total of 168 degrees of freedom.

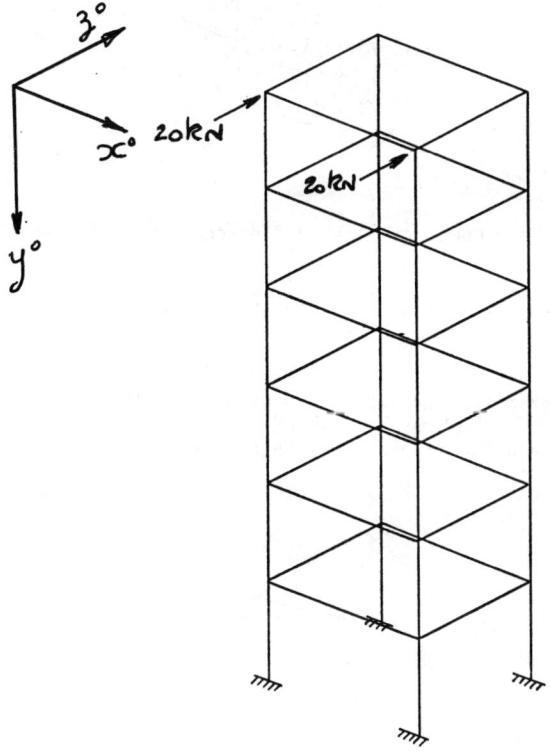

Fig. 9. Spiller's Tower.

Prior to processing, a screen dump of the tower was made, as shown in Fig. 10, and after processing, a screen dump of the deflected form of the tower was also made, as shown in Fig. 11.

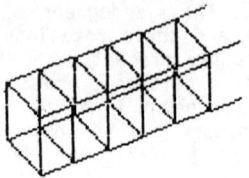

Fig. 10. Screen Dump of Spiller's Tower.

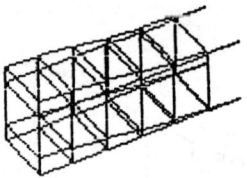

Fig. 11. Screen Dump of the Deflected Form of the Tower.

Comparison betwen Spiller's results and the microcomputer solution were found to be very good.

(4) <u>Microcomputer program for in-plane plate problems</u>. This program adopts the constant strain in-plane plate element of Turner et al, (1956), which has three corner nodes and two in-plane displacements per node, as shown in Fig. 12.

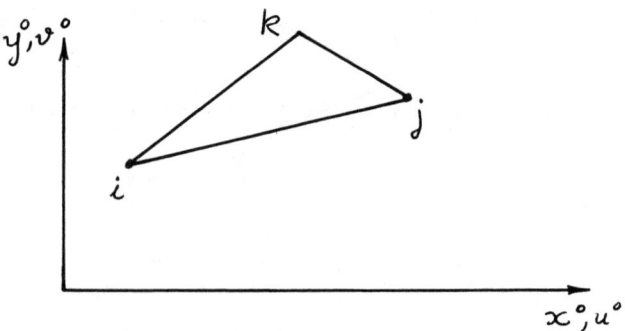

Fig. 12. In-plane Plate Element.

Two in-plane problems are used to demonstrate the capabilities of this program, namely, the transverse frame of a supertanker and a transverse section of a gravity dam, as shown in Figs. 13 and 14.

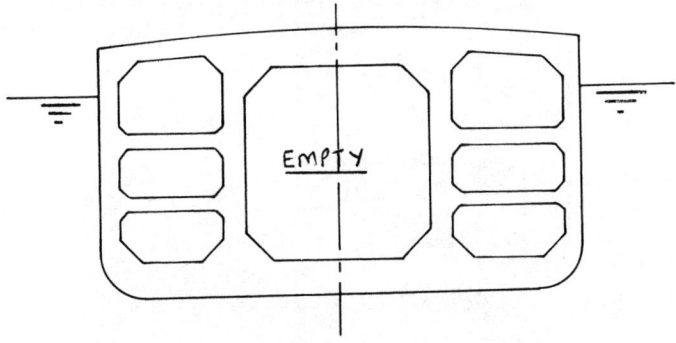

Fig. 13. Transverse Frame of a Supertanker.

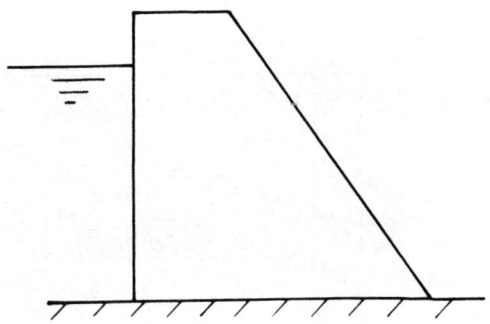

Fig. 14. Gravity Dam.

In the case of the supertanker, advantage was taken of its symmetry, by considering only one half of the section, as shown by the dump of Fig. 15, where the chosen mesh can also be seen. Figure 16 shows a screen dump of the deflected form of this framework, due to the external water pressure.

Figures 17 and 18 show the screen dumps of the gravity dam before and after processing, respectively.

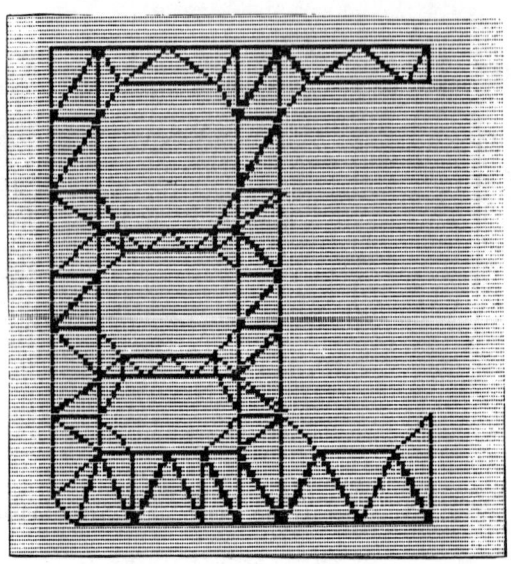

Fig. 15. Screen Dump of Supertanker Frame.

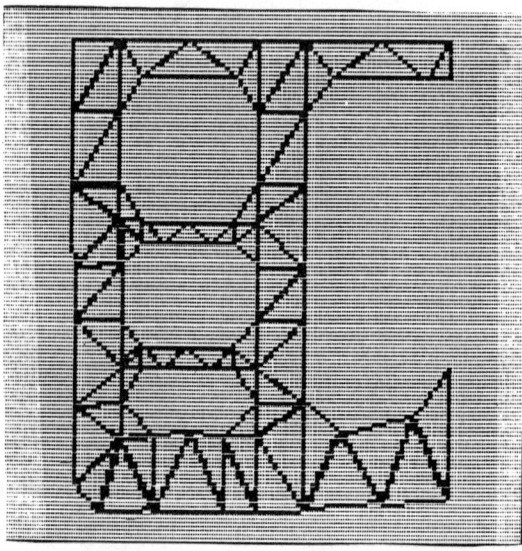

Fig. 16. Screen Dump of the Deflected Form of the Supertanker.

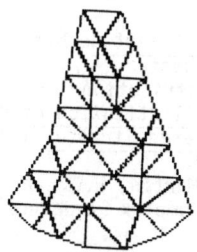

Fig. 17. Screen Dump of Gravity Dam.

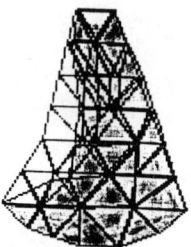

Fig. 18. Screen Dump of Deflected Form of Gravity Dam, (shaded area).

Screen Dumps. The screen dumps used in Figs. 2, 3, 4, 5, 10, 11, 17 and 18, were carried out with the assistance of a Miracle Systems screen dump, which took about 2 mins-12 s per screen dump. The screen dumps used in Figs. 15 and 16 were carried out with a Kempston printer interface and its firmware, and this took about 12 mins per screen dump. In all cases, the screens were dumped onto an inexpensive Brother HR-5 dot matrix printer.

CONCLUSIONS

The examples have shown that the expanded Sinclair QL is a formidable "number crunching" device, which has the storage capacity of many mainframe computers of a decade ago.

The examples have also shown that ther field of finite element methods is now opened up to smaller businesses, who cannot afford mainframe computers and their associated computer packages.

ACKNOWLEDGEMENTS

The author would like to thank his final year students, namely, Messrs. M.C. Cook, T.J. Goodridge, Anthony Pace and Andrew Phillips, for their assistance.

His thanks are extended to Mrs. L. Jenkinson for the considerable care and devotion she showed in typing the manuscript.

REFERENCES

Ross, C.T.F. (1985). Finite Element Methods in Structural Mechanics. Ellis Horwood Limited, Chichester.
Vedeler, G. (1947). The Distribution of Load in Longitudinal Strength Calculations. Trans. Royal Institution of Naval Architects, 89, 16-31.
Spillers, W.R. (1972). Automated Structural Analysis: An Introduction. Pergamon Press Inc., Oxford.
Turner, M.J., Clough, R.W., Martin, H.C. and Topp, L.J. (1956). Stiffness and Deflection Analysis of Complex Structures, J. Aero. Sci., 23, 805-823.

COMPUTER AIDED BRIDGES DESIGN

B. Marce and J. P. Chanard

Campenon Bernard, 92/98 Bvd V. Hugo, 92115 Clichy, France

SUMMARY

An extensive CAD software for bridge design has been developed at CAMPENON BERNARD. It enables the operator to build a realistic 3D model of the structure from wich structural software data files and drawings are partly or totally generated automatically.

INTRODUCTION

For CAMPENON BERNARD, a major French civil engineering contractor, the use of a CAD system was at first an answer to a drafting problem. Meanwhile the choice of a powerfull system was brought about by the wish to perform a smooth evolution to computer-aided design.

Drawings are nevertheless the main production from the design office. CAD system beeing mainly devoted to draftmen, the aim of the first developpement was to process data exchanges between drafting and design. Drawings, as a main data base for design, are transformed to a computer data base, easily and errorfree processed by structural analysis software.

But there is some differences between a computing model and a drafting model. Many precise details must be drafted, while they are unnecessary for structural analysis. Sometimes inconsistant with software simplification, they are of no mechanical consequence.

The aim of our developpements was to have the design draftman responsible for the preparation of a common model, under the control of the design engineer.

Such software should make the work of the draftsman easier, more precise and shorter while storing the necessary information to generate data files for structural computations.

The choice of bridge structures for this first attempt is hereafter explained, then the different steps of the drafting process are described and analysed.

THE CHOICE

- A common base between different models
- clear analysis of the design process
- ease of modelling
- programming effort and use of the software

These four criteria led to the choice of bridge structure. That type of structures had always been a major activity of our design office. There are still many bridges to build and a good design software should be usefull for a long time. A large bridge, to be built this year by our company, in Kuwait, confirmed our choice and speeded up the programming.

The process of a bridge study has been analysed precisely with people acting at different levels in multiples studies of that kind of structures.

It can be summarized as two parallel processes, one performed by the engineer, one or more draftsmen beeing in charge of the other one. Constant data exchanges is the price to pay for a complete accord between both results.

On the drafting part, the work begins with the lay-out of the structure in the given site in order to exactly define its geometry. The bridge is then divided into parts or segments and the different bearings located.

A first prestress scheme is defined with parts or elements added to the deck as bracings and prestress anchor blisters.

Making of drawings can start, then rebar placement and detailing using the former plans as reference drawings.

On the design side, the mechanical characteristics are first set. Section design and bearing location are modified in order to improve structural resistance and to minimise quantities. The prestress scheme is then designed and modified till the best results are obtained. Computations on the complete structure give final information on stresses in the bridge and allows the engineer to point out critical parts for him to design special reinforcement.

Data exchanges are numerous because that kind of work is an interactive process based on checking of geometry by draftsman and checking of structural behaviour by the engineer.

A bridge structure model can be compared to a ruled tube from section to section following a spatial axis. This tube is cut into segments to which particular parts are attached. Prestress cables are modelled by cylinders with variing axes.

Programming was not difficult, for the following reasons. First, the bridge structure is mainly linear which simplifies understanding of the problems which are liable to occur. The second reason was the opportunity to use three ready home-made softwares dealing with that kind of work:

-CP as a structures lay-out computation software from alphanumeric data files.

-CO as computation software for expected loss of prestress loads in cables.

-CDB or bar/structure analysis software specialized for bridges.

Bridge design, even for a small one always involves much work and requires a great volume of documentation. Details often have to clearly define typical parts. That kind of study needed a software that is able to reduce the work.

The availibility of a new **INTERGRAPH** software for concrete detailing provided us with a usefull solution to complete our design software.

I STRUCTURE LAY-OUT

The structure is positioned in space with the help of two plannar definitions, the site view and the profile line.

Site plan view is a projection of the reference axis of the structure upon an horizontal plane. It is defined by points of precise coordinates linked by simple elements (circles, lines) or by connection elements (conic, spirals). Elements are analytically defined or geometrically drawn by their particular properties as tangency and perpendicularity. Computations are very precised, the results are often to the millimeter even for radii of more than 1 kilometer.

The profile line gives the level of every point of the plan reference line. It usualy consists of straight lines and conics.

Construction lines are drafted in a 3D file, on two perpendicular planes.

On each curve, particular points are defined as indications of the major geometrical changes of the deck.

A 3D curve is automatically generated. More than a curve, points are placed in space. Every point is the location of piers or represents changes of the structure which leads to section modification. These points often mark a discontinuity in the construction process or precast element fabrication.

II SECTIONS DRAFTING (fig. 1)

Bridge sections while varying a lot, always still have some common characteristics between them.

A bridge section consists of slabs and webs. It can be open or closed with one or more openings. Symetrical or not, its shape is directly linked to its behavioural properties. It is one of the variables in the calculations, and cannot be fixed at the beginning.

For these reasons, we had to imagine an evolutionary process, free enough to allow any particularity while offering practical tools for drafting usual shapes.

Section generation

figure 1

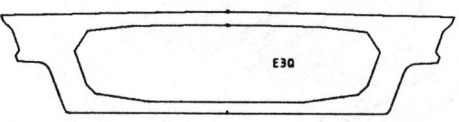

SECTION : E3Q		SECTION COURANTE PROCHE VSP		
CROSSFALL POINT		AXIS POINT		CENTROID
0.0000 2.6730		0.0000 2.6730		0.0000 1.4927
SURFACE 12.4734		ROTATION OF MAIN AXIS OF INERTIA 0.000 DEGREES		
INERTIA	V1	V2	SR	ZG
X 10.8715	-1.4927	1.1803	0.0000	0.0000
Y 186.4478	-6.1870	6.1870	0.0000	0.0000

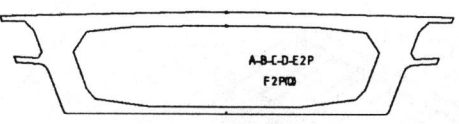

SECTION : A2P		SECTION COURANTE		
CROSSFALL POINT		AXIS POINT		CENTROID
0.0000 2.6730		0.0000 2.6730		0.0000 1.5221
SURFACE 10.5248		ROTATION OF MAIN AXIS OF INERTIA 0.000 DEGREES		
INERTIA	V1	V2	SR	ZG
X 9.4819	-1.5221	1.1509	0.0000	0.0000
Y 146.1496	-6.1870	6.1870	0.0000	0.0000

Deck generation

figure 2

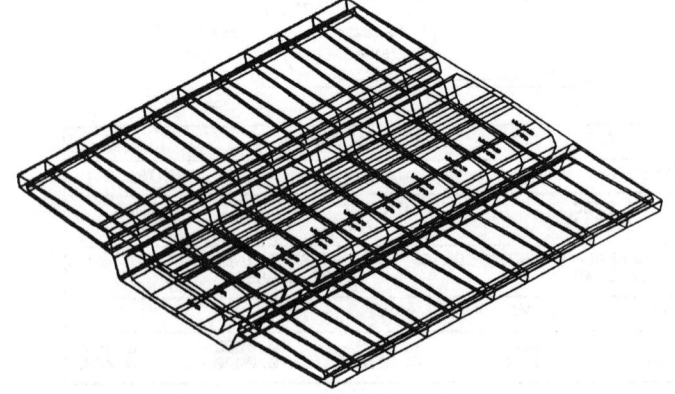

I - sections placement

II - volume generation

III - additive volume placement

Before they are recorded, different mechanical properties are computed and listed. Modifications are easy and quick, especially if these modifications are the usual geometrical changes applied to sections to improve their behavourial properties such as thickening of slabs and webs.

These sections are named and stored in a library. They can be recalled at any moment for any project.

III PLACING THE SECTIONS (fig. 2.I)

In addition to the mechanical and geometrical parameters, some more data linked to layout process are defined for each section. Attachment point to reference curve, superelevation points and theoretical mechanical axis for computation are defined. Some reference points can be added too, in order to identify, after the completion of the structural design process, the final coordinates of the different parts, which is usefull for construction.

Sections are placed, giving for each attachement point on the curve the following parameters:

- Name of the section : in some cases, two sections may be attached to the same point. If so, for each, an indication of wether it is left or right must be entered. It is allowed to make some break in continuity of the section.
- Crossfall of the section above horizontal line.

IV VOLUME GENERATION (fig. 2.II & 2.III)

From the positioned sections, volumes are automatically generated from one section to another. The usual variation is linear but it can also be parabolic or user defined. One restriction is that sections must be defined with the same number of points all along the project, even if some points are geometrically at the same place.

Erection of piers is done in the same manner. They are in fact very similar to the deck, in their design process.

V PRESTRESS CABLES (fig. 3.I)

Two types of prestressing techniques are used wich need totally different processes to be generated.

Cables placed externally to the structure are the easiest to design. Tendons are linked to concrete at some particular points, such as a deflacting block, wich modify their direction. The constitution of such a cable is made of lines linked by circular arcs at attachement points. It is often defined by theoretical points where lines cross, wich are also the points where loads concentrate. Circular arcs are determined as fillets between lines, with a given radius. The direction of the cable model is left to the draftman. Once the model is defined, all the different parts are linked together, and software is called upon to transform all this information into a coherent system. A facility is provided to the operator to perform difficult connections such as for non coplanar lines.

For internal cables, definition is totaly different. Some leading points are imposed. In sections, positions are often the same from cable to cable in the different sections. Geometrical interpolation between these points have to follow given rules. Ends near the anchorages are often the same too, in order to make design and construction easier and to reduce cost. For that reason, the user is helped as much as possible to easily define that kind of cable.

Imposed points are defined in a data file by their local coordinates inside the sections. Typical end points are studied and designed before the cable is defined. Interpolated with a 50 points-curve, they can be called for any cable.

Tendons are then generated by a batch job. They are aproximated by cubic parabolae. Imposed points between sections or new ones can be defined, some can be suppressed or moved to another place.

For both types, additional parameters are defined for each cable. The type of the cable, the different mechanical properties and the initial stressing load are input in order to get the final tension and expected loss. After modification, these results can be obtained interactively allowing the best definition to be found.

Cables placement

figure 3

I-Cables generation

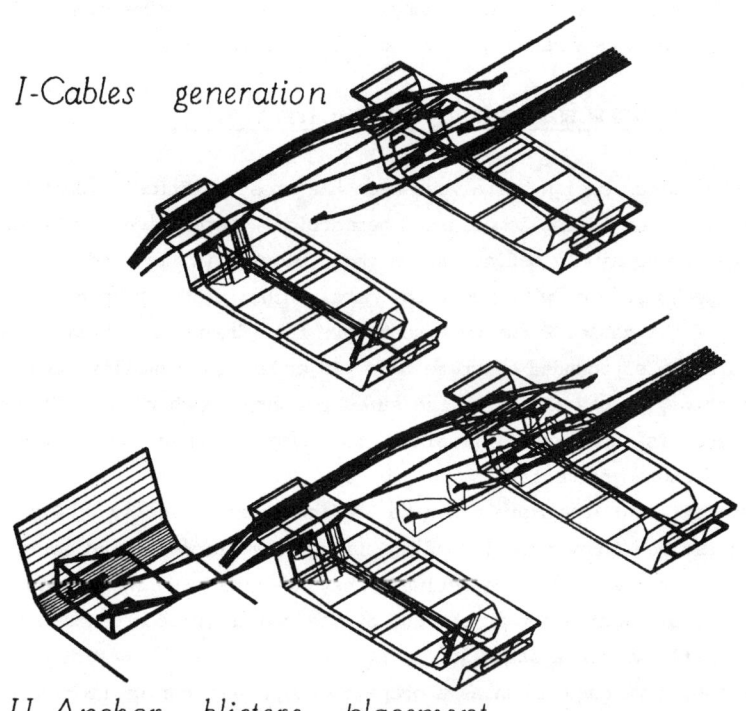

II-Anchor blisters placement

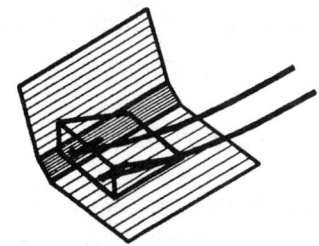 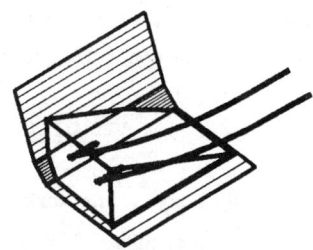

a-plaement   *b-boundaries adjustment*
III-Blisters generation - details

Cables are modelled by their central axis only. For spare economy and minimized response time, it is useless to model the sheath. But in particular points, for interference checking, an overall dimension tube can be automatically generated giving two points on the cable.

VI ANCHOR BLOCK DEFINITION (fig 3.II & 3.III)

Anchor block design has always been the most difficult part in bridge drafting, due to the complicated geometrical definition of these parts. If we try to simply define an anchor block, it is made of a dimension imposed face on wich rests the metal anchor plate, perpendicular to the axis of the cable. Pyramidal facets are the drawn to obtain the jonction with the surrounded concrete base. In order to simplify design and construction, shapes are often the sames for every anchor, even if the concrete base is different, leading to some simple geometrical modifications and adjustments.

Two different steps are taken to define these blocks . First, geometry is defined for each, including fixed dimension in front and variable facet on its side. Once defined, they are collected in a common library and automatically set at the end of the cables in accordance with a given data file within a batch job.

As they have been drawn as a graphic group, they can be reoriented after placement in order to improve access for jack. Once they are definitively set, variable facets are automatically adjusted to be linked to the existing concrete surface.

VII COMPUTING INPUT FILES GENERATION

Until then, the work performed by draftsmen has been identical to the one they should have done before, but much easier and quicker. As he is processing, much of the information is recorded for later use. With the help of the engineer, some parameters, directly linked to computation software as nodes and bars definition, sub-cutting and connections, internal as well as external, are defined.

Formwork drawing example
figure 4

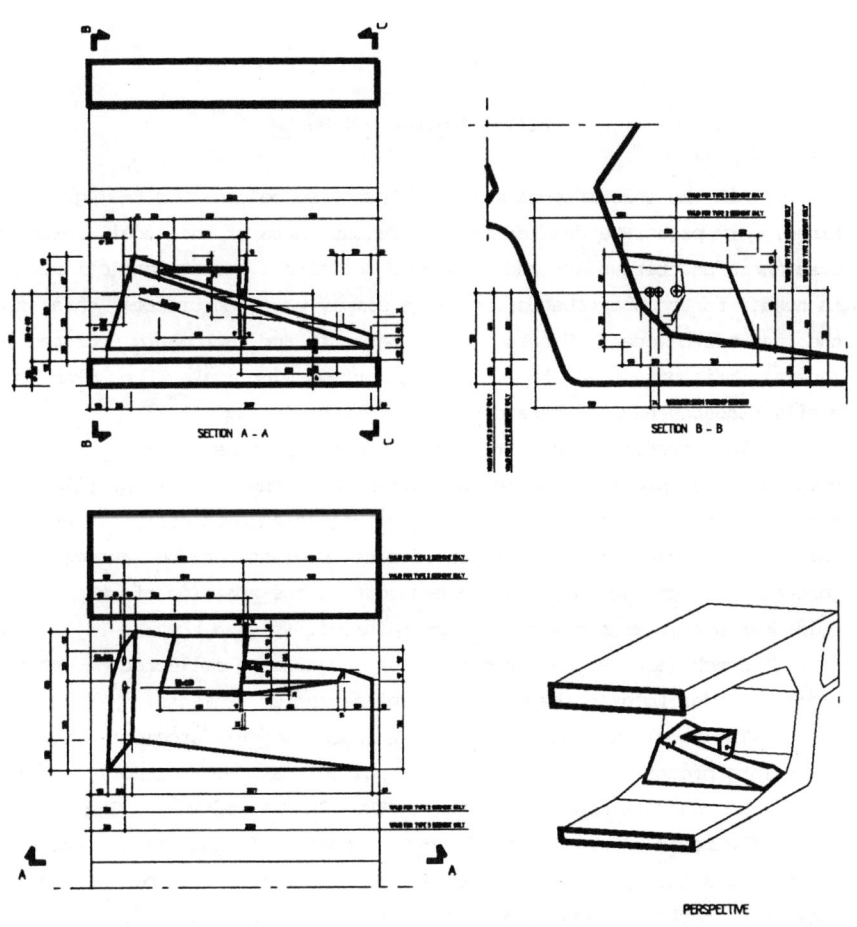

The software will automatically generate input data files for structural analysis software.

The engineer will have only to define external loads and get the results of the computation.

VIII GRAPHICAL EXTENSION

All the informations collected can also be used for the graphics. First, form plans are drafted from different parts of the model, automatic references and titles are added. No more difficult geometrical calculation is needed for complex shapes, software simply uses coordinates data from the real sized model. Hidden lines removal and automatic perspective generation is often used to add detailed views wich make the plan more easily readable and understandable by everybody. (fig. 4)

The drafting activity most aided by this facility is the preparation of prestress cables plans. On the longitudinal profile, for each point of the cable much information can be automatically written as name, local radius or slope. A set of section plans can be automatically generated to, giving for each defined section the position of the cables going through it with exact local coordinates. (fig. 5)

Bench marks set on each sections can also be collected on setting plans in order to help the making and placement of segments.

The Model is also used as a reference for reinforcement placement. No 2D interpretation of the model is required. Bars are directly defined inside the concrete model using the INTERGRAPH CDP software. The aim of this software is to provide an automatic check of the major rules of rebars placement in accordance with several major standards (ACI,CP100,BAEL). Freed from this, the draftsman can design better reinforcement. At the end of the work, sections and detail views are automatically generated, for assisting quantity takeoffs.

Report and bending schedules are drawn automatically too .With the help of interference checking, the draftman is able to draw more realistic plan of reinforcement.(fig. 6 & 7)

Prestressing annotation views

figure 5

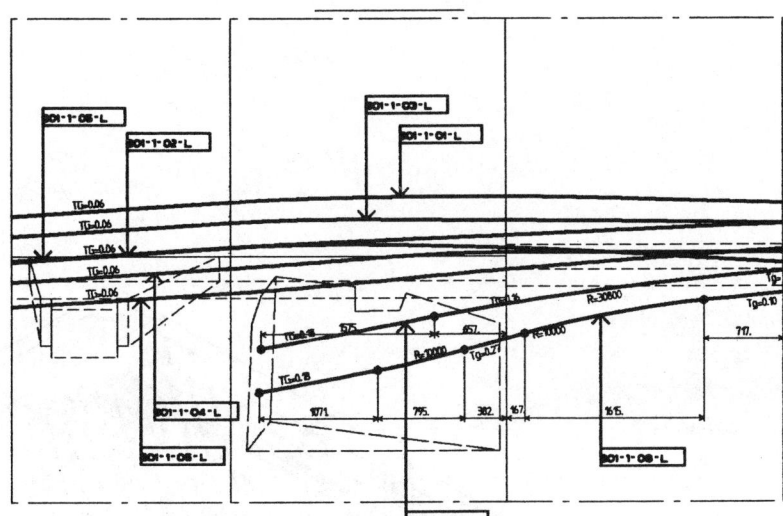

I-profile annotation

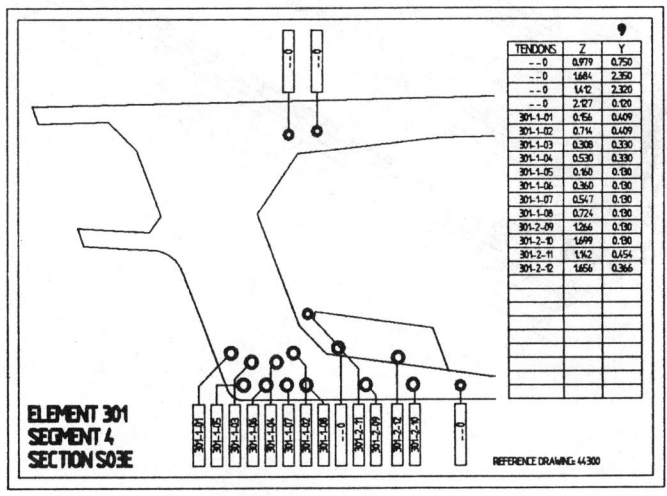

II-Automatic section extraction

Reinforcement placement
figure 6

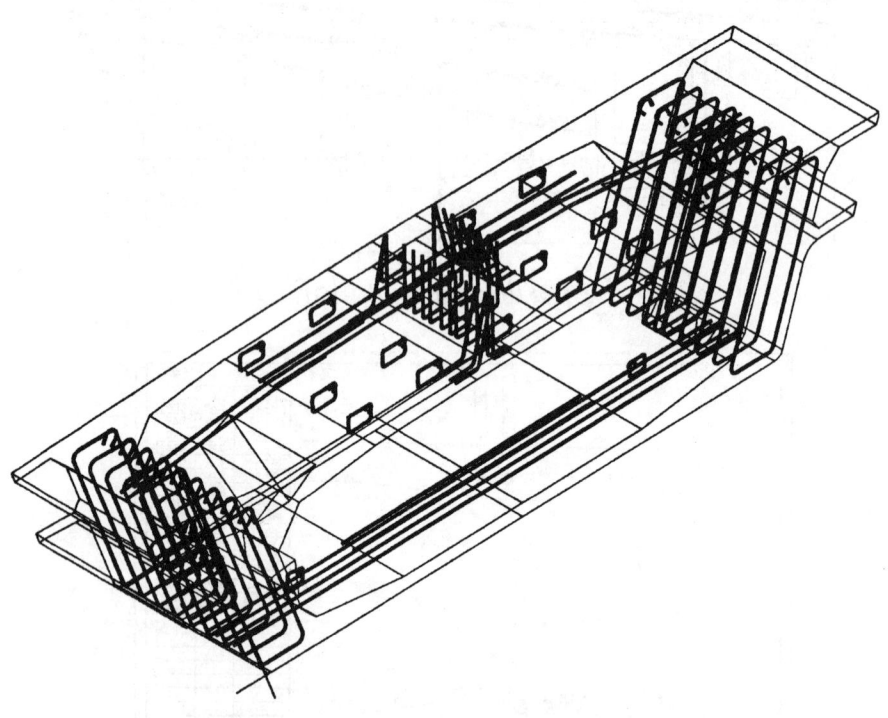

Report and detailing

figure 7

INDIVIDUAL BAR MARK ON FFI DRAWING	NUMBER	DIAMETER			BAR QUANTITY	BENDING SCHEDULE	BAR LENGTH	TOTAL LENGTH
		D	R	S				
a 1002	0001	16			18	(trapezoid shape, 2517 / 2517, 2.00, 784)	6784	12212
c 1002	0201	16			18	(U-shape, 2517, R=60)	3009	54162
d 1002	0301	25			34	(arch shape, 2534, 659, 598, 8.30)	3673	124882
e 1002	0401	16			72	(closed loop, 784/784, 267/267, 8.30)	2245	161640
f 1002	0451	16			8	(straight, 2400)	2400	19200

CONCLUSION

This major development needed more than one and a half year-man of programming. However, that important work has been done in understanding the basic softwares.

The first use of that software showed an important saving of time and more consistency in design.

We had given consideration wether we have to go further in automation of modelling process, eg. prestress optimisation. In fact, the bridges studied at the design office are too different from each other to find a common calculation method for geometrical optimisation and get the best results.

As of now, this software with the help and speed it provides, allows the enge neer to design a greater number variant models to select the best one.

LONG TERM STATIC ANALYSIS OF UNDERGROUND OPENINGS IN CREEPING ROCK

G. Borm

Institute of Soil and Rock Mechanics, University of Karlsruhe, FRG

ABSTRACT

If an underground opening is excavated under heavy rock pressure, the surface of the excavation deforms progressively with the lapse of time. Roof settlements, movements of the sidewalls, and raising of the invert are the obvious results. After excavation and supporting construction, the stress redistribution ceases after a few days, or months, or even years, until a new static equilibrium is reached.

Creep of rock causes progressively stressing of the support. The differential stresses at the cavity wall relax during time, while the rate of loading of the support and the rate of deformation in the rock mass decrease monotonously with time. For the simulation of discontinuous rock masses and localized internal slip surfaces, rheological joint elements are applied. Their slip directions can be constructed graphically from finite element analyses by the method of characteristics.

KEYWORDS

Computer aided rock engineering; underground excavations; salt rock; creep and relaxation; long term stability.

INTRODUCTION

The rock mass produces statical pressures by its self weight, whose intensity increases with growing depth. Other than in fluids, the rock pressure is a tensor, and one always means rock stress when speaking of rock pressure.

During mining excavations the primary state of stress equilibrium within the rock masses is disturbed. The restoration of a new state of equilibrium, of the so called secondary state of stress, causes considerable stress redistributions in the underground rock, which result in loading or deloading of the mine supports.

If the rock mass is only temporarily stable, the surface of the excavation deforms during the lapse of time; this can cause unwanted results such as: roof settlements, shifting of side walls, raising and expanding of inverts, damage or destruction of the lining, decreasing or increasing of anchor prestressings, or even rock bursts.

During construction and performance of mining excavations like shafts, tunnels, galleries, gate roads, rooms or caverns, the engineer is faced with the question of stability and durability of such structures. The evaluation of the time dependent stress redistribution in the rock mass and the hereby induced chronically loading of the support are investigated in the following.

ROCK PRESSURE IN ALPINE SALT CLAY

One of the best examples of pressurized rock mass is the Alpine salt clay. This rock breccia consists of a mixture of clay, sandstone, limestone and other constituents containing salt. Its high-grade stress sensitivity is extremely indicated at the gate roads and entries in raw salt clay. Due to the distinct viscoplasticity of the rock, it is necessary to re-rip it in relatively short intervals so that they remain passable within a period of time.

The creeping deformations are connected with stress rearrangements in the excavation surroundings, but are not necessarily always their cause. Resulting from this stress redistribution the rock mass in due time presses increasingly against the support and loads it chronically with normal, shear, and bending stresses.

Trapezoidal supports hardly adapt themselves to the principal stress trajectories and are therefore very sensitive towards the pressure of the rock surrounding it. The breaking down of such frame timberings due to the heavy rock pressure results in loosening and softening of the rock masses at the side walls. Arching supports adapt themselves comparatively better to the stress trajectories but are still relatively sensitive to normal loadings from the rock pressure.

Polygonous supports, which are flexible timberings with short props, adapt themselves excellently to the circular stress trajectories around the cavity. They develop high support resistances because they are less liable to bending than to axial forces. By exceeding the compressive strength of this wooden shell, the polygonous timbering fails as well. Due to the stress release of the arching rock and enforced by water, the rock swells into the gate entries and damages the invert as well as the rail tracks. Even a meter-thick concrete support cannot withstand permanently the pressure of the Alpine salt clay.

PROTECTIVE EXCAVATION METHODS

The most important fundamentals for protective tunnelling methods have been realized by Rabcewicz (1965) and Müller-Salzburg (1978), namely quick and close supports, advancement to circular profiles, closing of the bottom and strict consideration of the time factor. According to their concept, that the rock pressure effects all sides of an underground construction, a tunnel can be treated realistically as a closed embedded pipe and not as previously as an overburdened arch with vertical loads. Hence, the shapeless abutments of the earlier tunnelling methods are cancelled in favour of a statically more preferable quick closing of the bottom invert, and flexible shells replace the former plump tunnel arches.

While the ancient construction methods with their extreme support delays destroyed the capability of self support of the surrounding rock mass, the self support of the rock environment is largely conserved when protective tunnelling methods are applied with quick anchoring and shotcrete support (Fig.1).

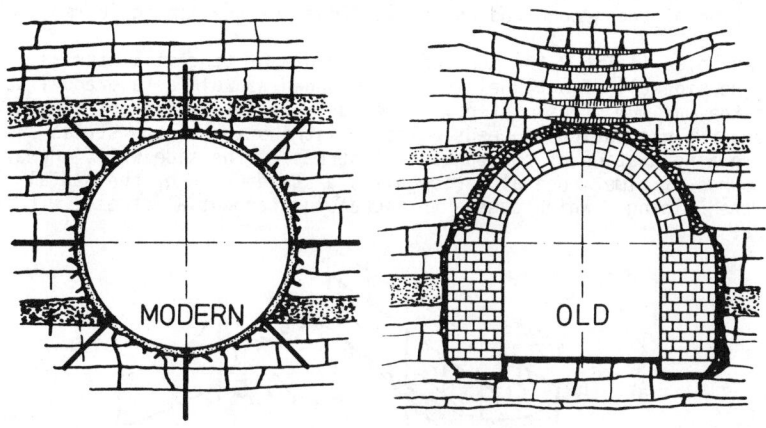

Fig. 1. Modern versus ancient tunnelling method
(after Müller and Fecker, 1978)

The effectiveness of protective tunnelling methods such as the New Austrian in a viscous rock is restricted to the prevention of loosening. In the only temporarily stable mining constructions it can therefore bring forth an economic and technical profit in stand-up time and reliability of operation.

STRESS RELAXATION OF ROCK MASS

The calculation of time dependent deformations and stresses according to the method of finite elements is generally proceeded as initial strain analysis, resulting in the relaxation of initial stress fields. The calculation process can also be rock mechanically interpreted in such a way that the chronical loading of a tunnel support by rock pressure results in an analogous manner from the relaxation of deviatoric stresses within the rock.

The deviatoric stress relaxation in a viscous or viscoplastic rock ground is not caused by creeping but on the contrary by its constraint. This resistance against deformation activates an increasing support pressure as time elapses, whose growth is determined by the retardation function and limited to the compressive strength of the support. While in an elastoplastic rock mass the self support of the ground can be activated by limited deformations whereby the loading of the support is kept to a minimum, the normal stress upon the support in a creeping rock is not stationary but continues to grow as long as the support can resist to.

APPLICATION OF THE RELAXATION THEORY

The guidelines for the calculation of shaft linings in unstable rock are commonly based upon a load acceptance due to horizontal rock stress, which is independent of the deformation of the ground. Consequently, they are not directly applicable to shaft construction in salt rock or in a frozen ground. Since the rock mass develops creep and relaxation abilities, the loading of the support by horizontal rock pressure depends largely on the time dependent deformation of the ground and on the stiffness of the lining (Borm, 1985).

As an example, in Fig.2 the monotonous decrease of tangential stress intensity at the sidewall of a tunnel is clearly shown as well as a gradual shiftening of the maximum stress intensity towards interior regions of the rock mass the more the excavation proceeds. The redistribution of the stress arch results in a relaxation of the tangential stress at the side wall. However, in the course of time, one also recognizes a steady rise of the radial stress upon the lining, which causes an increasing tangential stress within the support.

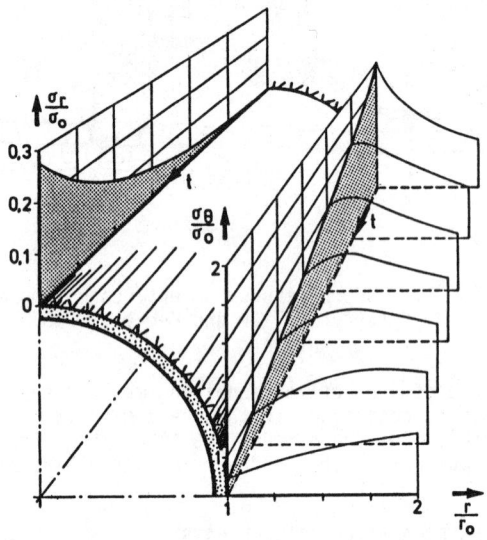

Fig. 2. Tangential rock stress relaxation and chronical loading of tunnel lining due to radial stress increase.

According to the material law, the monotonous reduction of stress differences lead to decreasing rates of convergency of the underground excavations as has been confirmed by in situ measurements in boreholes, shafts, rooms and other mining cavities. Without consideration of the relaxation behaviour one would assume and divert corresponding transiental creep laws upon evaluation of the convergency measurements. The application of these to other boundary value problems, however, could lead to false results or to erroneous conclusions of presumable stabilization of rock deformation and pressure.

In mining in great depth, it is of vital interest to know how supplementary pressures fade away in the course of time, when former extraction chambers are filled with goaf. Filling up cavities can considerably force the stress relaxation within the surrounding rock mass. In case of a relaxed, stationary state of stress in salinar rock, the rates of convergency are stationary as well, provided there is no deformational constraint in the excavation. Such a constraint resolves however from depositing of debris. This in turn will gradually be compressed by convergency of the rock masses and will develop a stress reaction according to the material law, which increasingly resists to further volumetric deformations. The growing of the internal pressure is decisively determined by the flexibility of the debris and is amplified by the increasing stiffness of the filling through compaction (Borm 1986).

Further examples of application of the relaxation theory of rock stress are: the time dependent compression of cavities filled with fossile raw materials in salt rock, stress measurements according to the prestressed hard inclusion method in viscous rock, or the relaxation of rebutment stresses in pillars, roofs, and side walls in room and pillar mining, which result in a rearrangement of the stress field in the underground and to the creation of a global stress arching around the entire pit outlay (Fig.3).

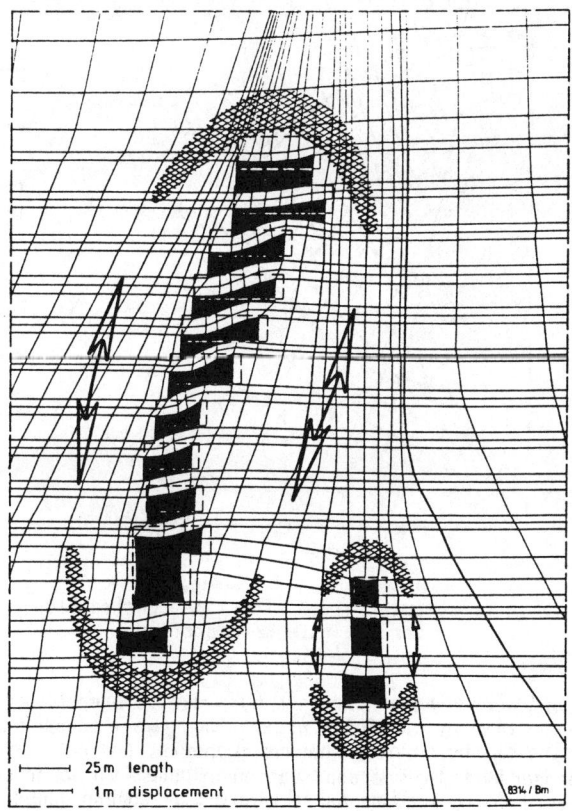

Fig. 3. Deformed finite element model of the vertical section of a mine outlay in salt rock: Shearing and global stress arching

SLIP LINE CONSTRUCTION

The rock of the Alpine salt clay mass is composed of very different geological constituents and is extremely heterogeneous; it deforms discontinuously and preferably along natural joints and weak regions. If the strength of the rock mass is exceeded, fracture proceeds by sudden or gradual destruction at the uppermost stressed shearing zones. Hence, in numerical analyses, discrete nonlinear joint elements are to be applied. The spatial orientation and expansion of the shearing surfaces, even for very complicated excavation geometries and heterogeneous geology, can easily be localized and visualized by computer aided graphical construction (Fig.4).

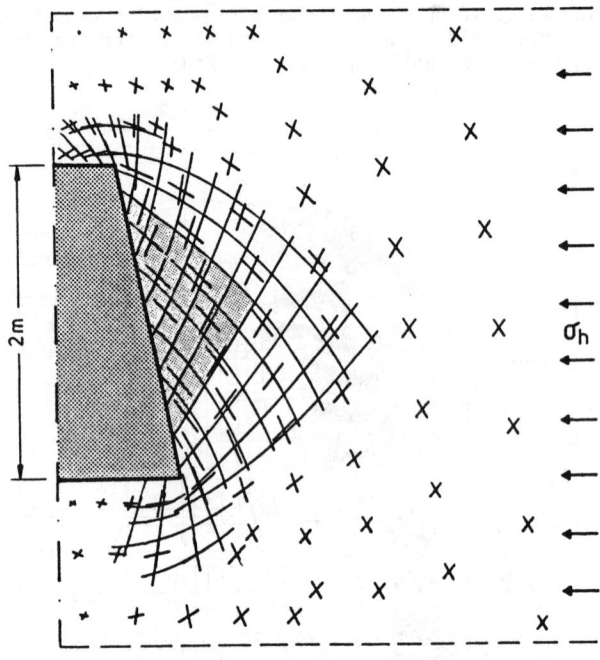

Fig.4. Computer aided slip line construction for the gate road profile

The loosening and weakening of the rock mass due to overstressing may be held up for a certain time by carefully excavating, well adapted cross sections, immediate closing of the invert, shaping supports, and rock bolting or grouting. According to the relaxation theory, the durability of the excavation depends primarily on the yielding and ultimate strength of the support as well as on those of the surrounding rock arch. The appropriate design and the performance of an optimum excavation and supporting layout can only be derived by thorough mining experience connected with computer aided calculations and measurements.

COMPUTER AIDED DESIGN OF THE SUPPORT

The constitutive parameters of the rock mass, the geological mapping, the geometrical and constructional data of the excavation layout are the basis of rock mechanical calculations, which in complicated cross sections and various stages of construction are commonly carried out by computer models according to the finite element method. They serve as a valuable tool for decision making in the evaluation of security, design and dimensioning of support and safety elements, in the prediction of deformations and stand-up time, and in the evaluation of the unsupported spans of the openings to be excavated (e.g. Fig.5).

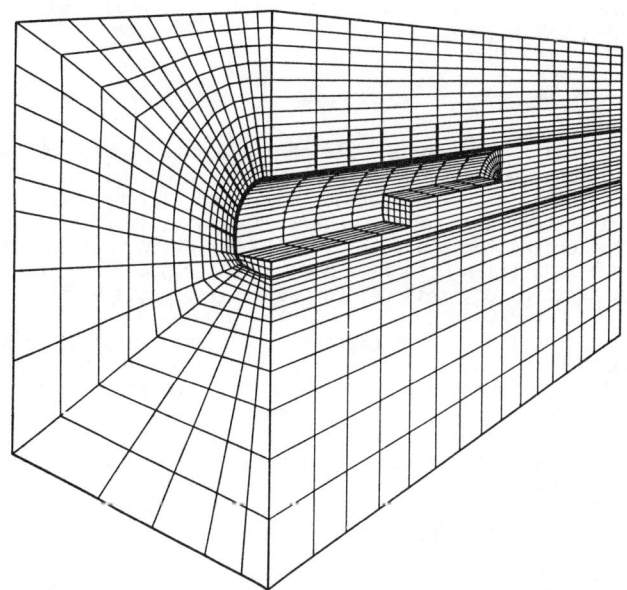

Fig. 5. Finite element model simulating stepwise excavation and support of a shallow tunnel

It is not a matter of calculation of some fictive safety faktors rather than of a reliable prediction of the chronical and spatial tendencies of rock deformations and stress rearrangements in order to optimize the excavation procedures, sequences, and support workings technically as well as economically.

A stiff lining in creeping rock effects short relaxation spans for the deviatoric rock stress, and thus induces fast increasing of rock pressure against the support. Under certain circumstances, the resultant stress can make extreme concrete dimensionings necessary. In the ancient tunnelling methods one tried to constrain the deformations of the rock mass as far as possible by using very stiff support elements, since they were principally considered as harmful loosenings. On the other hand, according to the New Austrian Tunneling Method, deformations to a certain degree appear to be necessary in order to activate stress redistributions within the environmental ground, so that the combined capability of the rock mass and the support is sufficient for stability. Such a stable state of stress with stagnancy of deformations will never be reached in a creeping rock mass even with a protective method of excavation, but on the other hand, a stationary state of stress can be achieved with stationary rates of deformation, which principally depend upon the constitutive behaviour of the rock, the intensity of the virgin stress, and the stiffness of the supporting system.

The support should at most have only so much resistance that the otherwise overstressed rock is constrained in flowing, loosening or fracturing, and its joints and slip surfaces remain closed. An immediate bolting after excavation is still the most effective support. It is sufficiently flexible and provides the necessary viscous resistivity in order to decelerate the rates of creeping convergencies and to hinder the rupture flow of the surrounding rock. The initially tensionless anchors fall themselves under stress by the restrained creep expansion of the rock masses, the more effectfully the closer and more regularly they are placed.

DISCUSSION

Alpine salt rock is the best example of pressurized rock, which is extremely creepable. Strong compression of the supports, bendings and destructions give evidence of the extraordinary stress developed. Every attempt to withstand the chronical deformation of the rock with massive stiff linings is in vain. The question arises for applicability of rock protecting tunnelling methods such as the New Austrian with flexible, circular profiles, shotcrete linings, and self supporting rock mass reinforced by systematic bolting.

In developing a stress relaxation theory of rock, which origins from initial strain approaches of finite element analyses and which is confirmed in practice as well as in laboratory investigations, the rock pressure on a support can mechanically be explained by the recovery of deviatoric stresses in the ground. Herewith, it seems to be proved that the New Austrian Tunnelling Concept cannot create a stable state of stress in creeping rock, in the presence of high supplementary stresses or in extreme depths, but it can well preserve a stationary state of stress and creeping, if it only succeeds in preventing potentially loosenings and weakenings by a flexible construction and rock bolting.

The main appliance of the relaxation theory, however, lies within the quantitative prediction of the time dependent convergencies, the stress redistributions and relaxations, the herewith connected chronically loading of supports even up to excess of ultimate strength, or in the case of debris, the assessment of its consolidation and bearing capacity.

With this, it will be possible to excavate in controlled manner and to maintain cavities within protection of the temporary self supporting rock arch also in very large depths with the help of measurements and computer calculations directed to the advantage of timely retardation of rock pressure.

ACKNOWLEDGEMENT

The author would like to express his gratitude to the German Research Society (DFG), Bonn, and Professor Dr.-Ing.O.Natau, chairman of Rock Mechanics at the Institute of Soil Mechanics and Rock Mechanics of the University of Karlsruhe for their kind support. The invitation to present this lecture to the Structural Analysis World Conference of the Institute for Industrial Technology Transfer (i.i.t.t.) in Paris 1986 is greatfully acknowledged.

REFERENCES

Borm, G. (1985). Wechselwirkung von Gebirgskriechen und Gebirgsdruckzunahme am Schachtausbau (Interaction of rock creeping and rock pressure upon shaft lining). Felsbau, 3, 146-151.

Borm, G. (1986). Zeitabhängige Kompression verfüllter Hohlräume im Salinar. (Time dependent compression of cavity fillings in salt rock). Felsbau, 4.

Müller-Salzburg, L. (1978). Der Felsbau, Band 3: Tunnelbau. Enke, Stuttgart.

Müller-Salzburg, L., and E. Fecker (1978). Grundgedanken und Grundsätze der Neuen Österreichischen Tunnelbauweise. In O. Natau and co-workers (Ed.), Grundlagen und Anwendungen der Felsmechanik, TransTech Publ., Clausthal.

Rabcewicz, L.v. (1965). Die Neue Österreichische Tunnelbauweise. Entstehung, Ausführungen und Erfahrungen. Bauingenieur, 40, 289-296.

Chapter 3
MICROCOMPUTER APPLICATIONS

VIBRATION OF SKELETAL STRUCTURES VIA A MICROCOMPUTER

C. T. F. Ross

Portsmouth Polytechnic, UK

ABSTRACT

Four microcomputer programs are described and applications of these programs are made to a number of skeletal structures, including the free vibration of two and three dimensional rigid-jointed frames, three dimensional pin-jointed trusses and grillages of complex shape. In the cases of the three dimensional rigid-jointed frame and the grillage, it was necessary to adopt eigenvalue economisers to reduce their dynamic degrees of freedom.

In all cases, the analysis was carried out by the finite element method, with the aid of an expanded Sinclair QL.

In the cases of the two dimensional rigid-jointed plane frame and the three dimensional pin-jointed truss, the eigenmodes were plotted on the screen and later, these were dumped on to an inexpensive dot matrix printer.

KEYWORDS

Microcomputer programs; finite elements; vibrations; frameworks; grillages.

INTRODUCTION

The four computer programs, which were written in Sinclair Super Basic, determined resonant frequencies and associated eigenmodes for the following types of structure:-

(a) Two dimensional rigid-jointed frames.

(b) Three dimensional pin-jointed trusses.

(c) Orthogonal and skew grids.

(d) Three dimensional rigid-jointed frames.

The present author discovered that when a 256 k bytes RAM pack was attached to the expansion port of a 128 k bytes Sinclair QL, the machine was capable of accepting a matrix, in BASIC, of order 237 x 237. Furthermore, if this RAM pack were replaced by one with a RAM size of 512 k bytes, the machine was capable of accepting a matrix of order 312 x 312. Thus, with such a lot of available RAM, it was possible to make serious applications of finite element methods to problems in structural vibrations. In all cases, the power method of solution, together with Aitken's acceleration was used to determine the eigenvalues and associated eigenmodes. One problem that did arise, because the power method was being used, was that when a symmetrical structure was encountered, there was a possibility that the system would have equal eigenvalues, and because of this, the algorithm would fail. This deficiency was overcome by making the co-ordinates of the free nodes of the structure slightly unsymmetrical, by less than 0.1%.

The degree of precision for the eigenvalues was set to 0.1%, but no degree of precision was set for the eigenmodes. It is a simple matter to increase or decrease the degree of precision, but if the latter is carried out, the computation time can increase significantly, and in any case, care must be taken to ensure that the degree of precision of the machine has not been exceeded.

In the case of the programs for the grillage and the three dimensional rigid-jointed frame, an eigenvalue economiser was adopted, (Irons, 1965). The eigenvalue economiser for the grillage program, allowed any node to have its rotational displacements eliminated, but not its out-of-plane translational displacement. The eigenvalue economiser for the three dimensional rigid-jointed frame program allowed any node to have either all its displacements eliminated or just the three rotational displacements, where in the latter case, only three translational displacements were left at that node.

A description of each of the four microcomputer programs will now be given, and to demonstrate their capabilities, applications will be made to some realistic structures.

The programs adopt elemental stiffness and mass matrices, as described by Ross (1985). All the programs allowed for a complex combination of concentrated nodal masses in addition to "distributed" masses.

(1) Vibration of rigid-jointed plane frames. This program adopts one dimensional elements, with two end nodes and three degrees of freedom per node. Two of these degrees of freedom were translational and one rotational. After the resonant frequencies and eigenmodes are determined, they are displayed on the screen, and these pictures can then be dumped on to an inexpensive dot matrix printer. Figure 1 shows a rigid-jointed plane frame, which is used to demonstrate the capabilities of this program.

The elements of this framework were assumed to have the following properties:-

Elemental length	=	1 m ± 0.001 m
Cross-sectional area	=	$1E-3 \text{ m}^2$
Second moment of area	=	$1E-7 \text{ m}^4$
Elastic modulus	=	$2E11 \text{ N/m}^2$
Density	=	7860 kg/m^3

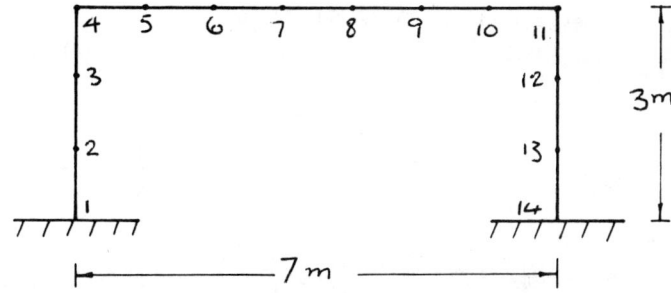

Fig. 1. Rigid-jointed plane frame.

Screen dumps of the first four eigenmodes and their associated resonant frequencies are shown in Figs. 2 to 5, where it can be seen that the first mode is a sway mode. The second and third modes appear to be beam modes, the former, symmetrical, and the latter, unsymmetrical. The fourth mode appears to be a combination of beam and column modes. From Figs. 2 to 5, it can be seen that the magnitude of the resonant frequencies increases quite rapidly.

eigenmode no.1 (1.873952 Hz)

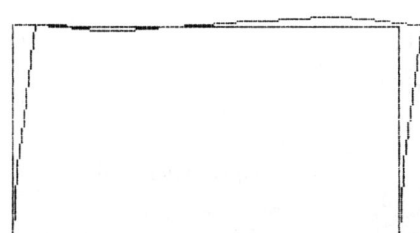

Fig. 2. First eigenmode.

eigenmode no.2 (2.784396 Hz)

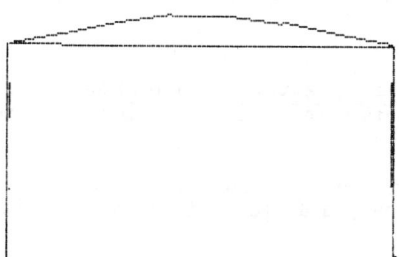

Fig. 3. Second eigenmode.

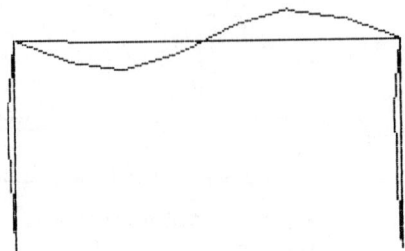

Fig. 4. Third eigenmode.

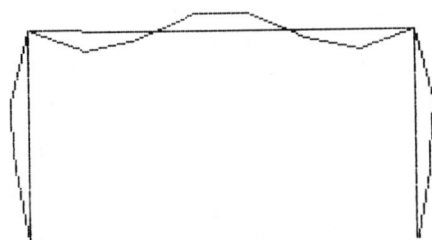

Fig. 5. Fourth eigenmode.

Solution of the problem took about 32 minutes, the bulk of the time being used to invert the 36 x 36 stiffness matrix. The total time taken to generate and assemble the 13 elemental stiffness and mass matrices, and also to shuffle out those parts of the system matrices that corresponded to zero displacements, was about 3 minutes. The time taken to invert the system stiffness matrix was about 22 minutes, and the time taken to determine the four resonant frequencies and their associated eigenmodes, was about 7 minutes.

(2) Vibration of a three dimensional pin-jointed truss. This program adopts one dimensional elements with two end nodes and three translational degrees of freedom per node.

After the resonant frequencies and eigenmodes are determined, these are displayed on the screen, and the picture can then be dumped onto a dot matrix printer.

Figure 6 shows the plan and front elevation of a Foppl truss, which is used to demonstrate the capabilities of the program.

The members of the truss were assumed to have the following properties:-

```
Cross-sectional area  =  1E-3 m²
Elastic modulus       =  2E11 N/m²
Density               =  7860 kg/m³
```

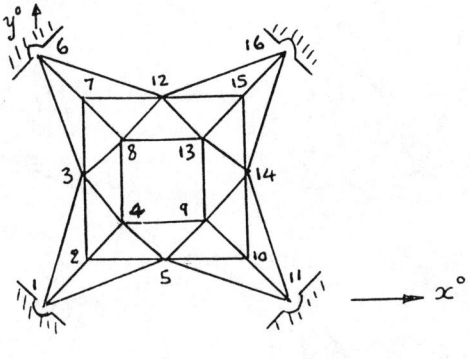

(a) Plan View

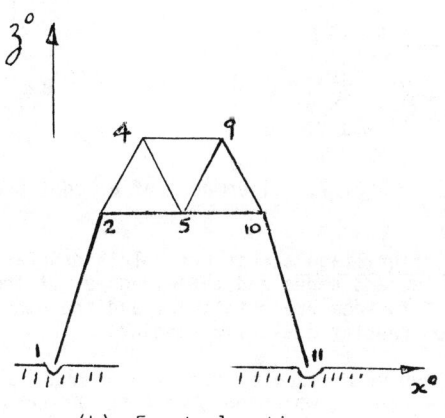

(b) Front elevation

Fig. 6. Foppl space truss.

Figure 7 shows a plan view of the first four eigenmodes of the truss, together with their associated resonant frequencies. It was decided to show these eigenmodes in plan view, as all the members of the truss were in view, but facilities exist to view the eigenmodes in three dimensions.

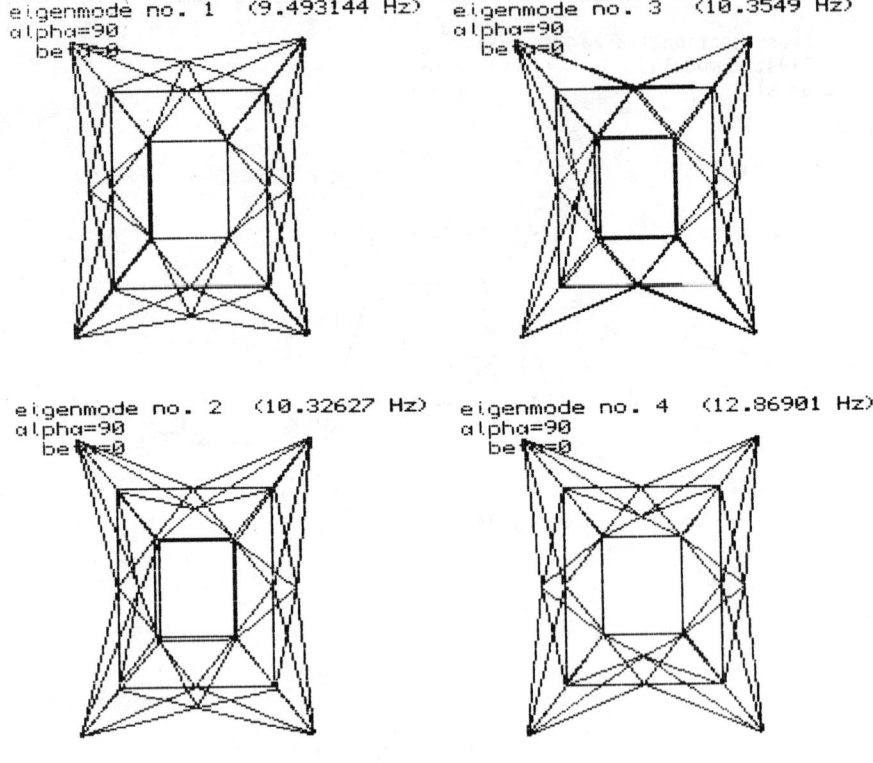

Fig. 7. Eigenmodes of a Foppl truss.

(3) <u>Vibration of grillage structures</u>. This program adopts one dimensional elements, with two end nodes and three degrees of freedom per node. Two of these degrees of freedom are rotational and the other degree of freedom was an out-of-plane translational displacement.

To allow the program to tackle large structures, an eigenvalue economiser was used, (Irons, 1965), which enabled both the rotational displacements to be eliminated, if required, but not the translational displacement. The program can tackle orthogonal or skew grids, and to demonstrate the capabilities of the program, the grids of Figs. 8 and 9 were analysed.

The properties of the skew grid, which was the same as that adopted by Venancio-Filho and Iguti, (1973), were:-

```
Cross-sectional area   = 0.004 m²
Second moment of area  = 1.25E-5 m⁴
Torsional constant     = 2.5E-5 m⁴ (assumed)
Elastic modulus        = 2E11 N/m²
Density                = 7860 kg/m³
```

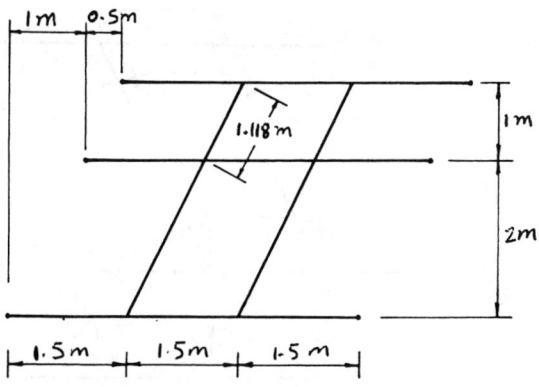

Fig. 8. Skew Grid.

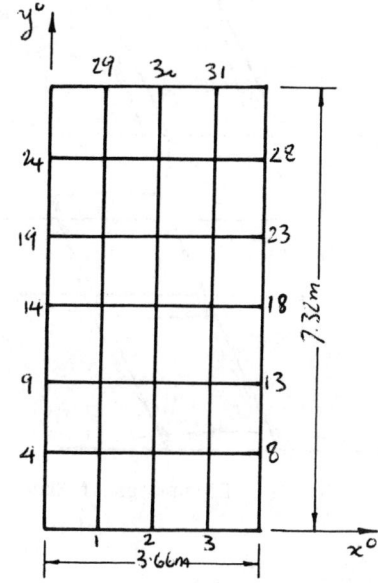

Fig. 9. Clamped-Supported Grid.

Figure 10 shows the first three eigenmodes, together with their associated resonant frequencies.

From Fig. 9, it can be seen that this grid was the same as that adopted by Clarkson, (1959), which was clamped along its longer edges and simply-supported along its shorter edges. It had the following properties:-

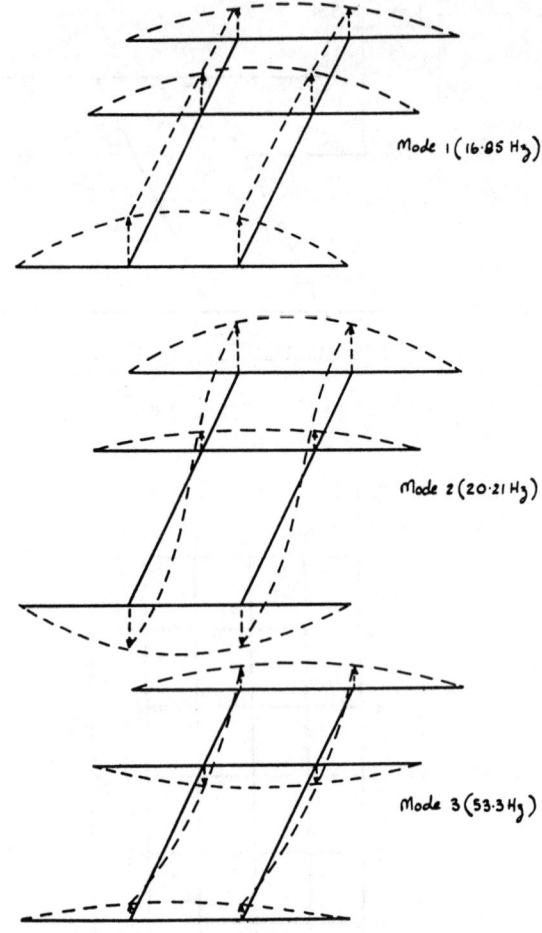

Fig. 10. Eigenmodes of Skew Grid.

Members in x° Direction

    Cross-sectional area = 7.55E-3 m^2
    Second moment of area = 5.83E-5 m^4
    Torsional constant = 5.83E-6 m^4

Members in y° Direction

    Cross-sectional area = 2.13E-3 m^2
    Second moment of area = 8.32E-6 m^4
    Torsional constant = 8.32E-7 m^4

For All Members

    Elastic modulus   = 2.07E11 N/m²
    Rigidity modulus = 7.96E10 N/m²
    Density   = 8055 kg/m³

Figure 11 shows the first two eigenmodes, and their associated resonant frequencies, for this grid.

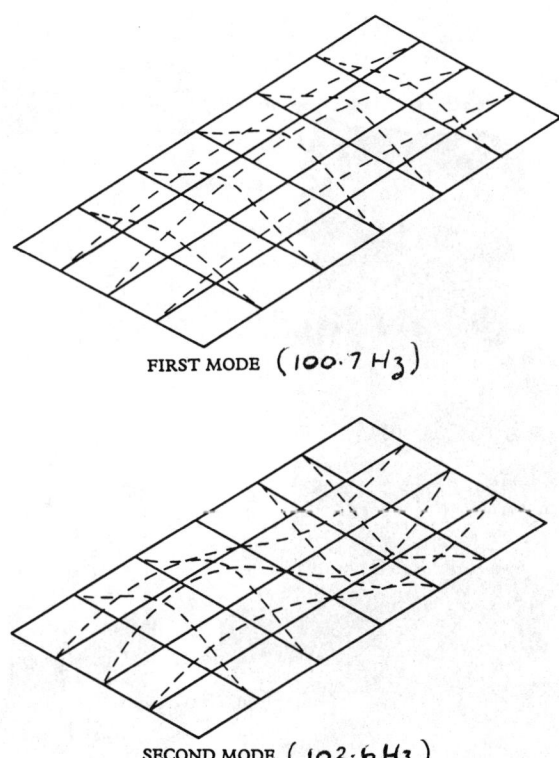

FIRST MODE (100.7 Hz)

SECOND MODE (102.6 Hz)

Fig. 11. Eigenmodes of Clamped-Supported Grillage.

(4) <u>Vibration of three-dimensional rigid-jointed frames</u>. This program adopted one dimensional elements, with two end nodes and six degrees of freedom per node. Three of these degrees of freedom were translational and three were rotational. Each element of the framework can have different sectional and material properties, if required. The program can tackle large frames of complex shape and with complex boundary conditions, but in order to allow for the solution of large structures, it was necessary to adopt an eigenvalue economiser, (Irons, 1965).

The eigenvalue economiser allowed either all the displacements at a node to be eliminated or just the rotational displacements.

To demonstrate the program, the brass tower of Fig. 12 was analysed, both by experiment and with the aid of the microcomputer program. As the tower was symmetrical and it would have some eigenvalues equal to each other, it was necessary to make the tower very slightly unsymmetrical, by feeding in errors of about 0.025 mm for the co-ordinates at the top of the tower, the height of the tower being about 75.6 cm.

Fig. 12. Model Tower and Vibrator.

This procedure appeared to work satisfactorily, as the first two resonant frequencies, which were theoretically equal, were in fact, nearly equal.

The tower had a total of 44 nodes, four of which were fixed, so that its dynamic degrees of freedom numbered 240. However, by careful use of the eigenvalue economiser, the resulting dynamic degrees of freedom were reduced from 240, down to a mere 42! The first two eigenmodes, which were of cantilever form, were similar, but 90° out-of-phase, and the third eigenmode was a "lozenging" type. Plots of the plan view of the first and third eigenmodes are given in Fig. 13, and Fig. 14 shows the variation of the fundamental resonant frequency with increasing mass, from both experimental observations and theoretical predictions, where the latter are shown by the full line.

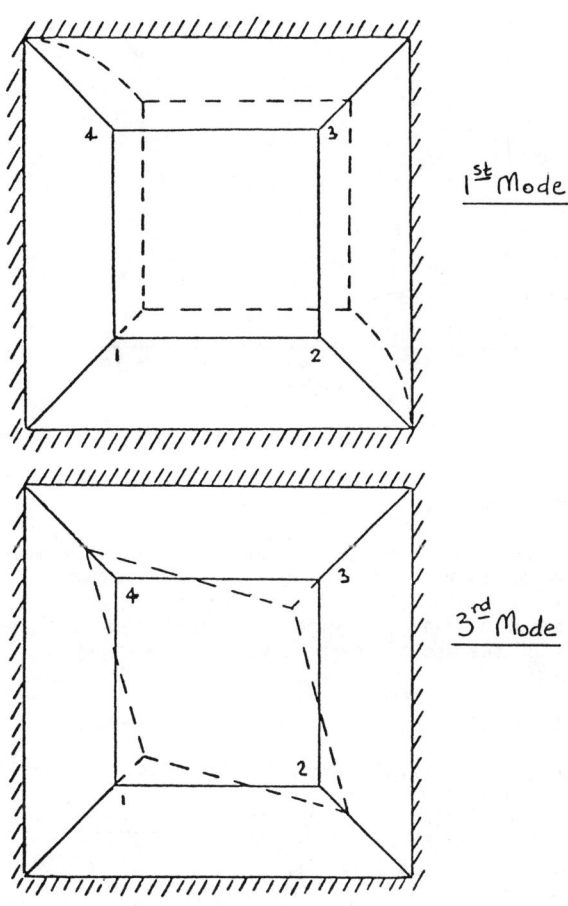

Fig. 13. Plan Views of Eigenmodes.

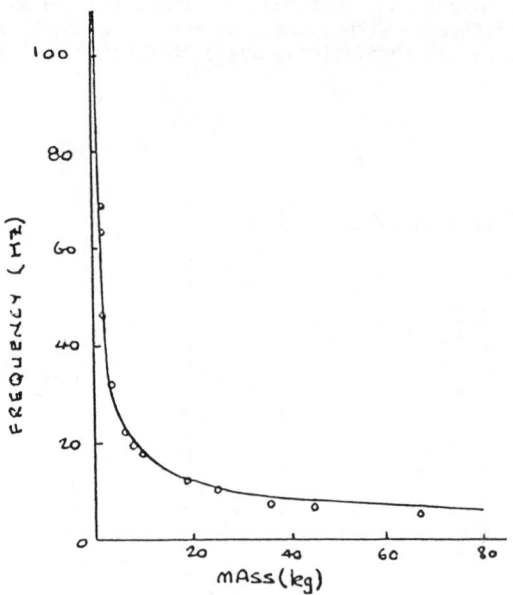

Fig. 14. Frequency-Mass Relationship.

CONCLUSIONS

The paper has shown that the dynamic analysis of large frameworks can be carried out on an expanded Sinclair QL microcomputer. It has also shown that the field of finite elements has been opened up to small companies, who cannot afford to purchase expensive mainframes and their associated software, through the use of inexpensive microcomputers.

REFERENCES

Irons, B. (1965). Structural Eigenvalue Problems: Elimination of Unwanted Variables. AIAA J.3, 961.
Ross, C.T.F. (1985). Finite Element Methods in Structural Mechanics. Ellis Horwood Limited, Chichester.
Venancio-Filho, F. and Iguti, F. (1973). Vibrations of Grids by the Finite Element Method. Computers and Structures, Pergamon Press. 3, 1331-1344.
Clarkson, J. (1959). Data Sheets for the Elastic Design of Flat Grillages Under Uniform Pressure. European Shipbuilding, No. 8.

ACKNOWLEDGEMENTS

The author would like to thank Mrs. L. Jenkinson for the care and devotion she showed in typing the manuscript.

ADAPTATION OF THE COMPUTER CODE STDYNL TO MICROCOMPUTERS AND TO VIBRATION IN SOILS BY DYNAMIC STRESS FUNCTION

Bulent A. Ovunc

University of Southwestern Louisiana, Lafayette, Louisiana 70504-0172, USA

ABSTRACT

The general purpose computer code STDYNL has been adapted to microcomputers. The preprocessor, processor and the postprocessor, which are the principal components of the code STDYNL are composed of independent modules. Each independent module has been generated separately by using the full capacity of the microcomputer, if necessary, and the outcome is stored in the corresponding location of the database. For the most efficient core assignment, the sizes of the arrays in the independent modules are entailed during the execution of each specific problem. Thus the code STDYNL is problem oriented, rather than program oriented. The first part of the code is related to the external data which describes the type of the type of the system in order to eliminate the superfluous freedoms, type of analysis, the geometry, the boundary conditions and constraints and the externally applied disturbances. The external data feeding is interactive and conversational with double checking on the input data. The second part is related to internal data which are obtained by the routines generating the meshes, joint coordinates, member identification array, connectivity array, axis transformation and characteristic matrices for the members and the system characteristic matrix. The external data can be checked, modified, if necessary at any point of the execution. Parts of the internally computed data may be considered as overlapping with the processor. The processor resolves the generalized coordinates of the given system, back substitutes generalized coordinates into the member characteristic matrices in order to determine the required states at any point of the given system. The postprocessor consists of modules which provide the results as numerical values or graphs. By assuming a proper value for the related parameter any intermediate or final results can be stored in the database for their interpretations. The results can be checked and if desired, the data stored in the database through the preprocessor can be modified. The execution can be restarted from the first point affected by the modification. All the modules of the code STDYNL are independently developed. They can be also incorporated in any other general purpose computer code. A specific driver routine, related to the type of the given system, is selected by the input for the first information in the external data of the preprocessor. The specific driver routine for the specific system type assambles all the necessary modules to analyze the type of the system in consideration.

KEYWORDS

Structural software, microcomputer application, processors, nonlinearity, elasto-plastic behavior, soil-structure interaction, dynamics, buckling.

INTRODUCTION

The engineering marketplace has been swamped recently by variety of softwares for microcomputers from most rudimentary to most sofisticated types. A plane frame program which has been based on an early article (Tezcan,1966) is composed of some three hundred statements and is the shortest and easiest to understand of the available methods (Ketchum, 1983). A simple software which includes earthwork, water distribution, frame analysis is available through SYSTEK (SYSTEK). The frame and truss package FATPAK, can handle large frames and trusses in two and three dimensions for applied loads and specified support displacements (FATPAK). A suite of finite element programs for Wang desktop computers has been developed, covering two and three dimensional, static and dynamic analysis of frameworks and plates. The software consists of a number of separate programs that can be applied on their own or as a part of a more complete program using a common database (SCIA). The RandMicas system has been made available for the IBM PC family. It is also compatible with most of the super micro and super mini systems (RandMicas). A comprehensive package is capable of performing both two and three dimensional analyses of structures comprised of beams, truss, thin shell elements. With complete implementation of AISC, AASHTO and ACI codes (STAAD-III). Most of the SOFTKIT programs have been made modular and menue driven. The structural analysis part creates a catalog of material properties, generates the meshes with an interactive graphics, includes linear and nonlinear analyses of plane and space framework (SOFTKIT). MODES-PC performs frequency and mode shape, time-histories and response spectrum analysis of typical systems (MODES-PC). The earthquake and static load analysis of three dimensional frames, buildings, trusses, bridges, dams and other complex structural systems can be obtained efficiently on microcomputers (SAP-80). The GIFTS which runs on variety of microcomputers, has wide range analysis, versatile modelling and loading and powerful graphics capabilities (GIFTS).

Herein, the adaptation of the general purpose code STDYNL to microcomputers is furnished. The preprocessor, processor and postprocessor of the code STDYNL are composed of independent modules. Each independent module has only one single dimensional array. The size of the only array is such that each module can occupy the entire core of the microcomputer. If a module has more than array, for a given problem the required size of each array is evaluated and two parameters defining the beginning and ending of each array. The arrays are stored in the single dimensional one from the ending of the previous array to the ending of the array in consideration. Therefore, the sizes of the arrays in the independent modules are entailled during the execution of each specific problem for the most efficient core assignments. The independent modules can be executed separately by reading the data from and writing the outcome to tha database. If necessary, and out-of-core scheme is used for the resolution of the generalized coordinates. A driver routine assambles all the required modules during the execution to minimize the CPU time. The code STDYNL is a medium capability program in which most of the modules are the results of the individual formulations proper to STDYNL (Ovunc 1983, 1985), such as: characteristic matrices for curved members (Tezcan and Ovunc, 1965), iteration procedures for nolinear elastic analyses (Tezcan and Ovunc, 1967, Ovunc, 1982b, 1982c), linear and nonlinear elasto-plastic analyses of high strength steel frameworks (Ovunc, 1968), dynamic analysis by continuous mass matrix method (Ovunc, 1974, 1978), effect of axial force on the dynamics (Ovunc, 1980), soil-structure interaction Ovunc, 1982, 1985), dynamic response time histories of continuous mass frameworks (Ovunc, 1979), frameworks dynamics under continuously distributed dynamic forces (Ovunc, 1986), boundary elements for plane stress and plate bending due to static and dynamics loadings (Ovunc, 1982a,1984, 1985b,1986). Moreover, the regular features such as: support settlements, known displacements, temperature variations etc., and regular modules such as plane stress, plate bending finite elements, etc., are also incorporated in the code STDYNL.

DEVELOPMENT

The improvements in terms of the increase in capacity and speed of the microcomputers have made their usage more attractive for the analysis of fairly large structural systems. Many general purpose programs have been adapted to microcomputers. Due to its modular nature, the code STDYNL (Ovunc, 1985) has been easily adapted to microcomputers.

The main skeleton of the code STDYNL which is composed of:

1. preprocessor, providing the input data to processor,

2. processor, performing the analysis

3. postprocessor, providing the output of the processor,

as in any general purpose program and remained the same in the adaptation to microcomputers.

1. PREPROCESSOR is the part of the code where the given structure is described to the machine by two types of data.

    a. EXTERNAL DATA which describes,

    i. type of the structure: plane or space truss or frame, plate, shell or any combination of these, in order to eliminate superfluous freedoms,

    ii. type of analysis: static: linear, nonlinear, etc., dynamic: steady state, transient, modal analysis, direct integration, various effects,

    iii. the geometry of the structure, boundary conditions, constraints,

    iv. externally applied disturbances: loads, settlements, support motions, temperature variations, etc.,.

The external data can be fed into the database by using data preparation forms for simple, small size problems. Whereas for complex, large size problems the independent module EXDAT can be used. The module EXDAT is interactive and conversational type. By a parameter fed at the beginning of EXDAT, the sequential order of data transfer to input file or database can be changed . So that the order of the input data can be adjusted to the reading sequences of various general purpose computer codes, to be executed in various micro, mini or main frame computers. The data fed through EXDAT may be checked by an independent GRAPH module and if necessary, may be modified.

    b. INTERNALLY COMPUTED DATA are obtained by the modules which generate:

        i. the meshes, numbering of the joints and members for large size complex problems,

        ii. code numbers array, which minimizes also the bandwidth,

        iii. member axes transformation matrices with respect to a fixed or moving global axes syste in order to accomodate various boundary conditions,

        iv. member characteristic matrices: stiffness, mass, etc,

        v. system characteristic matrices: stiffness, mass, etc, which are stored in single dimensional arrays with minimum bandwidth,

        vi. external loads: static or dynamic nodal or distributed loads,

The member stiffness matrices incorporated in the code STDYNL are for truss, beams, plane stress and plate bending members. They may be located out or within an elastic medium. For the static linear analysis, the axes transformation and stiffness matrices of the members and the related modules AXTRLN, SKLNEL, depend on the undeformed shape of the system and the member characteristics only. For a given system the axes transformation AXTRLN and stiffness SKLNEL matrices for members as well as the structure stiffness matrix STRST and the structure mass matrix for lumped mass method MASLMP are generated once and stored in the database. For the systems with material nonlinearity, the member stiffness matrix and its module SKLNPL depends on the final stress states after the loading. Similarly, for geometrical nonlinearity, the member axes transformation and stiffness matrices and their modules AXTRNL and SKNLEL oe SKNLPL depend on the deformed shape of the system. For the dynamic analysis by continuous mass matrix approach, the member stiffness matrix and its module SKDYCO depends on the magnitude of the natural circular frequency of the structural system. An iterative procedure is used for the static analysis of nonlinear system and for dynamic analysis by continuous mass matrix approach. Therefore the modules AXTRNL, SKLNPL, SKNLEL, SKNLPL, SKDYCN are recalled during each iteration depending on the type of the structural system and the structure stiffness matrix are regenerated. The structure stiffness matrix may be generated by the similtaneous use of three modules only: axes transformation AXTR.., member stiffness SK.... and structure stiffness STRST. modules stored in single dimensional array. The structure stiffness matrix may also be generated by a single module STRSTN, where already computed and stored values of the direction cosines and the stiffness matrices of the members are directly read from the database. If the size of the structure stiffness matrix exceeds the core capacity of the microcomputer, during the execution already genereted blocks of structure stiffness matrix by the multiple of the square of the band width are transfered to the database in order to clean the core for the next blocks.

The internally computed data can be checked and if necessay can be modified. Part of the internally computed data may be considered as overlapping with the processor.

2. PROCESSOR is composed of modules for;

        i. solution of the generalized coordinates which is obtained from

the system characteristic matrices in single dimensional arrays
by using direct solution algorithms based on Gauss elimination
Choleski factorization, skyline reduction or iterative solution,
algotithms based on Newton-Raphson, exhaustive search schemes
for finding final configuration of nonlinear deformed shapes or
for finding the eigenvalues,

ii. back substitution of the resolved generalized coordinates into
the member characteristic matrices in order to determine the end
reactions of the members, the variation of resisting forces and
moments, stresses within the member,

The module for the resolution of the generalized coordinated is the one that
requires the largest core allocation. The independent modules CHLREG,
CHLINT, CHLLRG may examplify some of the Choleski factorization procedures.
If the given problems are such that core allocations are less or equal to
the core capacity to accomodate simultaneously the modules for members axes
transformation module AXTR.., member stiffness matrix module SK...., tructure stiffness matrix module STRST., then the module CHLREG is used as a
subroutine for the solution of the generalized coordinates. The structure
stiffness matrix is brought in the module through the argument of the sub
routine. If the size of the problem in consideration is such that the core
capacity is sufficient enough to accomodate the structure siffness matrix,
then the module CHLINT is used independently. The structure stiffness matrix
is brought in the module CHLINT by reading directly from the database. For
problems whose structure stiffness matrix requires more than the core capacity, an out-of-core solution module CHLLRG is considered for the solution of
generalized coordinates. In the independent module CHLLRG the structure
stiffness matrix is read from the database by blocks of multiple of the
square of band width. Each block is factorized, then written back into the
database, so that the next block can be read in. In this case, due to the
slowness of the microcomputers, the CPU time surfaces as an important factor
to be thought about. Similar set of modules exist for skyline, Gauss elimination, etc.,. The exponent overflows and underflows in the magnitude of
some variables which appear in the exhaustive search procedure for extrac
tion of eigenvalues and in the iteration process of system with large geometrical nonlinearity have been circumvented without any lost in the accuracy
of these varaibles.

The variations of the resisting forces and moments within each member can be
computed by the back substitution modules. The stresses at critical points
can be evaluated. From the computed critical stresses, the safety and economy conditions can be checked for the members. If needed the sizes of the
members can be modified.

3. POSTPROCESSOR consists of displaying on the screen or printing on the
hard copies the results as numerical values or graphs. By assigning a
proper value to the related parameters any intermediate or final results
can be stored in the database for their interpretations. The results can
be checked. If needed, the external data stored in the database can be
modified by recalling the preprocessor and the execution can be restarted
from the first point affected by the modification.

A specific driver routine related to the type of the structural system, type
of the analysis, type of the externally applied loads is selected by the
first few data of the external data part of the preprocessor. For a specific
type of system, analysis, external loadings the specific driver routine

starts by assembling the required modules. The module CHLREG or CHLINT or CHLLRG or a similar one for the solution of the generalized coordinates is selected after the code numbers are generated by the module KODN, the maximum core allocation required for the problem under consideration are evaluated and compared with the core capacity of the machine used. For static analysis, the generalized coordinates are determined through the factorization process. For dynamic analysis, no matter whether lumped mass, consistent mass or continuous mass matrix is used, the terms of the mass matrix obtained by means of the kinetic energy can be added directly to the structure stiffness matrix. Then, the natural circular freuquencies and the corresponding modal shapes can be determined either by exhaustive serach method through the module CHLEIG or by some other modules.

All the modules in the code STDYNL are independently developed. Any new feature can be introduced in the code STDYNL either by modifying the related module or by adding a new module. Any desired module of STDYNL can be also incorporated in any other general purpose program.

The code STDYNL is written in FORTRAN. The BASIC version exists for static and partly for dynamic analyses.

METHODS OF ANALYSIS

Some of the significant methods particular to the code STDYNL are related to geometrical nonlinearity, plastic design, continuous mass matrix method and application of complex variable theory to the boundary element method.

Geometrical Nonlinearity

Various approaches have been developed for the analysis of structures with geometrical nonlinearity.

In the first approach the basic idea is to perform a standard linear analysis under the action of the given set of external loads and then calculate the member end reactions by using the deformed geometry. If the member end reactions at a joint are not in equilibrium with the given external loads, the out-of-balance forces are applied on to the new geometry to yield another set of deformation and forces. If the new member end reactions do not satisfy the joint equilibrium, the linear analysis continues with the latest geometry and the latest out-of-balance forces. This procedure is repeated until the equilibrium is reached at every joint. For the buckling of the structures, the original external loads are gradually increased and the equilibrium status is established at each time by following the process described above. The magnitude of the external loads causing the divergence in the unbalanced joint forces, in other words, producing excessive deformations at the joints is considered as the buckling load of the structure. The method has been applied to framed structures (Tezcan, Ovunc, 1967), to the high strength steel frameworks (Ovunc, 1968), Stress in the offshore pipeline during the laying process (Ovunc, Mallareddy, 1970), to the nonlinear analysis of elastic shell of revolutions (Ovunc, 1971). The method falls short in considering the thorough effect of the curvature of the member on the nonlinearity.

Another approach for the geometrical nonlinearity has been formulated to include the effect of the member curvature by considereing the following strain curvature relationship, v and w being the axial and transversal displacement of the member, respectively,

$$\varepsilon_z = \frac{\partial v}{\partial y} - z \frac{\partial^2 w}{\partial y^2} \Big/ (1 + (\frac{\partial w}{\partial y})^2)^{2/3}$$

in order to imrpove the effect of the curvature of the member. The improvement is included in the member stiffness matrix module SKNLCV (Ovunc,1981).

In the recently developed method for the geometrical nonlinearity, the equilibrium equations of an infinitesimal element are satisfied at any point on the deformed shape of the structure (Ovunc, 1982b, 1982c). At an arbitrary point of an infinitesimal element the strains and the stresses are along the Eulerian axes system, whereas the displacements v and w are refered to the Updated Lagrangian axes system. The axial and transversal displacements v and w are written in terms of a new variable ξ as follows (Fig. 1),

$v = v(\xi)$ and $w = w(\xi)$

where,

$\xi = y_v + v(\xi)$

By means of the differential geometry, the normal strain is expressed in terms of the displacements as,

$\varepsilon = \varepsilon_0 - \eta k_0 (1 + \varepsilon_0)$

where,

$$\varepsilon_0 = \frac{(1 + (w')^2)^{1/2}}{1 - v'}$$

$$k_0 = \frac{w''}{(1 + (w')^2)^{3/2}}$$

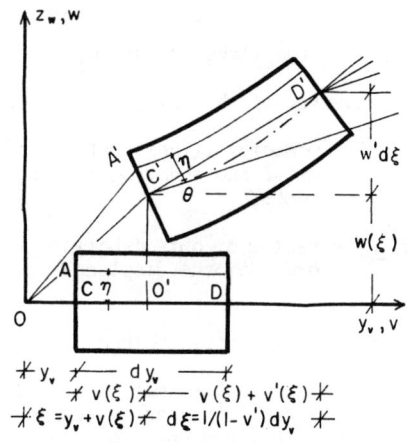

Fig. 1. Deformations

The equilibrium equations written on the deformed configuration of the infinitesimal element give,

$$\frac{dP}{d\xi} + k_0 (1 + (w')^2)^{\frac{1}{2}} V = 0$$

$$\frac{dV}{d\xi} - k_0 (1 + (w')^2)^{\frac{1}{2}} P = 0$$

$$\frac{dM}{d\xi} - (1 + (w')^2)^{\frac{1}{2}} V = 0$$

The displacements can be determined by considering the above differential equations with the force and moment resultants of the normal stresses at a cross section,

$$P = EA((1 + (w')^2)^{\frac{1}{2}} (1 - v') - 1)$$
$$M = EI \frac{w'}{(1 + (w')^2)} (1 - v')$$

and the boundary conditions in terms of the end displacements and rotations of the member. Then, the vector of the member end reactions $\{f\}$ can be evaluated.

At an intermediate iteration, the vector $\{f\}$ of the member end reactions is used to calculate the out-of-balance forces and moments at the joints of the structures. If all the out-of-balance forces and moments are of the negligible magnitudes, the intermediate iteration becomes the final iteration. Otherwise, further iterations are required to reduce the magnitudes of the out-of-balance forces and moments. If a next iteration is needed, the member stiffness matrix can be obtained from the vector $\{f\}$ of the member end reactions by writing the vector $\{f\}$ in the following form,

$$\{f_i\} = [k_{nl,i}] \{d_i\} + \{\Delta f_{i-1}\}$$

where, fir the i'the iteration,

$\{f_i\}$ = vector of the member end reactions,

$[k_{nl,i}]$ = member stiffness matrix including the effects of the strins due to axial and shearing forces, curvature and the slenderness ratio of member,

$\{\Delta f_{i-1}\}$ = vector of out-of-balance forces and moments related to the higher order of the displacements of the previous iteration.

Continuous Mass Matrix Method

In the continuous mass matrix method the equations of motion are satisfied not only at the joints as in lumped mass or consistent mass matrix methods, but at any arbitrary point of the structure (Ovunc, 1974, 1980, 1985a). In the continuous mass matrix method the equations of motion are written as,

$$[K_{dyn}]\{d\} = \{F(t)\}$$

where $[k_{dyn}]$ is the dynamic stiffness matrix.

In space a member has four independent vibrations: vibration due to axial displacement, torsional rotation and bending in two orthogonal palnes. For instance, the spatial part fo the deflection function for bending in vertical plane can be written as,

$$Z(y) = \{\phi(y)\}^T [L]^{-1} \{d\}$$

The matrix $[L]$ is obtained such that the spatial part of the deflection $Z(y)$ satisfies the boundary conditions of the member.

For the beam with constant moment of inertia vibrating in the vertical plane the interpolation function $\{\phi(y)\}$ depends on the assumptions,

a. vibration without any additional effect,

$$\{\phi(y)\}^T = (\sin\beta y \quad \cos\beta y \quad \sinh\beta y \quad \cosh\beta y)$$

b. vibration with the effect of compressive axial force,

$$\{\phi(y)\}^T = (\sin\beta_1 y \quad \cos\beta_1 y \quad \sinh\beta_2 y \quad \cosh\beta_2 y)$$

where, $\beta_{1,2} = ((\beta^4 + k^4)^{\frac{1}{2}} \pm k^2)^{\frac{1}{2}}$

$$\beta^4 = \frac{m}{EI_x}\omega^2 \quad \text{and} \quad k^2 = \frac{P}{2EI_x}$$

c. vibration with the effect of compressive axial force and soil-structure interaction, the nature of the interpolation function changes with the values of the parameters,

$$\beta^4 = \frac{1}{EI_x}[m\omega^2 - C p'] \gtrless 0 \quad \text{and} \quad k^2 = \frac{P}{2EI_x} > 0$$

i. if, $\beta^4 + k^4 > 0$, then,

$$\{\phi\}^T = (\sin\beta_1 y \quad \cos\beta_1 y \quad \sinh\beta_2 y \quad \cosh\beta_2 y)$$

where, $\beta_{1,2} = ((\beta^4 + k^4)^{\frac{1}{2}} \pm k^2)^{\frac{1}{2}}$

ii. if, $\beta^4 + k^4 = 0$, then,

$$\{\phi\}^T = (\sin ky \quad \cos ky \quad y \quad 1)$$

a transition stage yielding consistent mass matrix method,

iii. if, $\beta^4 + k^4 < 0$, then,

$$\{\phi\}^T = (\cosh\beta_1 y \cos\beta_2 y \quad \cosh\beta_1 y \sin\beta_2 y \quad \sinh\beta_1 y \cos\beta_2 y \quad \sinh\beta_1 y \sin\beta_2 y)$$

where, $\beta_{1,2} = 0.7071(\beta^2 \pm k^2)^{\frac{1}{2}}$

If the axial force is in tension β_1 and β_2 need to be interchanged.

The interpolation functions for members with variable moment inertias are also investigated (Ovunc, 1972). For member with linearly varying depth,

$$h = ny + m$$

the interpolation function $\{\phi\}$ is given by,

$$\{\phi\}^T = \frac{1}{\xi}(J_1(\alpha\xi) \quad Y_1(\alpha\xi) \quad I_1(\alpha\xi) \quad K_1(\alpha\xi))$$

where, $\xi = (ny + m)^{\frac{1}{2}}$, and $\alpha^4 = \frac{12\rho\omega^2}{Egn^4}$

The dynamic responses of the pipelines are analyzed by continuous mass matrix method by considereing the soil as a bounded plane in which the pipeline is placed (Ovunc, 1980, 1985c). The effects of various parameters are investigated for the free and forced vibration of the soil-structure system.

The forced vibrations of the structures are carried on either by modal analysis or by numerical integrations (Ovunc, 1979).

Boundary Element Method

The application of the complex variable method to plates under in-plane or transversal static loads provides a unique solution if the boundaries of the plates can be expressed in terms of a single parameter, or if the boundaries can be transformed by conformal mapping in to one which can be expressed in terms of a single parameter. An approximate solution has been given for plates whose boundaries can neither be expressed by a single parameter nor be transformed by conformal mapping (Ovunc, 1982a, 1983). The plates whose boundaries can not be mapped conveniently are divided into elements. Only the boundaries adjacent to two elements are discretized and the tractions at these discrete points are considered as the unknowns to be determined. The element characteristic matrices are obtained by means of the contour integrals. The unknown tractions at the discrete points along the common boundaries are determined from the continuity of the displacements at these discrete points.

The analysis is based on the determination of two complex potential functions per element whose expressions are uniquely obtained from the stress condition of the element along its boundaries. Therefore there is no need to select any interpolation function. The accuracy improves when the sizes of the elements increase. The plates having their boundaries do not require any special treatement. The computer code is the same as the one for finite element method, except the member stiffness matrix, load vector and the back substitution modules need to be modified. Since only the boundaries adjacent to two elements are to be divided to discrete points and the elements are to be of largest possible sizes, the number of the unknowns, the required storage area and the CPU time are very small compared to those of finite element method. The number of the terms in the series for the conformal mapping functions must be large enough to represent the mapped boundaries of the elemets properly. The corners of the elements are somewhat rounded due to the limited number of terms considered in the series of the conformal mapping functions.

The general dynamic displacement and deflection functions are obtained in complex domain for the in-plane and bending vibrations of plates (Ovunc, 1983a, 1985c, 1985d) Similar to Airy stress function the dynamic displacement or dynamic deflection function is composed of two complex potentials. The two complex potentials are uniquely determined from the boundary condition of the plates subjected to in-plane vibrations or bending vibrations: directly for plates with smooth boundaries, through the conformal mapping for plates whose boundaries can be mapped into those with smooth boundaries or by common boundary elements for the plates with irregular boundaries.

For the bending vibration of plates subjected to in-plane forces, the differential equation of motion obtained by decoupling the Von Karman field equations is a fourth order Helmholtz differential equation (Ovunc, 1985b). The general solution of the Helmholtz differential equation for the deflection of the plates constitutes the dynamic deflection functions. The natural circular frequencies and the corresponding modal shapes are evaluated from the free vibration of the plates. The forced vibration of the plates are obtained either by modal analysis or by numerical integration (Ovunc, 1984).

EXAMPLES OF APPLICATIONS

Various types of problems have been tested and analyzed by the code STDYNL. The stability of a parabolic dome has been investigated by using an iterative nonlinear analysis (Tezcan, Ovunc, 1967). The critical value of the concentrated load applied at the crest of the dome formed by arch ribs, has been evaluated and found to be 399.8 kips. The buckling of the dome primarily occurs because of the excessive outward deformations taking place at the crescent of the outside arch ribs.

A hemisphere under uniformly distributed load over the horizontal plane is considered as an example to the geometrically nonlinear analysis of elastic shells of revolution under axisymmetric loadings. the analysis has involved triangular and trapezoidal finite elements (Ovunc, 1971). The analysis has been performed for hemisphere on roller or fixed at the boundaries with or without flexibility properties.

The results obtained for the radial displacements along the bottom parallel is plotted in dimensionless coordinates. Where, R, t, E and p are the radius, thickness of the hemisphere, young modulus of the material and the load applied on the horizontal plane respectively (Fig.2).

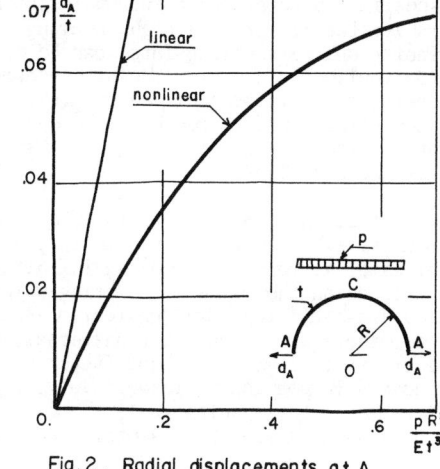

Fig. 2. Radial displacements at A.

A pipeline laying to a water depth of 85 m is considered as an example to a recently developed method for the geometrically nonlinear analysis (Ovunc, 1982b, 1982c). The pipeline rolls over the guidance tracks on the barge, slides freely on 100 m. length stinger and repses on an elastic soil at the sea floor. The lift-off angle of the pipeline from the barge is five degrees. The undeformed and deformed configurations of the pipeline under its own weight and the force applied at the barge are shown in the Figure 3. The variation of the shearing force with the variation of the tension applied to the pipeline at the barge is shown in the Figure 4. Since the pipeline slides freely on the deformed configuration of the stinger, the variations of the moment and shearing force within the part of

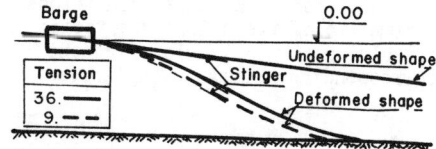

Fig. 3. Deformed configurations.

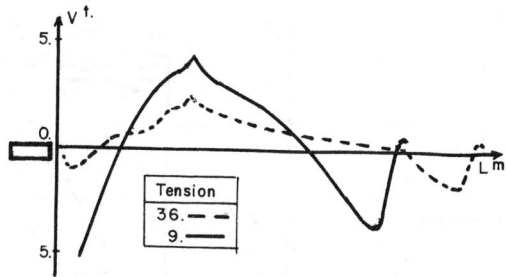

Fig. 4. Shearing forces diagrams.

of the pipeline supported by stinger are continuous. The discontinuity on the shearing force at the point where the pipeline leaves the stinger is undesirable since it creates high shearing stress around this point. The discontinuity on the shearing force can be eliminated either by increasing the tension applied to the pipeline at the barge or by increasing the length or decreasing the stiffness of the stinger. So that the pipeline lifts off from the stinger before reaching the end tip of it. The magnitudes of the moment and the shearing force are very small at the point where the pipeline touches the sea floor.

The effect of the member axial force and the surrounding elastic continuum for members embedded in elastic medium, are included in the differential equations of motion written on an infinitesimal element of the member. The static loads on the members vibrating within the plane of the externally applied dynamic forces are considered as distributed aom these members. Whereas, those acting on the transversal members are lumped at the ends of these transversal members. Load factors m and l are introduced on the distributed and lumped loads, respectively. When the distributed load factor m tends to zero, the results yield to those obtained by lumped mass matrix method. A nondimensional parameter is defined such that,

$$\alpha_n = \frac{(\omega_p)_n}{(\omega_0)_n}$$

where ω_p are ω_0 the natural frequencies of the n'th mode corresponding to structures with and without the effect of axial force and/or soil-structure interaction.

The characteristics of the effect of soil-structure interaction and the foundation model can be easily illustrated on three story frame on piles (Fig. 5). Two different boundary conditions, free and fixed, are considered at the bottom tip of the piles. The variation of the above defined ratio α_n, of a particular natural circular frequency of the frame supported on piles to the corresponding natural circular frequency of the three story frame

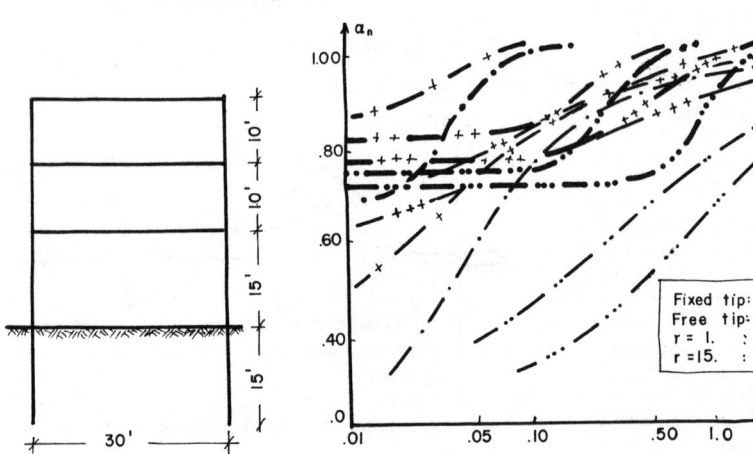

Fig.5. Three story frame.   Fig. 6. Variation of natural circular frequencies.

fixed at the base is plotted with respect to the variation of the soil characteristics. The variation of the rigidities of the members embedded in siol r, is also taken into account in the graph (Fig. 6). For frames on fixed tip piles, the variation of the natural circular frequencies is limited by the corresponding natural circular frequencies of of the four story frame without the effect of soil and the three story frame fixed at the ground level. Moreover the variation of a particular natural circular frequency remains within a limited range of the variation of the soil modulus. Whereas, the variation of the natural circular frequencies for frames on free tip piles covers a large range of the variation of soil modulus.

A sixteen story steel frame with and without shear walls up to sixth floor has its second floor beams pin connected to the colomns. The frame has been subjected to ground motion. The data for the ground motion has been taken from San Fernando Valley earthquake, February 9, 1971. First, second and third modal shapes are plotted for various load factors (Fig. 7). Under the earthquake motion, although the shear walls up to sixth floor reduce the floor displacements at lower floors, the roof displacements with or without shear walls are very close. The effect of member axial force becomes more pronounced when the loads are getting closer to their critical values. The first buckling mode occures as excessive horizontal displacements between the first and third floors, because of the pin connections of the second floor beams to the columns. The second buckling mode appears on the columns between the fourth and eleventh floors. By increasing the value of the load factor, the story to story displacements tend to zero at floors away from the buckling region of the frame.

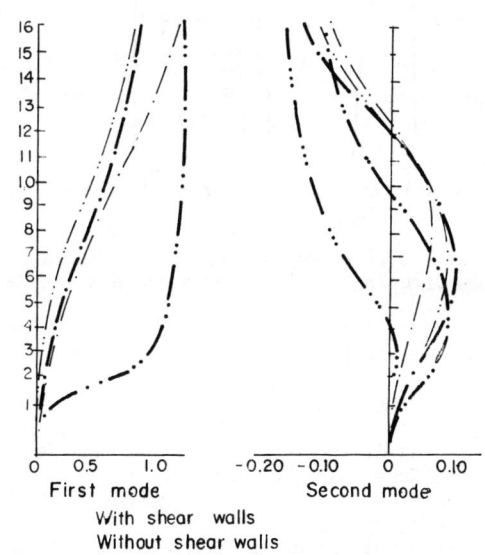

Fig. 7. Variation of floors displacements.

First mode / Second mode
With shear walls
Without shear walls

The beams of the main and cellar deck of an offshore platform are of size S57x18 and all the other members are pipes having their diameter varying from 17 in. to 42 in. (Fig. 8). The frame is assumed to be subjected to wave forces. The data for wave characteristics are collected from the information related to Gulf of Mexico. The bottom tip of the piles are assumed to be free. The variation of the modal shapes by the soil modulus are also shown (Fig. 8). The variation of the natural circular frequencies corresponding to the first and second sway and the first vertical displacement are plotted versus the variation of the soil modulus (Fig.9). The inclusion of the effect of the member axial force in the dynamic analysis reduces the magnitude of the natural circular frequencies. The variations of the natural circular frequencies with the increasing mass and static loads show that

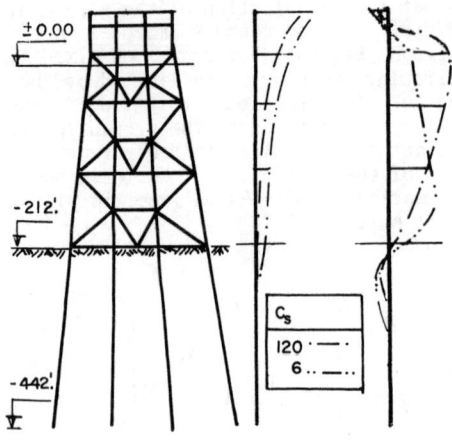

Fig. 8. Variation of modal shapes by soil modulus.

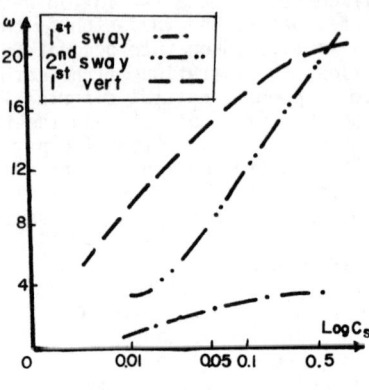

Fig. 9. Variation of frequencies with soil modulus

the natural circular frequencies including the effect of member axial force reduce much faster that that without the effect of member axial force.

REFERENCES

FATPAK. Structural Software Systems, 4440 Gateway Drive, Monroeville, PA. 15146.

GIFTS. CASA/GIFTS, Inc., Maryland Trade Center II, 7474 Greenway Center Drive, Greenbelt, Maryland 20770.

Ketchum, M. S. (1983). Frame program. ASCE Civil Engineering Magazine, December, pp. 61-63.

MODES-PC. Engineering and Educational Software, 1840 Arriba Drive, Monterey, Park, California 91754.

Ovunc, B. A. (1968). Nonlinear plastic analysis of high-strength steel plane and space frameworks. Proc., 8'th Congress IABSE, N. Y. pp. 583-596.

Ovunc, B. A. and Mallareddy, H. (1970). Stress analysis of offshore pipelines. 2'nd OTC. 1222, pp. 1727-1734.

Ovunc, B. A. (1971). Nonlinear analysis of elastic shells of revolution under axisymmetric loading. IASS, Bul. No. 43, pp. 9-16.

Ovunc, B. A. (1972). The dynamic analysis of space frameworks by frequency dependent stiffness matrix approach. Publ. IABSE, Vol. 32/2, pp. 137-154.

Ovunc. B. A. (1974). Dynamics of frameworks by continuous mass method. J. Compt. & Struc., Vol. 4, pp. 1061-1089.

Ovunc, B. A. (1978). In-plane vibration of plates by continuous mass matrix method. J. Compt. & Struc., Vol. 8, pp. 723-731.

Ovunc, B. A. (1979). Dynamic response time histories of continuous mass frameworks. Abst. Research in Progress, 16'th Midwestern Mechanics Conf. pp. 49-50.

Ovunc, B. A. (1980). Effect of axial force on frameworks dynamics. J. Comp. & Struc. Vol. 11, No. 5, pp. 389-395.

Ovunc, B. A. (1981). Stress in offshore pipelines. Abst. 3'rd. Int. Symp. on Freight Pipelines.

Ovunc, B. A. (1982) Effect of soil-structure interaction on the dynamics of structures. Proc., 3rd Int. Earthquake Microzonation Conf. pp. 821-830.

Ovunc, B. A. (1982a). Application of complex variable theory to the boundary element method. Proc., 4'th Int. Conf. on Boundary Element Methods in Engineering. pp.500-514.
Ovunc, B. A. (1982b). The geometrical nonlinearity of plane frameworks. Proc., Sino-American Symp. on Bridge and Structural Engineering, pp. 327-336.
Ovunc, B. A. (1982c). Design of offshore pipelines. Int. J. of Pipelines, No.2, pp.285-295.
Ovunc, B. A. and Voyadjis, G. Z. (1983). Application of complex variable theory to the free vibration of plates. Boundary Elements, Proc., 5'th int. Conf. Springer Verlag, pp. 709-713.
Ovunc, B. A. (1983a). New implementation of STDYNL. Handbook 4'th Int. Sem. on Finite Element Systems, Springer Verlag, pp. 443-450.
Ovunc, B. A. (1984). Forced bending vibration of plates by numerical integretion. Abst., 21'th Annual Meeting, SES, pp. 109-110.
Ovunc, B. A. (1985). STDYNL, a code for structural systems. in Structural Analysis Systems, The Int. Guidbooks, Edited by A. Niku-Lari, Pergamon Press, Vol. III, pp. 225-238.
Ovunc, B. A. (1985a). Soil-structure interaction and effect of axial force on the dynamics of offshore structures. J. Compt. & Struc. Vol. 21, No. 4, pp. 629-637.
Ovunc, B. A. (1985b). Free bending vibration and buckling of plates under uniform in-plane compressive forces. Boundary Elements VII, Vol. I, Springer Verlag, pp. 6-79, 6-88.
Ovunc, B. A. (1985c). Nonlinear free vibrations of plates. J. Compt. & Struc., Vol. 21, No. 5, pp. 887-891.
Ovunc, B. A. (1985d). Dynamic responses of buried pipelines. Proc., ASCE, Int. Conf. on Advances in Underground Pipeline Engineering.
Ovunc, B. A. (1986). Dynamic stress function for the vibration of plates. AIAA/ASME/ASCE/AHS, Structures, Structural Dynamics and Material Conf.
Ovunc, B. A. (1986a). Offshore platforms subjected to wave forces. ASCE, Dynamic Response of Coupled Civil Engineering Structures.
Ovunc, B. A. (1986b). Buckling of Large span frameworks under the effect of member axial force and soil-structure interaction. Proc., ASM'86, IASTED.
RandMicas. 17430 Campbell Road, Suite 114, Dallas, T 75252.
Sap-80. 1050 Leneve Place, El Cerrito, CA 94530.
STAAD III. Research Engineers, Inc. 303 Pavilions at Greentree, Marlton, N. J. 08053.
SCIA. Scientific Application Group, Attenrodestaat 6, B 3385 Meensel-Kiezegem, Belgium.
SOFTKIT. Kern International 433 Washington Street, Duxbury, MA 02331.
SYSTEK. SYSTEK Inc., P. O. Box 6234, Miss. State, MS. 39762
Tezcan, S. S. and Ovunc, B. A. (1965). Analysis of plane and space framework inluding curved member. Publ. IABSE, Vol. 25, pp. 339-352.
Tezcan, S. S. (1966). Computer analysis of plane and space structures. J. Structural Division, ASCE, pp. 143-173.
Tezcan, S. S. and Ovunc, B. B. (1967). An iteration method for the nonlinear buckling of framed structures. Space Structures, Edited by R. M. Davies. Part IV, No. 45, Blackwell Scientific Publications.

SAFEpm – STRUCTURAL ANALYSIS BY FINITE ELEMENTS ON POCKET MICROS

Josef Vykutil

VÍTKOVICE – Steel and Engineering Works of Klement Gottwald, Institute of Applied Mechanics, 611 00 Brno, Czechoslovakia

ABSTRACT

A package of programs SAFEpm for the elementary structural analysis (from beams to pressure vessels and box girder bridges) is available for students as well as engineers. SAFEpm consists of two programs BEAMSx using classical beam elements and of system of four programs MULTIx using straight two-node multipurpose elements. All programs are written in simple Basic and suitable for pocket micros or home computers. Listing of program MULTI2 is presented in this paper.

KEYWORDS

Structural analysis; beams; in-plane frames; orthotropic shells of revolution; finite element method; multipurpose elements; programs in Basic; pocket micros; home computers.

INTRODUCTION

Despite the invasion of Atari ST computers, majority of owners of home and pocket computers all over the world have only a fraction of their capacity. Some of them are or will be students and engineers engaged or interested in Structural Analysis by Finite Elements on these personal micros and for them the programs from package SAFEpm can serve as educational as well as professional ones.

The transfer of FEM technology and its integration in Computer Aided Engineering is one of the main goals of the Institute for Industrial Technology Transfer and guidebook series Structural Analysis Systems. One can hope that a SAFEpm Manual (with selfexplanatory theory, listings of programs and examples of use) could be useful for the extension of FEM throughout the world by using a great family of home computers as well as new pocket micros (e.g. Hewlett-Packard and Sharp). The students and engineers can now solve some structural analysis exercises and tasks not only at school and office, but also at home and outdoors.

PACKAGE OF PROGRAMS SAFEpm

A package of programs SAFEpm for linear elastostatic Structural Analysis by 1-D Finite Elements in 2-D mesh within poor memory (RAM) can be used for a number of in-plane skeletal and axisymmetrical shell structures. SAFEpm consists of two programs BEAMSx using beam elements with cubic function of deflection and system of four programs MULTIx using straight two-node MULTI-purpose elements with shear deformation and one-point integration of the stiffness matrix. Each program title has actual number of degrees of freedom per node used instead of letter x (Table 1).

TABLE 1 Package of programs SAFEpm

Programs SAFEpm for elementary structures (two-node finite elements in plane mesh)						
	BEAM elements		MULTI-purpose elements			
Program	BEAMS2	BEAMS3	MULTI2	MULTI3	MULTI5	MULTI6
Min. RAM	4Kb	10Kb	4Kb	10Kb	24Kb	32Kb

BEAMS2 - straight beams (4Kb is required for the program and data for 10 elements)
BEAMS3 - inplane beams and frames (minimum 6Kb RAM for educational purposes)
MULTI2 - Timoshenko beams and Mindlin orthotropic annular plates on elastic foundations (6Kb for 20 elements)
MUTLI3 - Timoshenko beams, arches, rings, simple frames and Reissner orthotropic shells of revolution with axisymmetric loading on elastic foundations (12Kb for 20 shell elements in two branches)
MULTI5 - Reissner smooth orthotropic shells of revolution with non-axisymmetric loading and simply supported circumferential segments of these shells (12Kb for 10 elements)
MULTI6 - Reissner orthotropic shells of revolution and their segments with simply supported end diaphragms (48Kb for simple box girder)

The theory of classical beam element is now covered in many textbooks and also in theoretical background for programs BEAMSx in SAFEpm Manual, in which FEM terminology and the different additional calculations of internal forces in classical displacement method and in FEM are particularly pointed out.

Many structural analysis techniques of great practical value are specific for each particular structure (i.e. displacement method for frames). The main advantage of the system of programs

MULTIx stems from the fact that a unified approach is used for
different types of structures, or otherwise, a 'one-element
library' is sufficient for a beam as well as orthotropic box
girder analysis. The presentation of *four* programs MULTIx is
justified by saving computer memory.

A beam with shear deformation and one-point integration was
first presented by Hughes (1977). A unification of in-plane
beam element and orthotropic shell element (Vykutil, 1981a) is
applied in program MULTI3. This axisymmetric shell element was
extended for the analysis of asymmetric bending of laminated
shells of revolution by the semianalytical approach (Vykutil,
1981b). Then the possibilities of multipurpose use of this semi-
element were shown (Oñate, 1983; Vykutil, 1984). The shell
element with six degrees of freedom per node was implemented
in program MULTI6 according to Kanok-Nukulchai (1979). The part
from 'SAFEpm booklet' devoted to basic system program MULTI2 for
novice user of FEM will be presented here to demonstrate the simplicity of the theory and the program and to indicate some possible applications.

ELEMENTARY THEORY FOR MULTI2

The vector of generalized strains ε for Mindlin circular plate
with axisymmetric loading includes the curvature κ_1 and shear
strain γ of Timoshenko beam and curvature κ_2 for circumferential
direction 2:

$$\varepsilon = \{\kappa_1, \kappa_2, \gamma\} = \{\beta_{,1} ; \beta/r ; w_{,1} + \beta\} \quad (1)$$

where $,_1$ defines the derivation with respect to longitudinal
(radial) mid-surface coordinate 1 ; β is rotation; w - deflection
and r - radius.
Vector of generalized stress resultants (forces) is obtainable by
using the relation

$$\sigma = \{M_1, M_2, Q\} = D\varepsilon \quad (2)$$

where **D** is a generalized stress-strain (elasticity) matrix. For
orthotropic material in directions 1 and 2, the thickness t in
direction 3 and unit width in direction 2, the appropriate matrix
D is

$$D = \begin{bmatrix} \dfrac{E_1 t^3}{12(1-\nu_1\nu_2)} & \dfrac{\nu_1 E_2 t^3}{12(1-\nu_1\nu_2)} & 0 \\ & \dfrac{E_2 t^3}{12(1-\nu_1\nu_2)} & 0 \\ \text{symm.} & & kE_{31}t \end{bmatrix} \quad (3)$$

in which E is the elastic modulus, ν - Poisson's ratio, k = 5/6
is shear correction factor.
The simplest approximations of deflection and rotation by shape
function **N** and unknown nodal parameters **u** are used:

$$\mathbf{f}_u = \begin{Bmatrix} w \\ \beta \end{Bmatrix} = \mathbf{Nu} = \begin{bmatrix} N_i & 0 & N_j & 0 \\ 0 & N_i & 0 & N_j \end{bmatrix} \{ w_i, \beta_i, w_j, \beta_j \} \quad (4)$$

where $N_i = 1-x/L$ and $N_j = x/L$ (the coordinate x in direction 1 starts in node i of the element with lenght L).
Using interpolation (4) in vector (1) yields another necessary matrix $\mathbf{B}$: $\boldsymbol{\varepsilon} = \mathbf{Bu}$. Thanks to the possibility and necessity of one-point integration of the element stiffness matrix $\mathbf{k}$ (Hughes, 1977), explicit stiffness terms are obtained by simple matrix multiplication:

$$\mathbf{k} = \int_0^L \int_0^b \mathbf{B}^T \mathbf{DB} r \, d\theta \, dx = r_c L \mathbf{B}_c^T \mathbf{DB}_c = r_c L \mathbf{B}_c^T \mathbf{S}_c \quad (5)$$

where $\mathbf{S}$ is called stress matrix and index c means evaluation in the centre (x=L/2) of the element.

The calculation of an element load vector $\mathbf{r}$ due to the surface load $\mathbf{f}_p$ must result into discretized nodal forces q_w and q_m (on lenght unit in direction 2) multiplied by the appropriate value r:

$$\mathbf{r} = \int_0^L \int_0^b \mathbf{N}^T \mathbf{f}_p r \, d\theta \, dx = \{ q_{wi} r_i \; ; \; q_{mi} r_i \; ; \; q_{wj} r_j \; ; \; q_{mi} r_j \} \quad (6)$$

Explicit load terms for uniform pressure p are

$$\mathbf{r} = \{ pL(2r_i + r_j)/6 \; ; \; 0 \; ; \; pL(r_i + 2r_j)/6 \; ; \; 0 \} \quad (7)$$

It should be noted that for the point load at the pole of the plate P(r=0) there is an exception; the used load term for this node must be $P/2\pi$ due to the integration of the stiffness matrix (5) with b = 1 (1 radian for plate).

An elastic (Winkler) foundation is considered by using this simplification: the foundation factor K_w in Newtons per cubic metre is used in (7) instead of p and the obtained values are added to the appropriate diagonal terms of the stiffness matrix (discretization to nodal springs).

The assembling of the stiffness matrix $\mathbf{K}$ and load vector $\mathbf{R}$ for the whole structure is required for the solution of unknown parameters $\mathbf{U}$ from the system of linear equations $\mathbf{KU} = \mathbf{R}$. Such assemblage for circular plate or straight beam is very simple: the appropriate diagonal submatrices $^m\mathbf{k}_{ii}$ (2 by 2) of stiffness matrix $^m\mathbf{k}$ of element number m are summed for common nodes (analogically also the load subvectors $^m\mathbf{r}_i$): (8)

$$\mathbf{K} = \begin{bmatrix} {}^1\mathbf{k}_{ii} & {}^1\mathbf{k}_{ij} & 0 & 0 & \cdot \\ {}^1\mathbf{k}_{ji} & {}^1\mathbf{k}_{jj} + {}^2\mathbf{k}_{ii} & {}^2\mathbf{k}_{ij} & 0 & \cdot \\ 0 & {}^2\mathbf{k}_{ji} & {}^2\mathbf{k}_{jj} + {}^3\mathbf{k}_{ii} & {}^3\mathbf{k}_{ij} & \cdot \\ \cdot & \cdot & \cdot & \cdot & \cdot \end{bmatrix} ; \; \mathbf{R} = \begin{Bmatrix} {}^1\mathbf{r}_i \\ {}^1\mathbf{r}_j + {}^2\mathbf{r}_i \\ {}^2\mathbf{r}_j + {}^3\mathbf{r}_i \\ \cdot \end{Bmatrix}$$

Only diagonal and upper submatrices (k_{ij}) are stored in memory.

The application of boundary conditions (prescribed parameters) is done numerically: the appropriate diagonal term of matrix **K** is multiplied by a great number (i.e. 1E20); then this value is premultiplied by the prescribed value of the parameter and imposed to the right-hand side. Finally, after the Gauss elimination of parameters **U**, the internal forces (2) for each element are calculated: **⌀** = **S**$_c$ **u**.

It must be pointed out that all introduced equations for the circular plate are valid for the beam (with rectangular cross-section with the width b) if $E_2 = 0$ and $r \equiv b$! Using this approach the bending (EI) and shear (GA) stiffnesses of the beam are found by the multiplication b·**D** in (5). The load vectors (6) and (7) are also valid for nodal line loads q across the width b and surface pressure p, respectively.

LISTING OF MULTI2

The presented theory is used in program MULTI2 for the unified analysis of orthotropic annular plates and of straight beams under nodal forces and / or pressure (axisymmetric for plates) resting on elastic springs. Program MULTI2 is written in simple Basic with trivial input and print statements - a user can improve those according to his hardware. The listing of program MULTI2 from Hewlett-Packard 85 is on the following page.

All arrays have dimensions for 10 elements. The necessary stiffnesses and loads are stored in arrays K and R. The thickness and radius (or the width for the beam) in the centre of each element in arrays H and B; the length of each element in array L. The description of the main loops of the program MULTI2:

```
lines  50- 60: zeroing of K and R
       80- 90: input of geometry (H, B, L) of each element
      120-210: assembling of stiffness K (8) using explicit terms
               of element stiffness matrix (5)
      240-320: input of the pressure and/or the foundation factor
               (for equally spaced elements) and storing of
               appropriate terms to R and/or K
      350-360: adding of the nodal line force to R
      390-400: input and application of the prescribed displa-
               cements
      410-460: Gauss forward elimination
      450-500: backward elimination
      520    : printing of the deflection and rotation in each
               node
      540-580: calculation and printing of the moments and shear
               force in the midside of each element.
```

USING OF MULTI2

Naturally the possibilities of all finite element programs are determinated by the programmer. But the scope of solvable problems

```
10 PRINT " MULTI2 : Mindlin circular plate or Timoshenko beam"
20 OPTION BASE 1@ ! c VITKOVICE 1985, author J.Vykutil
30 DIM K(22,4),R(22),H(10),B(10),L(10) ! for 10 elements
40 PRINT "No.of el. N" @ INPUT N@ PRINT N @ Q=N*2+2 ! Q=no.of eq
50 FOR I=1 TO Q @ K(I,1)=0 @ R(I)=0 @ FOR J=2 TO 4 @ K(I,J)=0
60 NEXT J @ NEXT I ! for each element :
70 PRINT "Thickness H,Mean radius (Width for beam) B,Length L"
80 FOR I=1 TO N @ INPUT H(I),B(I),L(I)@ PRINT H(I),B(I),L(I)
90 NEXT I ! for whole structure :
100 PRINT "Modul E1,E2(zero for beam),Shear modul G,Ratio N1"
110 INPUT E1,E2,G,N1@ PRINT E1,E2,G,N1 @ N2=N1*E2/E1
120 FOR J=1 TO N ! direct assembling of total stiffness
130 I=J*2-1 @ B=B(J) @ L=L(J) @ S=5*G*H(J)*B/6
140 D=H(J)^3*B/12/(1-N1*N2) @ D2=E2*D*L/4/B/B
150 K(I,1)=K(I,1)+S/L @ K(I,2)=K(I,2)-S/2
160 K(I,3)=K(I,3)-S/L @ K(I,4)=K(I,4)-S/2
170 K(I+1,1)=K(I+1,1)+E1*D*(1/L-N2/B)+D2+S*L/4
180 K(I+1,2)=K(I+1,2)+S/2
190 K(I+1,3)=K(I+1,3)-E1*D/L+D2+S*L/4
200 K(I+2,1)=K(I+2,1)+S/L @ K(I+2,2)=K(I+2,2)+S/2
210 K(I+3,1)=K(I+3,1)+E1*D*(1/L+N2/B)+D2+S*L/4 @ NEXT J
220 PRINT "No.of sections of equally spaced elements N"
230 PRINT "with pressure and/or foundation " @ INPUT N@ PRINT N
240 FOR J=1 TO N
250 PRINT "From node P1,with radius(width) B1,to P2,with B2"
260 INPUT P1,B1,P2,B2@ PRINT P1,B1,P2,B2
270 PRINT "Pressure P,Found.coeff. D2"
280 INPUT P,D2@ PRINT P,D2 @ D=(B2-B1)/(P2-P1)
290 FOR I=P1 TO P2-1 @ K=I*2-1 @ M1=L(I)*(3*B1+D)/6
300 M2=L(I)*(3*B1+2*D)/6 @ R(K)=R(K)+P*M1 @ R(K+2)=R(K+2)+P*M2
310 K(K,1)=K(K,1)+D2*M1 @ K(K+2,1)=K(K+2,1)+D2*M2 @ B1=B1+D
320 NEXT I @ NEXT J
330 PRINT "No.of nodal line forces N" @ INPUT N@ PRINT N
340 PRINT "Node I,Code K (force=1,moment=2),Value P"
350 FOR J=1 TO N @ INPUT I,K,P@ PRINT I,K,P
360 I=I*2-2+K @ R(I)=R(I)+P @ NEXT J
370 PRINT "No.of prescribed parameters N" @ INPUT N@ PRINT N
380 PRINT "Node I,Code K (deflection=1,rotation=2),Value P"
390 FOR J=1 TO N @ INPUT I,K,P@ PRINT I,K,P
400 I=I*2-2+K @ K(I,1)=K(I,1).E20 @ R(I)=K(I,1)*P @ NEXT J
410 FOR N=1 TO Q @ I=N ! Gauss elimination
420 FOR L=2 TO 4 @ I=I+1 @ IF K(N,L)=0 THEN 460
430 C=K(N,L)/K(N,1) @ J=0
440 FOR K=L TO 4 @ J=J+1 @ K(I,J)=K(I,J)-C*K(N,K) @ NEXT K
450 K(N,L)=C @ R(I)=R(I)-C*R(N)
460 NEXT L @ R(N)=R(N)/K(N,1) @ NEXT N
470 FOR N=Q-1 TO 1 STEP -1 @ L=N !.back elimination
480 FOR K=2 TO 4 @ L=L+1 @ IF K(N,K)=0 THEN 500
490 R(N)=R(N)-K(N,K)*R(L)
500 NEXT K @ NEXT N
510 PRINT "RESULTS" @ PRINT "Node no.,Deflection,Rotation"
520 FOR I=1 TO Q STEP 2 @ PRINT (I+1)/2,R(I),R(I+1) @ NEXT I
530 PRINT "Element no.,Moment long.,Moment circ.,Shear force"
540 FOR I=1 TO Q/2-1 @ J=I*2-1 @ C=H(I)^3/(12*1-N1*N2))
550 M1=C*(E1*(R(J+3)-R(J+1))/L(I)+N1*E2*(R(J+3)+R(J+1))/2/B(I))
560 M2=C*(N1*E2*(R(J+3)-R(J+1))/L(I)+E2*(R(J+3)+R(J+1))/2/B(I))
570 P=5*G*H(I)/6*(-(R(J)/L(I))+R(J+1)/2+R(J+2)/L(I)+R(J+3)/2)
580 PRINT I,M1,M2,P @ NEXT I @ END
```

mainly depends on the ability of the user to find simple, technically adequate, structural models.

Using program MULTI2, students can compare the deflection of clamped circular plate or beam under uniform pressure for different ratio t/l (Table 2). To obtain classical results without the influence of shear by programs MULTIx, a great value of input shear modulus ($E_{31}=E_1*1E4$) must be introduced.

TABLE 2 Influence of shear deformation on deflection

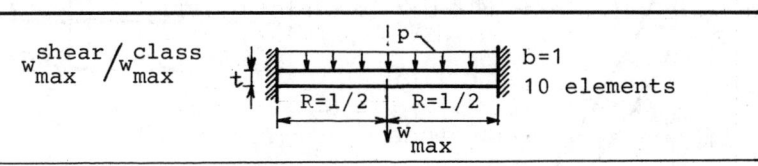

	BEAM		CIRCULAR PLATE	
t/l	$\nu=0.15$	$\nu=0.3$	$\nu=0.15$	$\nu=0.3$
0.025	1.00	1.00	1.01	1.01
0.05	1.02	1.02	1.04	1.05
0.1	1.10	1.11	1.15	1.19
0.15	1.24	1.27	1.34	1.42
0.2	1.43	1.49	1.54	1.74
0.25	1.68	1.77	1.95	2.15
	$w_{max}^{class}=\dfrac{8pl^4}{256Et^3}$		$w_{max}^{class}=\dfrac{3pl^4(1-\nu^2)}{256Et^3}$	

As an example from parametric study of simply supported square and circular plates under pressure on elastic foundations (Vykutil, 1982), the input data and some results of program MULTI2 for 5 elements are shown here:

```
line  40:    5
      80:  101.6,   50.8,  101.6
           101.6,  152.4,  101.6
           101.6,  254  ,  101.6
           101.6,  355.6,  101.6
           101.6,  457.2,  101.6
     110:  206843, 206843, 206843/2.6, .3
     230:  1
     260:  1 , 0 , 6 ,   508
     280:  68.95,  5.4287
     330:  0
     370:  2
     390:  1 , 2 , 0
           6 , 1 , 0
     520:  1    8.39058    9.05035E-25
     580:  1    1947559.7   1947559.7   -792.48093
```

A clamped circular cylindrical shell under internal pressure can be solved as beam on elastic foundation. A study of this problem is presented in Fig. 1. Program MULTI2 needs redimensioning in line 30 and less than 6Kb memory for 20 used elements.

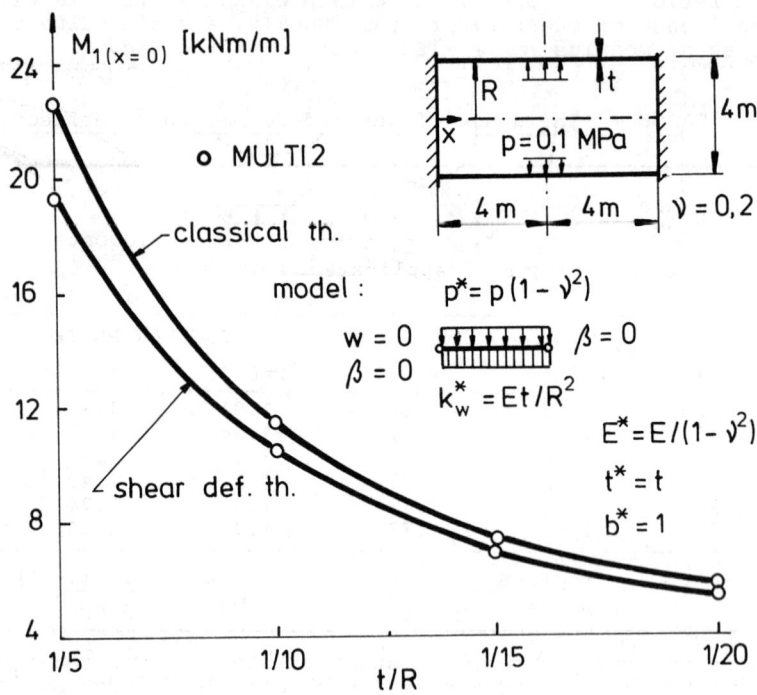

Fig. 1   Maximum moment in cylinder with pressure

CONCLUSION

The presented package SAFEpm is intended to meet academic and industrial needs in pocket micro-aided structural analysis. A wide range of structures suitable for MULTIx analysis is shown in Fig. 2.

SAFEpm could help to transfer FEM everywhere (even to your pocket).

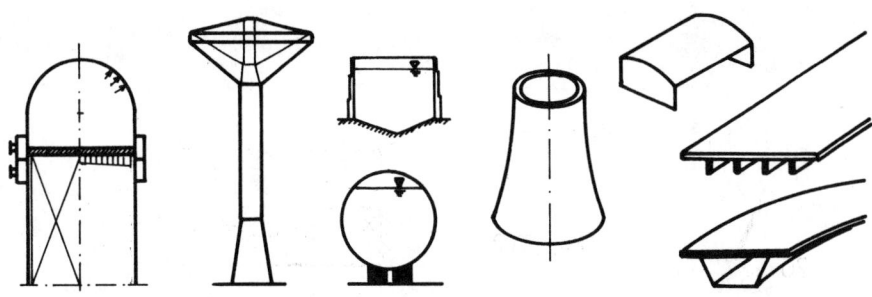

Fig. 2   Industrial applications of SAFEpm

ACKNOWLEDGEMENT

The author would like to express his gratitude to Professor
V. Křupka for his advice and to Dr. Niku-Lari for his support.

REFERENCES

Hughes, T. J. R., R. L. Taylor and W. Kanok-Nukulchai (1977).
   Int. j. numer. methods eng., 11, 1529-1543
Kanok-Nukulchai, W. (1979). *Int. j. numer. methods eng.*,13, 673-681
Oñate, E. and B. Suarez (1983). *Comp. Struct*, 17, 407-426
Vykutil, J. (1981a). *Int. j. numer. methods eng.*, 17, 1877-1881
Vykutil, J. and B. Svoboda (1981b). Analysis of laminated shells
   of revolution (in czech). *Proceedings 2nd Conf. Numerical Methods
   in Mechanics*, SAV Bratislava
Vykutil, J. (1982). *J. Eng. Mech. Div.*, *Proc. ASCE*, 108, 202-205
Vykutil, J. and V. Křupka (1984). A simplified approach to fi-
   nite element education. In J. Robinson (Ed.), *ART in FEM Techno-
   logy*, Robinson and Associates, England. pp. 271-280

UTILIZING THE GRAPHICS CAPABILITIES OF MICROCOMPUTERS FOR FEM PRE- AND POSTPROCESSING

J. F. Stelzer

Nuclear Research Centre (Kernforschungsanlage, KFA), D-5170 Juelich, FRG

ABSTRACT

It is reported about the way to subdivide rather coarse geometrical information, as e.g. coming from the CAD or the otherwise generated drawings into the finite element mesh. Interactivity and the continuous use of the graphics screen and plotters are necessary tools. A survey about different types of mesh display is given: wire frame mode, hidden line removal, hidden surface removal, continuous shading according to the cosine law for the generation of photo-alike pictures, colour filling to mark different property areas. Microcomputers are also unsurpassedly useful for the finite element postprocessing. The same features are applicable as well for temperature field results as well as for stress displays. Besides other possibilities most useful tools are: hidden line plots with contour lines on the remaining visible surfaces, and colouring the visible surfaces with colours between red (highest function value) and blue (lowest one). Unfortunately, this paper is printed in black and white, so the colour graphics pictures cannot shine in their splendour. However, the colouring with continuous colour transitions is the best way to illustrate stress and temperature patterns.

KEYWORDS

Finite elements; preprocessing; postprocessing; hidden line removal; hidden surface removal; continuous shading; colouring; contour lines.

INTRODUCTION

Microcomputers of today offer high-resolution screens and colour. Both are the presuppositions for good graphics. Computer graphics is the most important link between the computer's world of numbers and the engineer's visual thinking. For making structures visible many different graphical ways can be walked on. A first headline might be: vector graphics vs. pixel or raster graphics, a second one: hidden line removal vs. hidden surface removal, etc. However, it is not possible to decide which type is more advantageous. It just depends on the case. This will be shown in this context. Thus, according to our experiences, the full variety of the different methods should be present in the pre- and postprocessor.

The microcomputer should be completed to a full workstation by adding graphical devices. It is advicable to add a vector plotter for the vector graphics and a colour hardcopy with inkjet technique for the reproduction of pixel graphics.

About the use of graphics on computers the books of Newman and Sproull (1979) and Foley and van Dam (1982) give thorough information which were valuable for our developments. An important auxiliary means is the surface patching technique described by Stelzer (1984, 1986). A quick and reliable method for the removal of hidden lines in the vector mode was developed by Janssen (1983) which is preferred by the author. Some more information about a strategical conception for finite element software on microcomputers can be found in a publication by Stelzer (1984).

The prints of this paper dumped by a screen process are made with a screen with 512 x 360 pixels. The due colour hardcopy, however, has a resolution of 1024 x 1024 pixels. The dump driver developed by Wimmer (1985) can produce two sizes of pictures: small ones by dumping every pixel once, and greater pictures by dumping every pixel four times. Then the paper format is fully used. Before arriving at the details some slogans may now be listed.

Primary tools. Generating effective finite element graphics requires some primary tools. To account some: wire frame graphics, hidden line graphics, hidden surface features. The latter are both necessary for visual realism which yet can be improved by shading the surfaces according to Lambert's cosine law. It might be true that we step with this routine a little outside the finite element world more to the artists. However, such pictures offer photograph-alike images even of objects not yet existing in the reality.

Artistic aspect. In fact, images of this kind can be used in art or advertising. So, an artist could as well establish his object with an automatic FE mesh generator and produce very quickly a high quality photo-realistic picture.

Back to the engineer's environment. The result graphics tools with FEM should include, too: application of colour, and contour line features. Firstly, colour is very useful to mark different materials (material 1: red, 2: yellow, etc), see Fig.1. In the case of nonlinear relationships colour may be used to characterize regions still elastic and others which became already plastic. However, most powerful is the application of colour with temperature- and stress fields. Since the appearance of colour hardcopies the content of the screen can quickly be dumped on paper and added to the structural analysis report. Customers like the colour display very much because on the first look a stress distribution can be apprehended (stress peaks appear in red colour surrounded by a yellow court) and even people with no knowledge about stress fields at once understand what is going on and where the endangered points are. This is much more difficult with contour line plots.

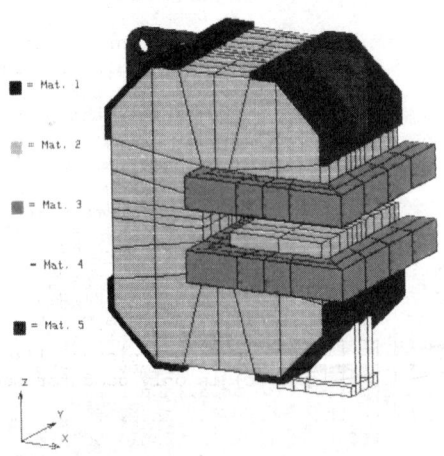

Fig. 1 Marking regions of different materials by colours

The next chapter will turn towards the preprocessing.

THE PREPROCESSING PROCEDURE

The goal of this program part is to offer the user maximum convenience with the data input, eventually coming from the CAD system concerning the topology, e.g. properties, boundary conditions and loads. The conception is to guide the user by questions, comments and menus. If a coupling shall be made between a temperature field calculation and a deformation and stress analysis it is necessary to call up after the temperature run the preprocessor another time for adjusting the mesh to the needs of the rigidity run (different degrees of freedom per node, properties etc). It must be specified from the beginning: whether the data are to be put in and stored manually; whether starting values, list of nodal points, list of material numbers, node coordinates, boundary conditions already exist and on which storage device; or whether modifications only shall be made on data already resident on the computer. In our program, if all the data already exist, a large menu appears offering most varied possibilities of modifying the mesh, but additionally:
- calculation of the storage space required and data check;
- calling up the mesh generator;
- front width minimization;
- input of boundary conditions;
- generating a graph;
- mesh transformation, translatory or rotatory;
- mesh extension by mirroring;
- combination of two bodies with the possibility of combining as many bodies as desired by means of repetition;
- insertion or removal of individual elements or nodes;
- checking the Jacobi determinants of every element.

By means of a series of pictures the generation of a FE mesh may be shown, see Figs. 1 and 2. Only a coarse mesh must be put in by hand, Fig. 1 a (six spatial 20-node elements). The graphic program draws bent lines in their real curved mode by employing the shape functions. Then, calling the mesh generator, the raw elements are subdivided in as many new elements as wanted, Fig. 1b. This process is run again using the shape functions according to Hinton and Owen (1979). Then as the next step the mirroring routine is called. The computer is told which plane may serve as mirror plane. The mesh shown as c) in Fig. 3 is made. The generation of this final mesh takes only a very short time. Of course, a picture like c) is only good for perceiving the mesh. However, it does not give a realistic view. How this can be made will be described in the next paragraph.

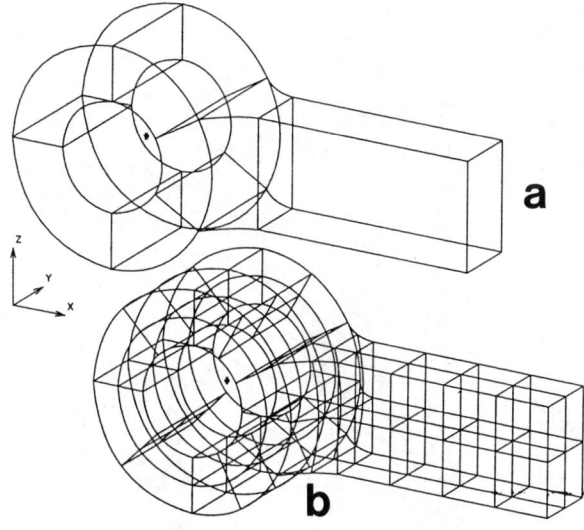

Fig. 2 Mesh refining by automatic subdivision

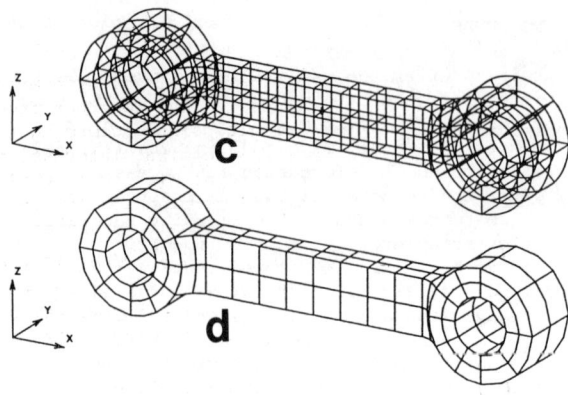

Fig. 3 Comparison of a wire frame- and hidden line plot.

Hidden Line removal. We can leave the task to extract the visible lines (or edges) or pieces of partly hidden lines to the computer. This technique has more than 20 years history starting with an algorithm by Roberts (1963). Today, such routines are short and speedy so that they can be used successfully even on microcomputers. Our favorit is the Janssen algorithm (1983). It can be speeded up considerably by the following measure: consider in turn every surface of every element by calculating its outward normal vector, and cancel then all edges of those surfaces the outward normal of which includes an angle greater than 90 degree related to the viewing vector coming from the observers point. A certain disadvantage is that this hidden line remover connects the points by straight lines. There is no easy possibility to introduce curved edges. Fig. 3d shows the hidden line plot to the generated mesh.

Problems of penetrating. Consider in this respect the Fig. 4. In this structure a tube and a quarter part of a torus are fit together. Because of the different types of possible penetrations it is very difficult to design an automatic routine for the generation of penetrated meshes. Our preprocessor offers the feature of omitting any second (or farther) point within a distance to a certain point. The distance is put in by the user. With this means two (or more) prepared meshes can be united. For the structure of Fig. 4 both parts were pregenerated solely, however, the coordinates along the penetrating lines were calculated analytically.

The same structure drawn in the hidden line mode can be seen in the Fig. 5. It is a trait of wire frame- and hidden line plots that they are precalculated in the vector mode. The picture is created with a black ink pen moved by the plotter from one paper coordinate to the next. The figures thus created are very exact and independent of the finite pixel resolution of the screen.

Hidden surface removal. In contrast to Fig. 5 now look at Fig. 7. This picture was produced by using a hidden surface algorithm

Fig. 4 (right) Wire frame presentation of a penetrated structure

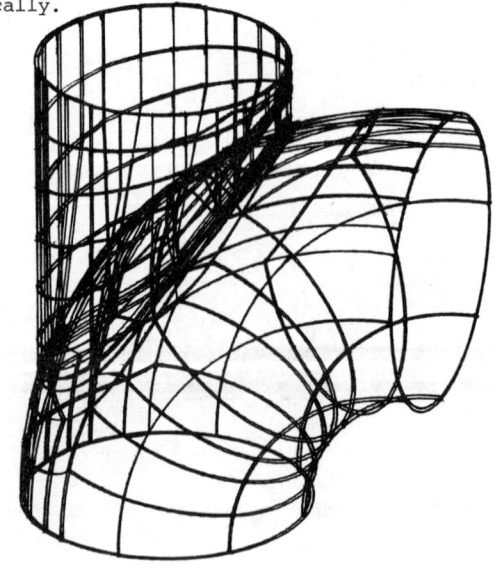

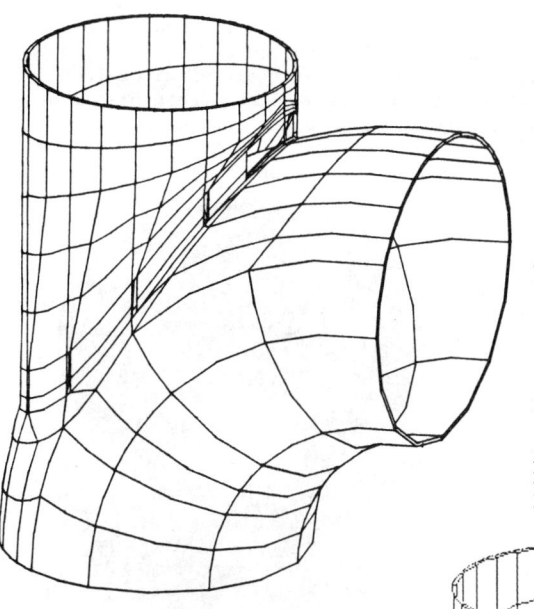

Fig. 5 Hidden line plot of the tube-torus structure (left)

It has curved lines. However, the lines are put together from many single points according to the pointwise pixel information of the screen. With this in mind the expensive high resolution screens have their advantage.

More realism by shading. If the visible surfaces are filled with colour the luminosity of which is adjusted according to the cosine of the angle between the surface normal and the light beam direction, then very realistic images of bodies can be produced, see the Figs. 6 and 8. Moreover, arbitrary colours can be applied.

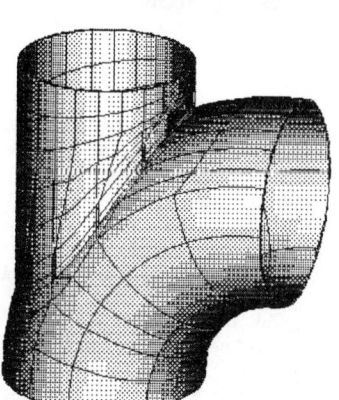

Fig. 6 Filled and shaded hidden surface plot

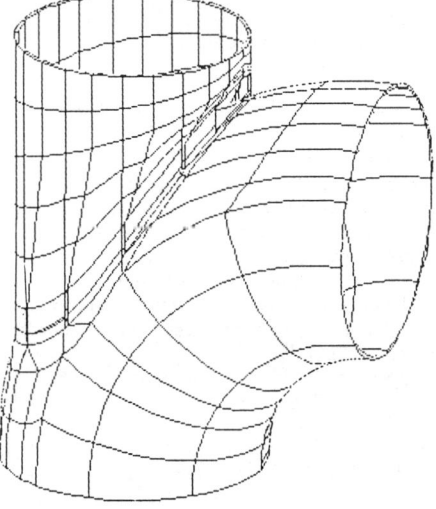

Fig. 7 Plot generated with the hidden surface routine

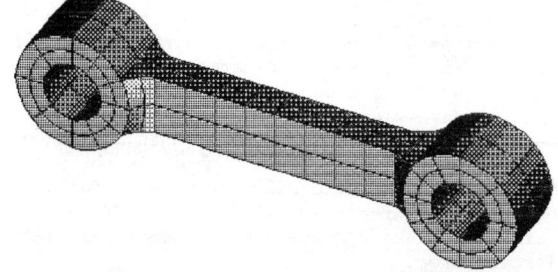

Fig. 8 (left) Filled and shaded hidden surface plot

Design of an algorithm for hidden surface removal. The main idea is the so-called Z-sorting (see Newman and Sproull or Foley and van Dam). The element surfaces or parts hereof are drawn in the sequence of their distance from the eye point, beginning with the farmost one. In this way the screen pixels get new informations again and again, overwriting the past ones unless no new hiding surfaces are in between eye point and surface. In Fig. 9 two intermediate states during the generation of such a plot are shown.

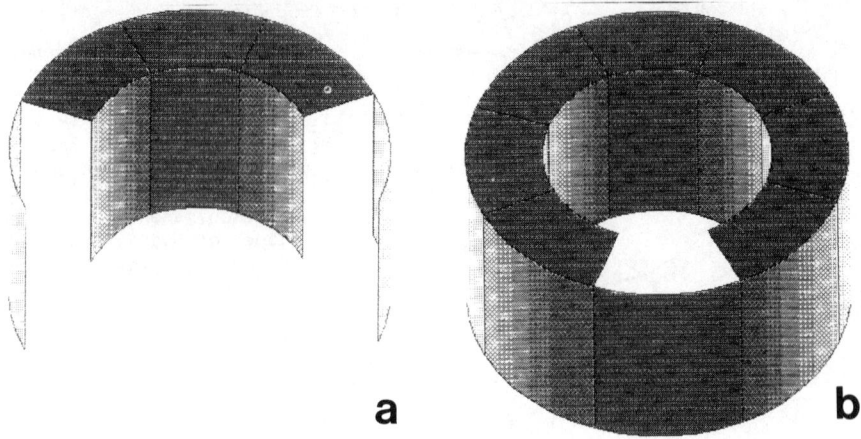

Fig. 9 Two intermediate states during the generation of a hidden surface plot

Yet before the plotting can take place some preparating measures are necessary which will be dealt with in the following outlines.

Establishing an information matrix. In this matrix the essential graphics information is written. At the beginning the number of its rows is equal the product of element numbers and surfaces per element, and it has four columns. The entries of a row are: 1) element number, 2) surface number, 3) distance between eye point and surface, 4) cosine of the angle between surface normal and eye vector.

Sorting out internal surfaces. Surfaces located inside a structure show the quality that they are common to two adjacent elements. They easily can be recognized by the fact that the sum of the appropriate node numbers must be equal because to both surfaces belong the same points. Consequently, if there are two surfaces with equal node number sums both must be expelled. Experience showed that it is advisable to weight the maximum node number by multiplying it by a large number. The information matrix is then reduced by redimensioning to the surviving number of surfaces.

Determining the angles between surface normals and eye vector. For every surface the normal vector in the centre point indicating element-outwards is calculated. Then the cosine of the angle between the normal- and the eye vector is determined and stored in the 4th column of the information matrix. When calculating the normal vector a precaution is necessary. To calculate the normal vector the equation of the surface plane must be established using three node points of this surface. However, if these three points are taken randomly it could happen that they lie on a straight line which is not seldom with isoparametric elements. Consequently, the calculation will fail. We exclude this effect by first determining three times with three different node sets the appropriate plane areas and take for the normal vector calculation that set which spans the largest area.

Expelling looking-off surfaces. Surfaces the normals of which indicate off from the observer's position are a priori invisible and thrown out. Experience showed that it is not advisable to use the angle of 90 degree between eye- and normal vector as the measure of invisibility, but to enhance this region by about 10 degree.Thus also parts of curved surfaces entering the visible region can be regarded using the special patch technique described below. The information matrix is now shrinked again.

Calculating the distances. The aspects might be generated in parallel projection. The eye point is elsewhere on a viewing sphere described by two angles, the azimuth and the height inclination. Advantageously the radius of the viewing sphere is established as the twofold of the maximum structure extend. In parallel projection the eye "point" is in fact a tangential plane at the sphere. The distances between every surface centre and the eye plane is calculated and stored in the 3rd column of the information matrix. This matrix is then sorted in descendent order according to the distances.

Patching and plotting. The patching was developed by Stelzer (1984). Hereby, any surface is subdivided in an eligible amount of stripes with which an due amount of patches is generated. This subdividing is accomplished in the natural coordinate system. The corner nodes of the patches are transformed using the shape functions to the world coordinate system and from there into the projection coordinates of the screen. If a patch edge coincidices with a part of a surface edge, being then an element border, too, then this edge is drawn during the plot process. Thus, a sufficient fine patching effects well-curved element edges. During the plotting, it is started with the farmost patch in the farmost surface.

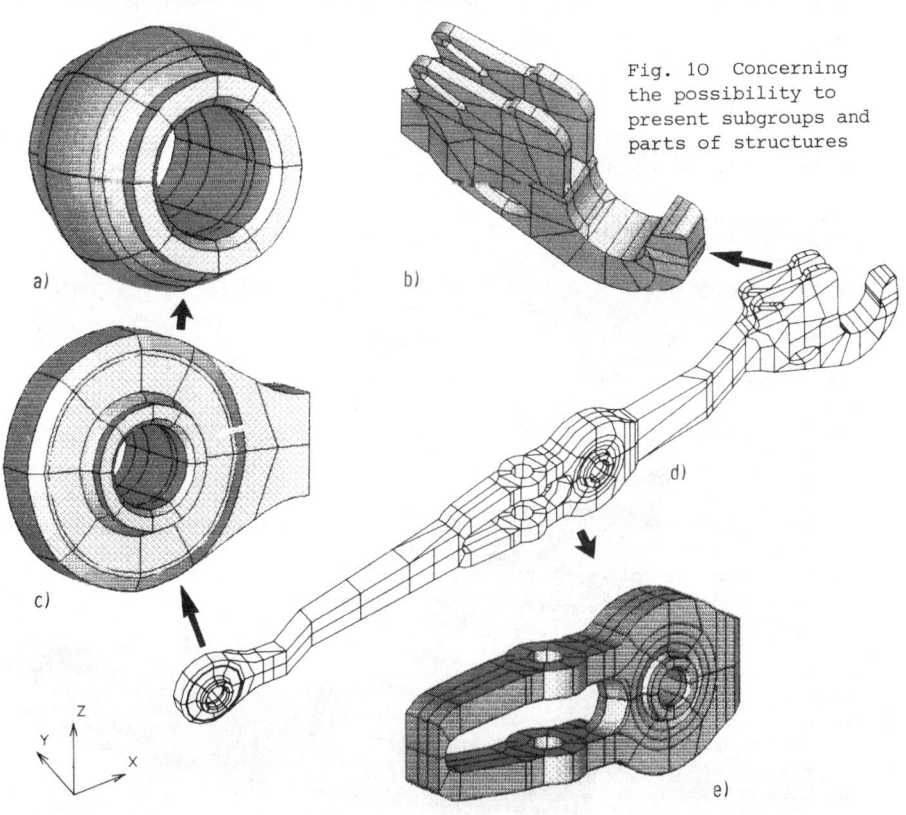

Fig. 10 Concerning the possibility to present subgroups and parts of structures

Filling and shading. For every patch midst the normal vector is calculated, too. The filling with colour of every patch is accomplished more or less intensively, according to the cosine between normal- and eye vector. So values between 0 and 1 are obtained, and just this value is used for the *luminosity* number which controls the intensity of filling with colour of a polygon. If the patching is sufficiently fine then continuous transitions of shading are achieved ("smooth shading"). In Fig. 10 a more elaborate example is shown. In the centre the hidden line picture of a tractor lever can be seen. Around it some subgroups are arranged showing the perfection of this kind of structure presentation.

Of course, the preprocessing contains more features like input of boundary conditions, loads, properties with appropriate graphics representations, too. However, because of confining reasons these things might be omitted. Also the number crunching with stiffness calculations, load vector establishment and equations solution needs not be mentioned. The other step of finite element calculation where graphics are indispensable is the result presentation during the postprocessing phase.

GRAPHICAL POSTPROCESSING OF FINITE ELEMENT ANALYSIS

Let us start with the result display of temperature fields. The classic method is the application of isothermal lines. In the case of 3-D structures these lines are drawn upon the remaining visible surfaces, or the visible parts hereof. However, the quickest and thorough insight into the temperature rel-

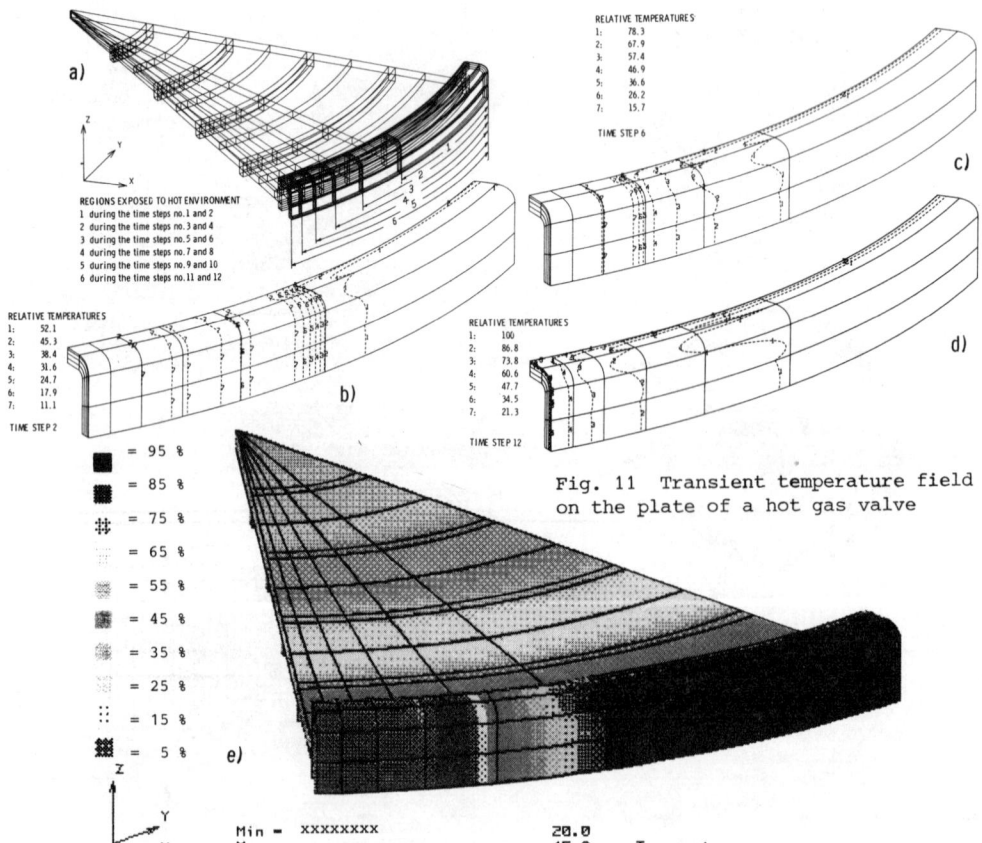

Fig. 11 Transient temperature field on the plate of a hot gas valve

ationships accomplishes the colour representation. Fig. 11 gives an example showing the results of a transient temperature field. The valve plate is gradually drawn out of its cooled rest position, and increasing parts of its surface are exposed to a hot gas environment. The figure gives also the possibility to compare contour line- and colour representation.

Which colours? The computer assigns to the different colours certain numbers: the spectrum begins with red (=0) and ends again with red (=1). In between are e.g. the colours with the following numbers: yellow = 0.16667, green = 0.3333, cyan = 0.5, blue = 0.6667, magenta = 0.83333. It is very appropriate to associate to the highest variable value (here temperature) the colour red =0, and to the lowest one blue = 0.66667. This matchs also the human association of colours and temperatures (red tap gives hot water, blue tap cold water). Consequently it is useful to employ the whole colour spectrum between blue and red for the temperatures between the lowest and highest value. Analogously it may be proceeded with stresses.

Smooth colouring. Continuous colour transitions are accomplished by the already mentioned patching technique, see Stelzer (1984). For the midpoint of every patch the function value is calculated by using the node temperatures and the shape functions. This patch is then filled with the colour belonging to the due function value. A sufficient fine patching delivers the continuous colour transitions we are accustomed to from thermography pictures or stress optics. Below an example.

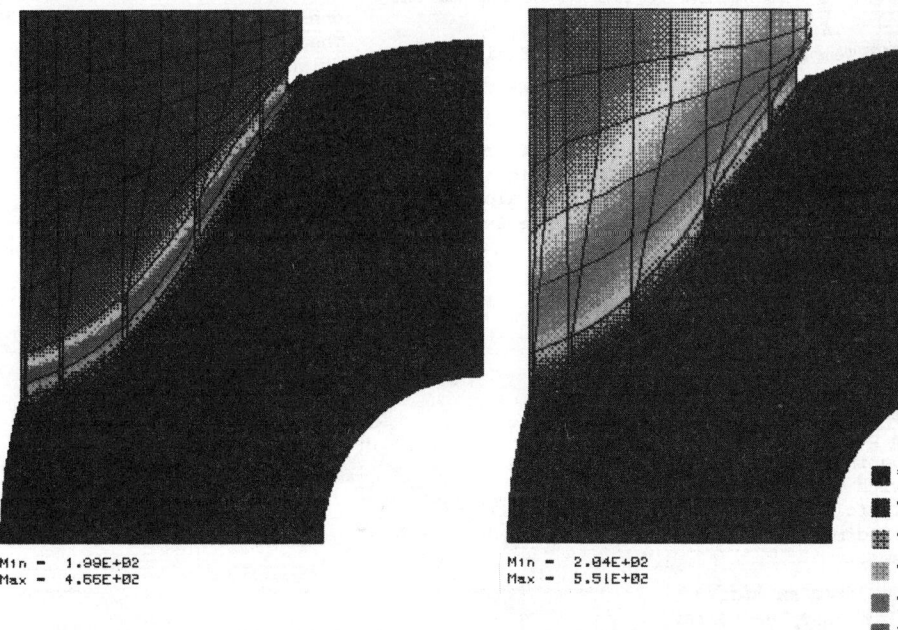

Fig. 12 Two temperature fields during the heating-up phase.
Left: after the 7th step of the time integration (steepest local temperature gradient), right: final balanced state

The tube-torus structure of Fig. 4 was object of a coupled temperature field and stress calculation. From a certain time point on hot fluid flows through the torus heating it up rather quickly. The attached tube follows with delay causing shear stresses in the transition zone. Sought for was the location and the amount of the intermediate maximum thermal stress. In Fig. 12 the time point of the highest stresses is shown (steep temperature gradient in a very close area) as well as the final state.

Generating patterns of time-dependent temperature fields. This is another useful feature which should not be missed in a FE postprocessor. The user selects an amount of node points the temperatures of which shall be plotted as a function of time. In this way the Fig. 13 was produced. In this picture one can see that the steepest temperature gradient occurs at 250 seconds. Only for this time step the stresses need to be calculated. Furthermore can be seen that the settled state is reached after one hour, approximately. The temperature distributions of the both pictures in Fig. 12 belong

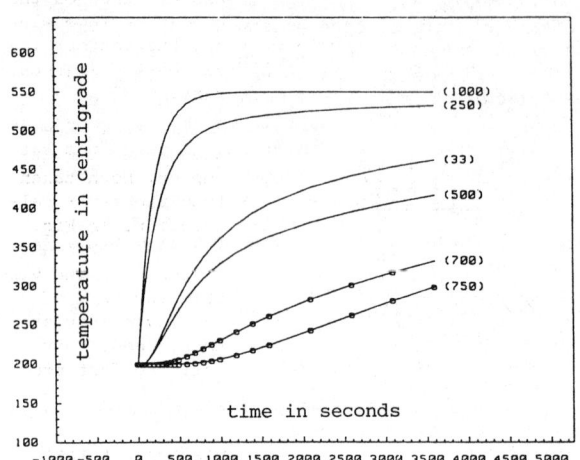

Fig.13 Temperatures as a function of time at different node points

to the time steps at 250 and 3600 s.

Colour display of stress fields. The tractor lever may be used again. In Fig. 14 the hook with a piece of its neck is to be seen where higher stresses occur in the upper left and lower right alongside edges. As an example for 2-D relationships the stresses on a flange surface are shown, see Fig. 15. The flange periphery is clamped. It is loaded by uniform pressure and additionally by three point loads with 120 degree distance, as shown in the contour line plot of Figure 15. Please pay attention to the continuous transitions with the colours, exactly following swelling or diminishing stresses.

Contour lines on hidden line and -surface plots. Effective isoline features are indispensable in FE postprocessors. In the method we developed the shape functions are employed to find the

Fig.14 Distribution of the reference stresses in a tractor lever hook

sought positions of the function values. In the same way as with the patching by a double transformation the contour lines on spatially curved surfaces can be drawn into the parallel projection image. Naturally, a combination of the

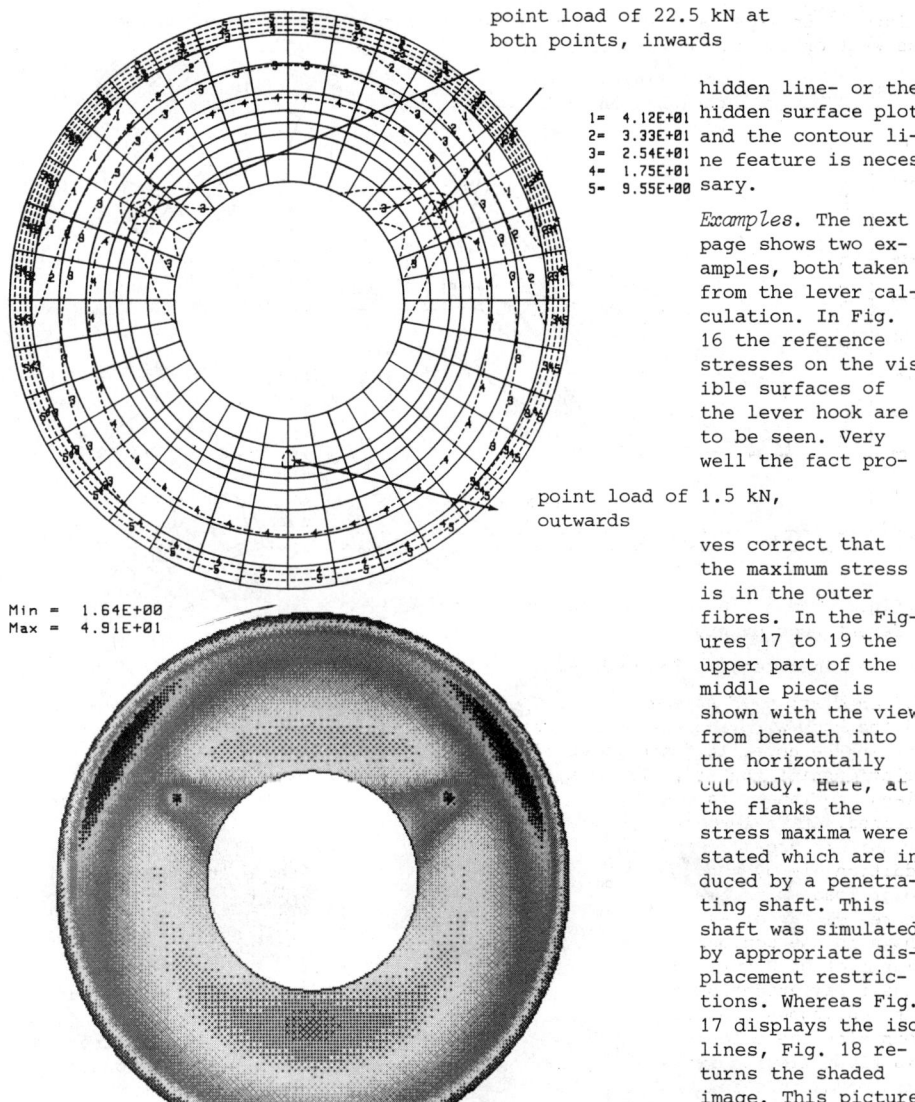

point load of 22.5 kN at both points, inwards

1= 4.12E+01
2= 3.33E+01
3= 2.54E+01
4= 1.75E+01
5= 9.55E+00

point load of 1.5 kN, outwards

Min = 1.64E+00
Max = 4.91E+01

- 4.83E+01
- 4.36E+01
- 3.89E+01
- 3.41E+01
- 2.94E+01
- 2.46E+01
- 1.99E+01
- 1.51E+01
- 1.04E+01
- 5.63E+00

Fig. 15 Reference stress distribution on the surface of a flange as a consequence of pressure- and nodal loads; contour lines (above) and colour (below)

hidden line- or the hidden surface plot and the contour line feature is necessary.

Examples. The next page shows two examples, both taken from the lever calculation. In Fig. 16 the reference stresses on the visible surfaces of the lever hook are to be seen. Very well the fact proves correct that the maximum stress is in the outer fibres. In the Figures 17 to 19 the upper part of the middle piece is shown with the view from beneath into the horizontally cut body. Here, at the flanks the stress maxima were stated which are induced by a penetrating shaft. This shaft was simulated by appropriate displacement restrictions. Whereas Fig. 17 displays the isolines, Fig. 18 returns the shaded image. This picture was embodied to interprete the somewhat complicated content of the Fig. 17. Finally, the Fig. 19 exhibits the due stress colour plot.

Combination of deformation display with hidden line- and hidden surface plot. Our postprocessor foresees, moreover, to draw pictures in the hidden line mode, simultaneously respecting the nodal displacements, see the tractor lever in the deformed state,

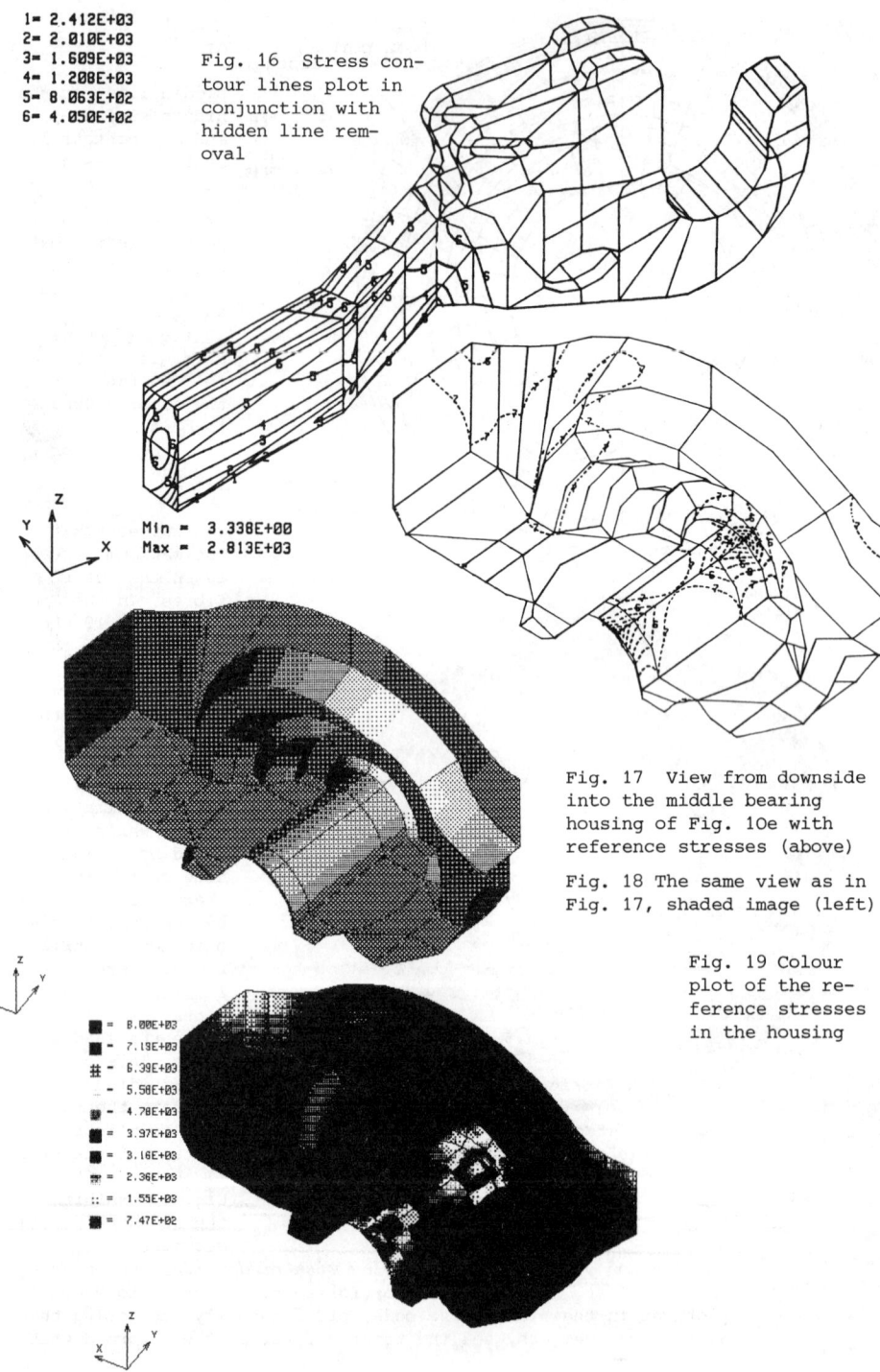

Fig. 16 Stress contour lines plot in conjunction with hidden line removal

Fig. 17 View from downside into the middle bearing housing of Fig. 10e with reference stresses (above)

Fig. 18 The same view as in Fig. 17, shaded image (left)

Fig. 19 Colour plot of the reference stresses in the housing

Fig. 20. As an example of a deformed structure plotted in the hidden surface mode inclusively shading may serve the magnet of Fig.1 again, see Fig. 21. It is loaded by its own weight and fixed in the suspension eyes.

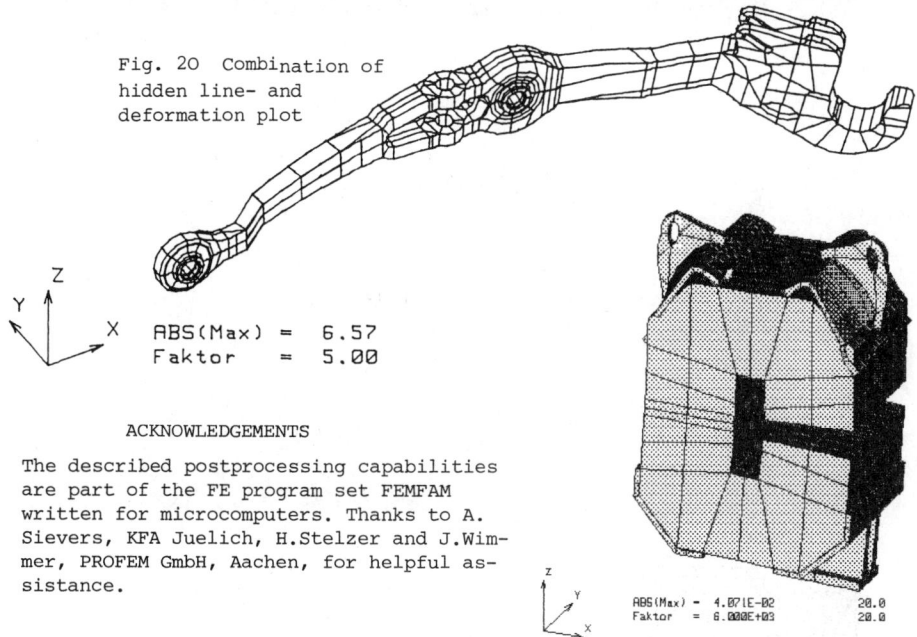

Fig. 20 Combination of hidden line- and deformation plot

Fig. 21 A deformation plot in the shaded mode

ACKNOWLEDGEMENTS

The described postprocessing capabilities are part of the FE program set FEMFAM written for microcomputers. Thanks to A. Sievers, KFA Juelich, H.Stelzer and J.Wimmer, PROFEM GmbH, Aachen, for helpful assistance.

REFERENCES

Newman,W.M. and R.F.Sproull (1979).Priciples of Interactive Computer Graphics. McGraw-Hill, London

Foley,J.D., and A.van Dam (1982). Fundamentals of Interactive Computer Graphics. Addison-Wesley, Reading

Stelzer,J.F. (1984). A Simple but Effective Method to Produce Colour FEM Result Presentations. Eng.Comp., vol.1, no.3, 227-231

Stelzer,J.F. (1986) Microcomputers in Engineering, ed.B.A.Schrefler, R.W.Lewis. Pineridge Press, Swansea, 219-230

Janssen,T.L. (1983). A Simple Efficient Hidden Line Algorithm. Computers & Structures, vol.17, no.4, 563-571

Stelzer, J.F. (1984). Considerations and Strategies in Developing Finite Element Software for Desktop Computers. Eng.Comp., vol.1, no.2, 1o6-124

Wimmer, J. (1985). Color Dump. Internal Report of the PROFEM GmbH, Salvatorstr.32, D-5100 Aachen

Hinton,E. and D.R.J.Owen (1979). An Introduction to Finite Element Computations, Pineridge Press, Swansea, 328-346

Roberts, L.G. (1963). Machine Perception of 3-D Solids. TR315, Lincoln Labs, MIT, Cambridge, Mass.

SUBJECT INDEX

Analysis
  dynamic, 93
  finite element, 3
  kinematic, 93
  nonlinear, 133
  response spectrum, 167
  stress, 109
  structural, 247
  thermal, 109
Animations, 35
ANSYS, 51
Automatic
  conversion to special FE- and CAD-software-packages, 35
  load stepping, 133
  solution, 133

Baseplate, 167
Beams, 247
Boundary elements, 35
BRAVO, 93, 93
Bridge design, 191

CAD, 51
  software, 35
CAD/CAM, 3, 15
CASTEM, 25
CA.ST.OR, 109
Civil engineering, 3
Colouring, 257
Computational geometry, 15
Computer-aided rock engineering, 207
Conformal mapping, 35
Contact, 133
Continuous shading, 257
Contour lines, 257
Creep, 207

Depth complexity, 15
Distortion - integral equations, 77
Dynamic analysis, 93

Electric design, 93
Elastic-plastic material, 133
Electromagnetic fields, 61
Electronic design, 93
Equilibrium models
  in closed meshes, 35
Expected running time, 15

Finite elements, 35, 179, 219, 257
  analysis, 3
  method, 247
  modelling, 87
Forging, 149
FORGE2, 149
Frameworks, 179, 219
Friction, 133

GET3D, 61
GRAFEM, 93
Graphics, 3, 25
Grillages, 179, 219

Hard-software supported education, 35
Hidden line removal, 257
Hidden surface
  elimination, 15
  removal, 257
Home computers, 247
Hot forming, 149

IFAD, 93
Implicit scheme, 133
In-plane
  frames, 247
  plates, 179

Input commands
  simplified, 35
Instrumentation cabinet, 167
Integral equations, 77
Interactive graphics, 15
  and color, 87

Kinematic analysis, 93

Long term stability, 207
Lower bound, 15

Mechanical design, 3
Meshing, 25, 61
  generation, 87
Metal forming processes, 133
Microcomputers, 3
  programs, 179, 219
Modal analysis, 167
Multipurpose elements, 247

NlogN algorithm, 15
Nonlinear analysis, 133
Nuclear qualification, 167

Optimisation procedures, 35
Orthotropic shells of revolution, 247

Parallel processing, 87
Plastic materials, 77

Pocket micros, 247
Postprocessing, 87, 257
Postprocessors, 25
Preprocessing, 257
Preprocessors, 25
Programs
  Basic, 247

Relaxation, 207
Response spectrum analysis, 167

SAFEpm, 247
Salt rock, 207
Scan-line methods, 15
Solid modelling, 35
STDYNL, 231
Steel construction, 3
Stress analysis, 109

Tangent stiffness, 133
Thermal analysis, 109

Underground excavations, 207

Vibrations, 219

Workstation
  engineer's, 35

Z-buffer, 15